Journalism Workbook

A *manual of tasks and resources*

Brendan Hennessy and F W Hodgson

Focal Press

Focal Press
An imprint of Butterworth-Heinemann Ltd
Linacre House, Jordan Hill, Oxford OX2 8DP

Ⓡ A member of the Reed Elsevier plc group

OXFORD   LONDON   BOSTON
MUNICH   NEW DELHI   SINGAPORE   SYDNEY
TOKYO   TORONTO   WELLINGTON

First published 1995

British Library Cataloguing in Publication Data
Hennessy, Brendan
  Journalism Workbook: A Manual of Tasks and
  Resources
  I. Title II. Hodgson, F. W.
  070.4

ISBN 0 7506 2075 7

Composition by Scribe Design, Gillingham, Kent
Printed and bound in Great Britain

Contents

Acknowledgements

The writing of *Journalism Workbook* owes a good deal to the feedback in letters and questionnaires from the many users – students as well as lecturers – of the titles in the Butterworth-Heinemann Media Series, now in its Focal Press livery. It is from them that the germ of an idea for a special sort of workbook for journalism courses originated and took root.

Many experts both in the series and outside have since lent their time and advice to the authors in their quest to get the book right for its niche. There are some special people I would like to thank, however: Martin Keene for his ideas and his permission (along with that of the Press Association) to use the pictures on pages 70 and 71; Toby Melville of the *Bristol Evening Post* and Justin Lloyd of the *Yorkshire Evening Post* for permission to use their pictures on page 72, and special thanks to Rob Selwood, Chief Executive of the NCTJ, for drawing my attention to the work of these two young photographers and for showing an interest in the project.

I also wish to thank the editor of the *Manchester Evening News* for the picture of the MEN newsroom used in Chapter 1, and the editors of *The Sun*, *The Independent*, *The Guardian*, the *News of the World*, *Brighton Evening Argus*, *Croydon Advertiser,* and *Campaign* magazine for permission to print pages from their publications to demonstrate aspects of page design.

F. W. Hodgson, Editor, Media Series
March 1995

Illustrations

Introduction

THERE are many training routes in journalism in Britain today. To the traditional courses conducted by the National Council for the Training of Journalists and the many Higher National Diplomas in journalism and its fringe areas have been added in recent years the industry-based National Vocational Qualifications (NVQs). Spurred on by NVQs and their demand for trained lecturers and assessors at those centres undertaking them, in-house training schemes have become more widely available among the main newspaper companies, and also better organized. Some offer their own specialized diplomas as well as NVQs in an attempt to attract the best entrants to their staff.

Meanwhile, the media have penetrated the academic world on a broad front with more universities offering degrees in media studies, and finally in journalism itself. This has made Britain increasingly sought after by Commonwealth and other overseas students seeking qualifications rooted in British practice and has greatly increased the numbers of journalism students in the country as well as trainee journalists. Correspondence courses and learning packs are winging their way abroad in a new wave, bringing more overseas students than ever within the orbit of British journalism training.

Media studies degrees were originally much concerned with the psychology of language and communication and the morality of the press, all valid aspects of study. In recent years they, too, have increased their vocational content in film, PR, broadcasting and print journalism – in what one assumes must be response to student demand – and are becoming more commonly chosen as first degrees by graduates entering the industry's training schemes. Syllabuses, however, should be carefully scrutinized for content by those students looking to take up careers in the media.

Textbooks have to take account of this burgeoning activity. In a world in which journalism and its techniques are increasingly under the microscope, the Focal Press Journalism Manuals, published by Butterworth-Heinemann, break new ground with *Journalism Workbook*, a manual of hands-on tasks covering all aspects of practice.

Here is a book that will be a boon not only to in-house tutors and trainees but to students on journalism and media studies courses and those grappling with learning packs, or simply their own burning ambition, who have yet to work 'in the field.'

The authors take each area of practice and demonstrate with the use of practically based, assignments the world of work that awaits young journalists in the early years of their careers. Each assignment is designed to spin off a number of tasks which are spelt out in the form of briefings. With these are notes and book references to help the trainee or student tackle them and also further their knowledge of the particular area of practice. Students are recomended to study the background texts to hone their skills.

The exercises can be used on courses or as a self-administered extension of course work carried out under the guidance of tutors or lecturers. Above all, they are intended to help tutors and students by providing models for further course work based upon the skills required of their staffs by today's newspapers and magazines.

Assignments range from reporting and news writing to feature writing, subediting and headline writing and press photography. Assignments on page planning and design are included to help journalism students and trainees understand the principles by which newspapers are put together and targeted on their audiences, and to give a flavour of the more esoteric world of the production journalist.

General questions of the relationship between newspapers and their readers and the place of the press in society are not neglected. Workshop projects and study programmes outline ways in which students and trainees, working in groups or singly, can study and analyse newspaper content, build up readership profiles and consider methods of practice, social attitudes, press regulation and press economics.

The book outlines ways in which vocational training can be extended through research into the press and its methods by means of debate, seminars and the submission of long papers on a chosen press subject.

The chapter on sources and the appendix on books, publications and organizations are designed to make young journalists confident in identifying and acquiring – and knowing where to look for – information needed for the many tasks with which they are likely to be faced.

The authors finally consider the thorny subject of marking and assessment, including self-assessment, and suggest ways in which the assignments, projects and study programmes in this book – or ones derived from the models given – can be used to measure achievement within the parameters of the training programmes for which they are used.

Journalism Workbook is not a textbook as such but rather a guide on how to utilize textbooks alongside fieldwork and the requirements of syllabuses in the process of learning to be a journalist. Practical work in the field plus sound theoretical instruction are both necessary to the young journalist starting out. This book is offered as the bridge between the two.

For the benefit of those concerned with particular aspects, each chapter has an introductory outline covering its area of practice and has been made as self-contained and easy-of-reference as possible.

1

Reporting

A WIDE range of work awaits the young reporter starting a first job on a local paper. The smaller the paper the more varied the work, for an editor with a modest budget will be less able to call upon specialists for particular tasks, and in emergencies quite important jobs can fall upon young shoulders. This is one of the valuable aspects of training on a local paper.

Training begins from day one with the fledgeling news gatherer being assigned to accompany a senior journalist in the coverage of jobs. As training proceeds, some of the first solo assignments you will get might appear simple but it would be wrong to assume that they are easy. The correct approach in dealing with people and care in finding and checking information applies to the reporting of weddings and funerals on your local weekly no less than it does to interviewing a celebrity or working as a lobby correspondent in parliament.

Some simple newsgathering jobs can be a minefield for the unwary. Failure to understand this can damage a newspaper's relations with people and lose a wanted story. It can also bring a quick end to the career of a young reporter however good they are with words.

Reporting is a twofold activity – news gathering and news writing. Both are of equal importance since without the techniques necessary to gather and verify news an ability in to write it would be of little avail, while skilled news gatherers would come unstuck if they could not communicate properly with the reader.

NEWS GATHERING

THE techniques of gathering news – how to find it and how to authenticate it – are taught by a combination of instruction, example and

Figure I   Hub of a busy newspaper – a corner of the newsroom at the *Manchester Evening News*

experience during the early stages of in-house training. In the case of students on pre-training courses, instruction has to predominate but a good deal can be done through simulated exercises of the type given in this book.

For those taking either route, the assignments that follow demonstrate the wide spectrum of a reporter's work and the demands editors are likely to make. With each assignment are notes to help the student and trainee reporter arrive at the right responses and give guidance with self-assessment.

NEWS WRITING

WHILE this is not a how-to-be-a-reporter textbook, a word at this stage about news writing will be helpful for those about to tackle these assignments.

Each reporting job originates in the news room (see Figure 1) and is set out in a briefing given to the reporter by the news editor or chief

2   THE SUN, Saturday, January 14, 1995

EURO-REBELS TELL MAJOR WHERE TO STICK HIS WHIP

'It's all for one and one for all'
— JOHN WILKINSON

By PASCOE WATSON

FIVE of the nine MPs who lost the Tory whip for rebelling over Europe last night snubbed John Major's efforts to woo them back.

They vowed they would only return to the party if their fellow rebels are taken back as well.

One of the five, John Wilkinson, declared loyally: "It is one for all and all for one."

The nine were kicked out before Christmas for failing to back the Government in a vote to give more taxpayers' cash to Brussels. But the Premier decided five should be forgiven for supporting him in this week's key vote on the composition of Commons committees.

He ordered a hush-hush operation to win over Mr Wilkinson, Sir Teddy Taylor, Sir Richard Body, Nicholas Budgen and Richard Shepherd.

Mr Major wanted senior Tory MPs to act as "nurses" to privately persuade them to return.

The four other rebels — Teresa Gorman, Christopher Gill, Tony Marlow and Michael Cartiss — did not back the Government on Wednesday, and are still out in the cold.

But all nine insist they will only go back as a whole. Mr Wilkinson said:

"We were all dismissed in an irrational way.

"The correct thing to do now is for all nine friends and colleagues to be invited back."

Mr Budgen said: "It would pose real problems if they tried to divide this group of nine by inviting some back and not the others."

Mrs Gorman said: "I would be exceedingly surprised about the manhood of any of my male colleagues who didn't refuse an invitation to rejoin at this stage."

"We are one group of people who have been foolishly treated by the very immature group of people running the country at the moment."

At least two of the rebels are threatening more trouble for Mr Major over the new Euro fishing deal allowing Spanish craft into our waters.

Sir Richard Body and Mr Marlow both indicated they may refuse to back the Government in next Wednesday's vote.

The Sun Says — Page Six

PM SETS SIGHTS ON 21st CENTURY

John Major yesterday shrugged off polls showing the Government's popularity at an all-time low — and summoned ministers to a summit to plan for the next century.

A spokesman said the talks at Chequers were about "promoting Britain's long-term interests."

Top security ... but terrorists say Full Sutton jail is too tough

IRA MEN SUE

Continued from Page One

their cells at Full Sutton, near York, since aerosol can "bombs" were found being heated in ovens on Christmas Day.

Between them they are serving 98 years for plotting to kill Princess Anne and John Major, shooting three policemen and other offences.

The four — Birmingham-born Feilim O'Hadhmaill, Michael O'Brien and Damien McComb from Belfast and Patrick Kelly, of Co Laoise, Eire — first complained last month.

In a letter to a newspaper they whined about their "claustrophobic" Special Secure Unit.

INSULT

They moaned that it was not run like a five-star hotel and that they had suffered long-term "physical and psychological" damage.

Now they have engaged top London solicitors Benedict Birnberg, who also act for Moors Murderer Ian Brady.

Their writ seeks damages for alleged negligence and wrongful actions by staff at Full Sutton and Parkhurst Jail, where some were previously held.

MP Mr Cran, of the Tory backbench Northern Ireland committee, said: "I am disgusted.

"To hear them whinge about prison conditions makes my blood boil — but to sue for damages is the final straw."

Stan Walpole, chairman of the Prison Officers Association branch at Full Sutton, said: "I am utterly gobsmacked.

"Even to contemplate giving them legal aid to sue the department holding them is an insult."

Last night the Legal Aid Board said: "Anyone, including prisoners, is entitled to apply.

"Whether aid is granted depends on whether we decide the applicant has a good prospect of winning."

The Prison Service said: "We understand a writ has been issued. There is nothing more we can say."

Kelly, 42, is serving 25 years for planning to bomb the Lord Mayor's Show and shooting a London bobby.

O'Hadhmaill, 36, got 25 years after being caught with Semtex.

McComb, 32, is doing 30 years for plotting to kill the Prime Minister and other VIPs.

O'Brien, 29, an accomplice of Paul Magee, who killed Special Constable Glen Goodman, is serving 18 years.

The Sun Says — Page Six

McComb .. death plot

Kelly ... 25-year term

O'Hadhmaill .. Semtex

O'Brien ... accomplice

NORM GUNS FOR GLENDA

SACKED Chancellor Norman Lamont plans to stand against film star MP Glenda Jackson at the next election.

He heads the Tory shortlist of candidates for the Labour actress's seat in trendy Hampstead, North London.

Mr Lamont's current constituency of Kingston-upon-Thames, Surrey, is to be abolished.

Ford puts up prices

FORD is putting up car prices by an average of 2.1 per cent from Wednesday.

The Fiesta 1.1 will cost £7,250, up from £7,095, and the Mondeo 1.8LX is up from £12,445 to £12,700.

Ford's new 1995 Escort starts at £9,495 for a basic 1.3 Encore.

ROCKET HITS SKY TV MAN

A SKY TV newsman was hit in the face by shrapnel when a shell exploded near his crew in Grozny yesterday.

Yuri Tunev, 29 — a soundman for Sky News — was wounded as the Kremlin launched another bid to finally seize the capital of rebel republic Chechnya.

Men in their 60s and teenage boys are among Chechen rebels fighting to keep control of the city.

Figure 2   News presentation tabloid style – a typical page 2 from *The Sun*

reporter. The briefing specifies the task, includes any necessary known information, suggests certain lines of inquiry, and in most cases nominates the length required and the copy deadline.

The reporter, having gathered the facts and information needed, should start writing the story by identifying and encapsulating the essential facts in the first paragraph – the intro. It should be short, pithy and aimed at grabbing the reader's attention. It should tell the reader what the story is about. It should be important and newsworthy enough to form the basis of the headline, which will be put on to the story at a later stage by the subeditor.

The next few paragraphs should justify and qualify the intro, explaining for the reader any references made or quotations used, and enlarging upon or explaining any points used by the reporter in writing the intro.

Where there are several good news points do not try to cram them all in the intro. Identify what in your opinion is the best one (or ones) to lead off with and bring the others into the second or third paragraphs in the course of 'standing up' your intro.

Thereafter the facts of the story and the supporting quotations, information and qualifications should be unfolded in logical progression, the more important and newsworthy coming first and the less newsworthy towards the end.

It is tempting to keep a pithy piece of information as a last paragraph, or pay-off, but beware! In the rush towards edition times it is useful, when time is short, if a story can be cut easily from the end if it turns out to be too long, or if other things encroach upon its space in the page. Your pay-off might fall off the bottom!

Inevitably the reporter's daily work will provide exceptions to the above approach to writing up a story. You might be called upon to contribute to a shopping guide, or cover a play or concert, to write an item for the weekly gossip column. Here, the hard objective approach to news has to yield to the subjective approach of feature writing where comment and opinion can be expected. Here, as will be seen in the two chapters on feature writing, a softer approach to the writing has to be used, with regard being given to colour, pace and persuasion.

You will find the notes given with the following assignments a useful guide where special circumstances apply to a story.

WEDDINGS can make news on a local weekly paper. Many offices have special forms to be filled in by a couple who want their big day included in the weddings column. Writing up the column is one of the first jobs given to a beginner.

Assignment 1

Here is the sort of information a typical wedding form might give:

Bride: Cindy Carstairs, aged 25, an SRN at Townshire General Hospital, younger daughter of Mr John Carstairs, of 14 Combermere Road, Old Town, and Mrs Helen Watson, of Frinton-on-Sea, Essex.

Bridegroom: John Walters, aged 27, computer engineer, only son of Dr and Mrs Bruce Walters, of The Manse, Dike Road, New Town.

Bridesmaids: Tallulah Carstairs, the bride's sister, and Clara Walters, cousin of the groom.

Best man: Charlie Vickers, rugby club colleague of the groom and captain of Old Town Rugby Union Club.

Place: St John's Church, Old Town.

Clergy: the Rev Clarence Jones.

Time: Saturday, 12 June at 2 pm.

Telephone contact: Bride's father: Old Town 893440

Special comments: Bride wearing a hundred-year-old wedding dress embroidered in 1898 by her great great grandmother. Bridegroom has a Royal Humane Society award for saving a boy from drowning three years ago at Saltcliffe-on-Sea. Groom's father is a well-known GP in Old Town.

TASK 1 *Use the information on the wedding form to write a 150-word account of the Carstairs-Walters wedding as the lead story to a column of weddings. The paper's press deadline is Tuesday afternoon.*

TASK 2 *Explain briefly what steps you would take to:*
(a) Check that the wedding has taken place exactly as planned.
(b) Identify the names on a wedding group picture it is proposed to use.
Notes: Remember that friends and family will spot instantly any misspelling of a name and may well land you with your first complaint to the editor. Editors can write apologies and publish corrections but they do not warm to young reporters who cause the problem. See Harris and Spark: *Practical Newspaper Reporting* 2nd Edition (Focal Press, 1993) page 153.

FUNERAL REPORTS can be equally important on a local weekly paper. Checking out the facts of the life of a deceased person and, even more, compiling lists of mourners and talking to relatives calls for a great deal of tact and understanding on the part of the trainee reporter to whom such assignments usually fall. Here there is no help as with wedding forms. The assignment is invariably an exercise in personal contact of the most delicate kind.

Assignment 2

Imagine the circumstances of the funeral in your town of a well-known ex-mayor who has a distinguished military record and, from the facts you have been able to glean, prepare the following:

TASK 1   *Write a 250-word account giving the principal mourners.*

TASK 2   *Describe in 300 words how you would research the life story of the person.*

TASK 3   *Describe in 300 words the dress and social protocols you would expect to have to observe in your role as a respresentative of your paper at assignments such as the above.*

Notes: With local personalities the office cuttings library is an invaluable source of information, but do not rest on cuttings alone. There may be a unique fact awaiting disclosure that will interest your readers more than anything else. Ask around. Also, check Harris and Spark, pages 222–6, on looking things up.

MAKING CALLS calls should not be regarded as an irksome routine. They are, after all, the means by which a reporter keeps in touch with contacts, and it is from contacts that some important news stories start their journey into the newspaper. Regular – but not bothersome – chats with your more important contacts are important. Even the most ordinary conversation by telephone or face to face can turn up the unexpected.

Assignment 3

A game of snooker at the police club with a friendly inspector one evening may not produce much on the criminal front but when the inspector casually mentions that a colleague, a long-serving sergeant, has caught a monster carp in the old stew-pond of a nearby ruined abbey that was not thought to contain any worthwhile fish, your ears prick up.

How much did it weigh?

Is it a record?

Did the sergeant know it was there and had he planned to catch it?

Has it got a pet name?

How experienced an angler is the officer?

What other monster carp have been caught in the area?

What did it feel like as he hauled it in?

TASK 1   *Assume that you have followed up the inspector's tip-off. From what you have found, write up a 400-word news story about the sergeant and his carp.*

TASK 2   *Suggest what picture possibilities the story has and what liaison you would establish with the picture desk.*

TASK 3   *Explain in 300 words how you went about getting the information and background to build the inspector's tip-off into a news story.*

Notes: A good little story for a reporter who likes digging around for background and an example of the value of talking regularly to your contacts (Harris and Spark, pages 8–9).

Assignment 4

The local barber is a useful contact in a reporter's area. Your chap, a notorious gossip, mentions while snipping your hair that a customer's wife in the town has inherited a painting she thinks might be valuable. It had been lying for years in her father-in-law's attic.

You get the woman's address and pay her a call. She is quite happy to talk about the picture and you discover from her:

(a) The father-in-law hated the picture and couldn't stand it on the wall.
(b) It consists of a rather decorous Victorian nude bathing in a rural setting.
(c) The woman and her husband are short of money.
(d) She has written to Sotheby's asking about the signature on the bottom of the painting.

TASK 1   *From the above interview and from other inquiries that you decide to make write a 400-word news story.*

TASK 2   *Write a three-paragraph version of the story for a national daily paper as if you were the local stringer.*

TASK 3   *Describe in 300 words how you went about fleshing out the story from the facts you have been given by the woman.*

Notes: This is a good example of a story that could only come from a tip-off. See news sources in Harris and Spark, pages 8–9.

HANDOUTS: Newspaper offices are the favourite recipients of publicity handouts from the press offices of companies and celebrities hoping for various reasons to catch the eye of editors. Some have been poorly targeted in terms of readership market and stand little chance of getting beyond the news editor's in-tray.

The newsdesk tries to sort through this daily influx of paper and the ones more likely to interest readers are given to a reporter – often quite a junior one – to see if there is a worthwhile a story to be distilled from the contents. Some important stories originate in this way.

Assignment 5

The following printed handout is received from a company with their headquarters and a factory in the paper's circulation area:

Hybrid Homes have scored a first in this country with their new three-bedroomed self-erect bungalow, the Matchwood house, which is being unveiled to the press at the company's headquarters in Old Town on Friday, 16 July.

The bungalow, which has been designed by the company's architect, Mr James Brickhouse, is intended to shorten building time by more than 80 per cent. It is delivered in kit form to site in sections and can be put up by three people in less than a week. The plumbing comes in fully assembled units and the windows are ready glazed. The only extra is the electric wiring, which is left to customer's choice.

Help with site preparation is provided by the manufacturers and the general specifications are designed to comply with current building regulations.

The Matchwood house is the first prefabricated house to be made and marketed by a UK company since 1955.

Hybrid Homes are proud to announce that the Government of Botswana has already ordered 10,000 of the bungalows, and that two other Third World countries are considering placing orders. A recent sales tour in Africa showed that a high potential sale for the house existed in countries suffering from serious shortages of housing stock.

It is also hoped to win sales for the Matchwood house as holiday homes and as cheap housing for cash-strapped councils. The price in this country, to be announced on Friday, is likely to be less than £26,000 a unit, delivered to site.

Mr Brickhouse is also the designer of the company's top selling Shower-me unit bathroom, which won an award at last year's Top Homes exhibition at Earl's Court.

Success with the Matchwood house is likely to mean more jobs at the company's Old Town factory which last year shed a third of its labour force.

TASK I *Discuss in about 300 words the sort of inquiries you would want to make from the company or its press officer or from any other sources to harden the story's local interest*

TASK 2 *Prepare and write a 400-word news story for the local evening paper from the above handout and such inquiries you needed to make about its contents.*

TASK 3 *Write a memo to the news desk with ideas for illustrating the story.*

Notes: Handouts are much under-estimated as news sources in some offices but reading through them does consume valuable time; sheer weight and numbers can set up editor resistance. Learn to skim read by taking in the first few words on each line. The publicity being sought by the writer may be of no concern to the paper but there could be a pearl of information in paragraph forty-nine that your readers would want to have. Or it could be the first inkling of an important news story affecting the circulation area.

SPEECHES of all kinds are made publicly by all manner of people, many of them aimed at catching the eye or ear of the local paper. Some, sadly, are given space because of who the speaker is rather than what they have to say. They should not be neglected as assignments, however, even though some may seem sadly deficient in quotable material. Try to be patient if you have the time; the gem of the piece may come at the end.

 **Assignment 6**

The local MP, Nicholas Droppitt, is in full flood in defence of the Government's record in a speech he is making at the opening of the new sports and leisure centre in New Town. He has not provided a preliminary handout and the reporter, who has just rushed in from a previous engagement, struggles to take a shorthand note of what sounds to be pretty routine stuff. This is the gist of it:

> You cannot say that this Government has consistently broken its promises. Take the thorny issue of EEC directives. The Prime Minister has fought for, and made it clear to his EEC colleagues, as he said he would, that he is not prepared to accept restrictions that hamper the sort of free trade for which the Common Market was created.
>
> The EEC is a forum in which one fights for, and seeks support for, one's national policies. Only by rigorous lobbying and persuasion can this support from other members be gained. I put it to you that on no major issue affecting the products of this country has Britain – and by Britain I mean the Government – yielded on issues that affect the livelihood of our workers or the health and welfare of our people.
>
> [The worthy member drones on for while and the reporter's notetaking languishes...but suddenly he pricks up his ears. The Member is saying....] I can tell you this – that it is as a direct intervention from Britain that the Commission at Brussels has agreed to the use of EEC funds as subsidies for the provision of homes in areas that have less than an agreed percentage of housing stock available to meet the needs of people on council waiting lists.
>
> The Townshire conurbation is precisely the sort of area to which I refer. I can go further than this. I can tell you that a grant of EEC funds is in the pipeline for housing purposes in the Townshire conurbation.
>
> Do you know what this will mean? It will mean not only shorter waiting lists for homes; it will mean more jobs as house-building, after five years of stagnation, takes off in Townshire....

A routine opening ceremony has come alive. Whether he intended to or not, the MP has leaked an important piece of news for the area.

TASK 1   *Write up the coverage of the opening ceremony highlighting the MP's disclosures.*

TASK 2   *Explain what illustrations would you try to set up for the story.*

TASK 3   *Discuss in 300 words what further inquiries/interviews, etc. you would set in motion to harden up and develop the story.*

Notes: If a newspaper operates in a local or regional market then issues concerning readers in the circulation area are important, especially those affecting people's lives and jobs (Harris & Spark, pages 172-9).

NOT all news events are so conveniently arranged in advance as speeches, meetings, handouts, press conferences and weddings. **THE UNEXPECTED** is an inevitable ingredient of news and can call for resource, and often speed, from the reporter.

Assignment 7

A boy of 12 has rescued a child of 6 from a mud-hole at a seaside town as the tide was coming in. Someone telephones the paper and you are sent to get the facts. You have little to go on and realize that by the time you arrive on the scene you are going to have to tell the story through other people's words, and in particular the words of those people you are able to find in time for your edition deadline.

You manage to line up interviews with the following:

1   The boy. Fortunately it is a Saturday so he is not at school. His parents naturally insist on being present.
2   His parents.
3   His teacher.
4   A middle-aged couple who saw the rescue but were non-swimmers and could not help.
5   A young girl who tried to help.
6   The police.

With your deadline near you have no time for further inquiries. In fact you have to telephone the story to copytakers straight from your notes.

TASK 1   *Explain what sort of background material you would look for to go with the story and how you would go about finding it.*

TASK 2   *Simulating in your mind the news situation, write a 400-word story using the above sources.*

TASK 3   *Explain what you would do about photographic coverage for the story.*

2c Display 081-668 4111 The Advertiser, Friday, December 30, 1994

Real-life Shirley Valentine settles for love and life in Greece

Innate goodness: Mixalis.

IT'S a long way from the concrete jungle of Croydon to the sun-soaked shores of Greece.

For a quick package holiday it requires only packing a swimsuit and hopping on a plane.

But to move there for good, as Croydon woman Liz Stolls has, requires a leap in culture too.

And to settle into the old-fashioned role of the Greek woman almost certainly requires another attraction; love.

Indeed, Liz Stolls' shift to the village of Lesbos is the romantic and remarkable tale of a holiday romance that led to marriage and a whole new lifestyle.

Shown next Tuesday on Carlton (7.30pm) 'Love Story' traces Liz's path as a real-life Shirley Valentine.

Ironically, Liz, now 41, did not even want to go to Greece and was certainly not looking for a holiday fling.

She said: "I'd never had a holiday romance. I always thought they were a waste of time. It was either sex or you would get your heart broken so what was the point?"

Liz and her friend settled on Greece from the glossy travel brochures and decided on the island of Lesbos.

Once there, Liz embarked on a passionate affair with local dancer/waiter Mixalis Kostis.

She said: "From the first time I talked to him I could sense an innate goodness; something that had been missing at four in the morning lying on the carpet after dinner parties in London."

At the end of the two-week vacation, in 1987, Liz went home. But even throwing herself into her new dream job as head of PR at Sadlers Wells could not get Mixali out of her mind.

Two months later she left the critics at the year's biggest premiere and flew back to Lesbos.

At first glance it would seem a recipe for disaster. He was from a remote mountain village where his family herded sheep and grew olives. Liz came from the world of smart dinner parties and international dance.

Liz's father Peter Stolls, of Lower Addiscombe Road, Croydon, said: "He's from a peasant background. He has a different religion, he comes from a foreign country and he's not as well educated. It was a risky business."

But with so much at stake, not least her pride, Liz surmounted the difficulties of language and lifestyle.

The couple married in traditional Greek style and are still happily wed, with their daughters Anastasia and Katarina.

Mr Stolls, who visits about once a year with his wife Eithne, said: "They seem pretty happy. They've proved their point."

Liz said: "There are times when I think I am going to chuck it all in and run home. Then I remember what it was about Mixalis and life on Lesbos that made me leave London behind. I couldn't recommend it to anyone unless they had the strength of character to give up a lot and worked very hard at it."

Risky business: Liz.

2 SECOND THOUGHTS

In this week's second section of The Advertiser:

CUP PRICES

PALACE'S attempt to cut admission prices for their FA Cup third round tie against Lincoln City on Sunday, January 8, has been turned down by the Football Association, following Lincoln's initial rejection of Palace's proposal to charge £12 (adults) and £6 (juveniles and senior citizens):
See page 23

TOP MEN

TODAY we offer Crystal Palace fans the chance to choose their Player of the Year on our exclusive phone-vote line. He may be a player who has made most progress or has been the most consistent performer; the choice is yours. Results of the poll will be published next week:
See Page 26

LOOKING BACK

AS 1994 draws to a close, we reflect in words and pictures on some of the key events and developments that have shaped our lives both individually and as a community over the past 12 months:
See pages 35-38

GHOST STORY

AN enterprising venture turns eerie at the Brierley Cloisters, as the spirit of the Black Monk takes exception to events. Revel in the creepy goings-on in this spine-chiller by SHIREEN DUCHI:
See page 39

BLUE MURDER

WIMBLEDON Theatre plays host to a night of top alternative comedy on Monday, January 9 in *The Screaming Blue Murder Show* ... the biggest names on the comedy circuit, including Jo Brand, Lee Evans, Harry Hill and Kevin Day:
See page 41

NEWS Digest

Free workshop

A SERIES of free workshops to help people looking for work are starting up next month. The JOBHELP workshops cover job searching, skill assessment, interview preparation and CV presentation, and are open to anybody. A new group starts on January 17 at East Croydon United Reformed Church, Addiscombe Grove, and will run every Tuesday and Friday from 10am-noon for five weeks. The scheme runs independently of the DSS or Employment Service. Further information is available from Sheila Kemble on 081-686 0650.

Party for cash

NEW Year's Eve revellers at Stanley Halls in South Norwood will be partying in a good cause by helping raise cash for an African Caribbean centre for Croydon. Members of the borough's black community have already raised £1,000 for the centre and the hunt for premises is under way. Tickets for tomorrow's family event cost £10, or £2 for under-12s. More information from 081-771 3008.

Punched for £1

TEENAGE thugs punched a boy to the ground for the sake of £1. The two boys, aged around 15, demanded the coin from a 16-year-old Croydon boy as he walked along Thornton Heath High Street on Tuesday. After asking for more cash, the pair punched the victim and pushed him to the ground.

Mugger failed

A MAN tried to drag a woman into a garden after grabbing her as she walked along Peaks Hill, Purley, late last Thursday. The victim managed to struggle free and her attacker fled.

Nineteen new arrivals add extra cheer at Christmas

By Jenny Forsyth

NINETEEN bundles of joy brought parents the ultimate cute and cuddly Christmas gift.

The babies, born on Christmas Day at Mayday University and East Surrey Hospitals, were an extra special festive bonus to their mothers and fathers.

The first Croydon baby to share Jesus' birthdate was Kady Miller, weighing 7lb 1oz when she was born only half-an-hour into Christmas Day.

Mother Tracie Miller, 30, of Unity Close, New Addington, said: "I feel chuffed about it and my family is complete. She is beautiful, lovely, a real cutie.

"I am feeling on top of the world. It is the best Christmas present I could have hoped for."

At Mayday University Hospital, Thornton Heath, it was a boom day in the maternity ward.

Seventeen babies, nine boys and eight girls, were delivered there during the day, compared to the daily norm of around 12.

And at East Surrey Hospital a further two babies were born to Warlingham families.

Delighted first-time grandmother Karen Tighe watched as her daughter Nicola cradled newborn Chloe in her arms.

Nicola Tighe, 21, of Waverley Road, South Norwood, gave birth to the tiny 6lb 2oz baby at 9.46am.

Nicola's mother Mrs Karen Tighe said: "She debated whether or not to call her

> "I am feeling on top of the world. It is the best Christmas present I could have hoped for."
>
> Tracie Miller

Holly because of the day but she decided not to.

"Nicola's well-pleased. She's a really lovely baby."

Policeman Nick Witham, of Crowborough Drive, Warlingham said he was overjoyed to have his new junior.

Wife Elaine gave birth to a girl weighing 6lbs 5oz. They have named her Sophie.

New grandfather Jim Witham said: "It's the first baby and they're overjoyed. The fact she was born on Christmas day is an added bonus."

Just in time: Tiny Kady Miller was the first Christmas baby in Croydon, born at 12.32am. [Photo: X942670/4 by Kevin Shaw

THIS CHRISTMAS, SPEND NOTHING ON YOUR PARTNER.

Christmas is for surprises. Tell your loved one you haven't spent a penny on them and watch their face. Then tell them about the Network SouthCentral '2 for 1' Christmas Cheap Day Return, which allows another adult (or child) to travel free when you buy an adult '2 for 1' ticket. Tell them they're going shopping with you. Then watch their face. For full details, please call at your local Network SouthCentral rail station or telephone 01273 206755.

Network SouthCentral

Offer valid from 17 December 1994 to 6 January 1995.

Dedicated fundraiser wins top Rotary award

A FUNDRAISER has been presented with a major international award for his charity work.

Peter Dawes was given the Rotary Club's international Paul Harris Fellowship, joining previous winners such as the Princess Royal and Mother Theresa.

He was nominated by the Coulsdon Manor Rotary Club in honour of his dedicated work for others, even though he is not a Rotarian.

The prestigious award has only been given to four Coulsdon Manor Rotarians in the past decade.

Mr Dawes was picked for his work raising money for the Coulsdon Parish Church of St John in Canons Hill and the Centre for the Retired in Old Coulsdon.

The 86-year-old, who lives in Bradmore Way, Old Coulsdon, has organized charitable events for about five years with the help of his wife Vera, and has raised more than £10,000.

During the summer he arranged a special 10th birthday fete for the Centre for the Retired at its base in Bradmore Green.

Coulsdon Manor Rotary Club president Tony Sales made the surprise presentation at the club's Christmas dinner at the Coulsdon Manor Hotel.

He paid tribute to Mr Dawes' "tangible and significant contribution to the life of the local community".

Mr Dawes said of the award: "It's a great honour really. I hadn't heard of the fellowship before and it's only since I looked into it that I realized that it's the Rotary International top award."

Mr Dawes became involved in fundraising when St John's Church needed money for an extension.

He said: "I thought it would be nice to put on some sort of entertainment. We arranged concerts and they were a success.

"These have developed to become something for the community of Old Coulsdon, not just for those who go to St John's."

The fete organized for the Centre for the Retired also turned into a village event, raising £2,500.

The Paul Harris Fellowship award takes its name from the founder of the Rotarian movement and has been awarded to scientists, politicians, entertainers, sportsmen and women and others around the world.

Among holders of the fellowship are opera star Luciano Pavarotti, Mother Theresa, Jonas Salk, the inventor of the polio vaccination, and the Princess Royal.

Rotary clubs across the world can nominate anybody for a Fellowship who they feel deserves recognition.

In this country, the nominations are handled by Rotary International Britain & Ireland (RIBI), before being passed to the international headquarters in America.

Mr Sale said: "Peter is a most worthy addition to this group and we are delighted to be able to honour his work in this way."

Discount fares scheme lacks the support of two boroughs

TWO Tory boroughs have been branded "selfish and parasitical" for adopting a stance which will scupper plans to give pensioners and disabled free travel on British Rail trains in London.

The attack from deputy leader of Croydon Council, Coun Jerry Fitzpatrick (Lab, Addiscombe) came after Wandsworth and Westminster Councils refused to back an extension of the existing concessionary fares scheme, despite the fact that its cost is expected to drop next year.

The capital's 30 other boroughs are in favour of the move.

Wandsworth and Westminster have also come under attack from charities representing the elderly, who have described their decision as incomprehensible.

The charities, including Age Concern and the Greater London Forum for the Elderly, will step up pressure on Westminster and Wandsworth to reconsider their decision.

But if the scheme is to be extended there will have to be unanimous agreement among London boroughs and there is no sign of movement from Wandsworth.

The present concessionary scheme gives pensioners and the disabled free travel on buses and the Tube and half price tickets on British Rail.

Coun Fitzpatrick said an extremely good deal had been worked out for next year which would see the costs of the scheme going down, even if the price of the extension is included.

Croydon Council's contribution drops from £5.281 million to £5.258 million.

He said: "This is typical of the selfish and parasitical approach of these two Tory councils. They are trying to get all the benefits they can without considering the interests of people of London as a whole."

A spokeswoman for Wandsworth Council said it was not supporting the extension because it did not agree with cost calculations made by the London Committee on Accessible Transport, which oversees the concessionary scheme.

The council was also concerned the extension did not target people with specific difficulties.

Snatched baby re-united with foster parents

A BABY snatched by his 16-year-old mother was re-united with his foster parents for Christmas.

Detectives acting on a tip-off found the five-month-old baby alive and well at an address in Shrublands on Thursday (December 22) afternoon.

The discovery came two weeks after police appealed to Advertiser readers for information.

The baby was taken from foster parents in Sutton as his mum, from New Addington, visited him on December 5.

Police combed New Addington for the boy, visiting around a dozen addresses in the area and interviewing his mum's friends and family.

Det Sgt Nigel Edwards, of Sutton CID, said: "The baby is fine, fit and healthy.

"It was a relief it had been rescued. We are very pleased the inquiry came to a satisfactory conclusion, especially just before Christmas.

"The foster parents were very upset when it was taken and were very, very happy that he was safe and well."

The baby was placed with foster parents after he was put on Croydon Council's at risk register.

Det Sgt Edwards said since the incident involved the boy's natural parents and happened in the UK, the only charge that could be brought would be removing a child from a place of safety which carried a maximum penalty of six months' imprisonment.

No charges have yet been made in connection with the baby's disappearance.

Imperial pub measures nipped as spirits go metric

BRUSSELS Bureaucrats and the Government will change the way we drink in the New Year when they oust imperial measures in favour of the metric system.

From New Year's Day spirits will go metric with the 'nip' or one-sixth of a gill being axed in favour of the larger 25 millilitre (ml) measure which is 1.5 per cent larger.

Wine drinkers will also face the metric music with glasses measuring 125ml or 175ml, bad news for restaurants who will have to state how large measures are on menus.

The changeover from the outdated Imperial system will be gradually phased in over the next few years.

Red-letter days to watch out for are October 1 next year which will see the end of the gallon, yard and pint and January 1 in the year 2000 which will mark the demise of the pound and ounce.

By the turn of the century only the faithful pint for beer and cider and milk and the mile for roads will still be in use. The metric system had, in fact, been in force since the year 1897.

And adopting more of it will make life easier for Croydon Trading Standards inspectors. They have to take along a boxful of equipment when testing measures because they are never sure whether they will come up against metric.

BUMPER'S BARGAINS
ADVERTISE FREE NO LIMIT
Only in the Croydon Advertiser

Figure 3 How a suburban weekly does it – a well-filled news page from the *Croydon Advertiser*

Notes: Speed and fast thinking are the essence of this sort of story, with a fairly close deadline. Even though you may be confident of telephoning copy from notes you need to know when to cut off your inquiries and file for the edition. It is likely that you can add matter for a later edition if there is time and the story warrants it. (Harris and Spark, pages 12–19.)

LOCAL TALKING POINTS: An effective local paper cannot afford to neglect issues that have become talking points in the area and should try to cover as wide a cross-section as possible of matters that are arousing public debate. Letters to the editor are often a good guide to what people are concerned or worried about.

Democracy through elected representatives on local councils is often not enough to get things done, or at least get things started; the activities of local campaigns and pressure groups need to be followed – and they can make good copy. The fact that they may court press publicity is no bad thing, for a newspaper is itself part of the process of democracy.

Assignment 8

Here is a typical local talking point that might occur in your area: the villagers have had enough of Long Lane, Blackton, the local accident black spot. There have been three fatal accidents in a year where the road bends as it enters the village. The road surface is poor; putting up a 'black spot' sign seems to have done no good, the 30 mph sign is hidden by trees. The road, according to the villagers, is unfit for the use it is getting. Cars have finished up three times in the past two years in the garden of one of the houses.

There have been debates by the council's roads committee on what further can be tried, but no decisions. Now the village has formed an action committee to get something done. The committee has been on to your editor and you are sent to Blackton to do a piece for your weekly paper on the problem.

TASK 1 *Plan a briefing for yourself on the various aspects of the problem, listing likely sources of opinion and information.*

TASK 2 *Simulating the circumstances from the above information, write a 750-word 'news special' on the black spot of Blackton.*

Notes: This is not a job to be rushed. There are bound to be two (or even more) sides to the problem. The editor will undoubtedly have given you time to take soundings. What you are engaged upon is a piece of investigative journalism or, if you like, news-in-depth reporting. It may well be your first introduction to this important area of reporting and the result could be useful to your career. One hopes, too, it will produce results for the community.

See Harris and Spark, pages 25–33, 15–19 (sources), 36–48 (interviewing); also Brendan Hennessy: *Writing Feature Articles* 2nd Edition (Focal Press, 1993) on interviewing, chapters 9 and 13.

LOCAL GOVERNMENT means, in Britain, the running of local services (and collection and spending of local taxes) by tiers of authorities consisting, in descending order, of county councils, district councils and parish councils. The councils are elected bodies in the same way that Parliament is an elected body, and they have certain paid officials to whom work is delegated.

For the local residents relations with the council in their area involve dealing with the appropriate department at the town hall – the housing department, highways, planning, libraries, leisure, finance departments and so on. The departments are each controlled by an appropriate council committee on which various of the elected councillors serve. The committees in their turn report to and are answerable to the full council.

For a newspaper covering the area what happens at the town hall is of vital interest to their readers and so they obtain each month published copies of the council's minutes to find out what is being done, and they attend meetings of the council and many of the committees to report on the debates that take place and the decisions taken.

Assignment 9

You discover from reading the minutes that your local council, at its upcoming meeting, is to consider a long-awaited recommendation from the amenities committee, about the future of a piece of waste land on the edge of the town which was formerly common land. They say it should be offered for sale by tender because of problems of development. The committee's deliberations are not open to the press or public but you know that there will be a vigorous debate in full council about the land and its use. The Labour minority on the council have being trying to whip up public support for a plan to keep the land as a council-owned playing field. You attend the council meeting, which is in the evening, prepared for fireworks.

TASK 1 *Write up the council debate and the decision taken, giving the sort of speeches and points of view you would expect on this matter of great local interest. Interested people and local bodies are present in the public gallery of the council chamber, although they are not allowed to speak. It could be a noisy debate.*

TASK 2 *Assuming that the council have accepted the committee's recommendations to sell the land, write a follow-up piece for the following day's edition based on six simulated interviews with townspeople to try to gauge reaction to the council's decision.*

Notes: Your paper, in its editorial voice, might have a partisan attitude to this matter but in reporting it you should try to give a fair account of the debate and avoid comment. The follow-up-piece should give an opportunity for local council tax payers to take the matter further by voicing their views about the council and its decision, either for or against. You could take an imaginary straw poll of people in, say, a shopping precinct to try to get a balance of for and against.

INDUSTRIAL REPORTING means broadly stories to do with jobs and industrial activity, and very often with the relations between unions and managements. Because such reporting needs to be well informed, editors often employ specialist industrial reporters who do nothing else. Such a luxury is seldom available on a small evening paper or weekly and young reporters might find themselves pitched into some local union–management confrontation – a strike for example – where careful organizing of sources and resources is needed and treading on toes avoided if possible.

 **Assignment 10**

Women operatives have downed tools at the local sportswear factory allegedly over the activities of a male foreman who has cut their teabreaks and taken a hard line over holiday and sick-time arrangements. The trouble has lasted three days and the editor wants a wrap-up for page one of the evening paper's main edition, which is three hours away from its last copy deadline.

TASK 1 *In 300 words, list the sources you would need to consult, and the persons you would try to talk to to get to the facts of this sort of* *dispute, and explain how you would go about this to produce copy in the time available.*

TASK 2   *Imagine that in this case you have discovered that:*

(a) *The firm takes the view that the foreman is only doing his job in accordance with company policy.*

(b) *The union have sent in an official negotiator to bring the sides together.*

(c) *There are rumours of a private bust-up between the foreman and the woman shop steward.*

(d) *There is a story in cuttings saying that the company's recent annual figures had a reference to a downturn in sportwear sales.*

(e) *The trouble on the shop floor has been simmering for longer than the company admits, according to workers you have spoken to.*

From what you have discovered, write a 400-word account of the 'tea-break strike', taking care to preserve a balance between sides in what is still an unresolved dispute.

TASK 3   *Write a 200-word ordered account for a national tabloid of what they want to call 'the strike in a teacup'.*

Twenty minutes before copy deadline you are told by the local union that the stoppage has spread to the warehouse staff and van drivers of the company and that they are considering making it official if a meeting being held with the company at that moment fails.

TASK 4   *File a 150-word new intro for your story for your local paper and mark it at the end: 'Subeditors – please lift rest of story as needed.'*

TASK 5   *When you can (your own paper must come first), give the national tabloid an update for your ordered story.*

In mid-afternoon your contact at the factory telephones to say that the women operatives who originally walked out have received dismissal notices from the management and have set up pickets at the factory's two gates.

TASK 6   *Rewrite your 'teabreak strike' story in 600 words for the late edition of your evening paper taking in the later material.*

TASK 7 *When you can, send an updated 200-word rewrite of your story to the national taboid.*

Notes: It does not pay to take sides in an industrial dispute. There is often more to it than meets the eye and a poorly informed, prejudiced account gets editors into trouble. On the other hand, talking to people and careful beavering for information can give the story better context and make it more comprehensible to the readers, especially those in whose area it is taking place.

COURT REPORTING is an important source of news but is bugged with legal restrictions about what a reporter can and cannot do, as the following assignment shows.

Assignment 11

Three local desperadoes have been caught red-handed burgling a house in which an elderly couple are found tied to their beds. The three have already appeared in court before the local magistrates and pleaded not guilty and been remanded in custody (the police having objected to bail) without formal evidence being given apart from that of arrest. You have reported this bare fact, giving their names.

You are told on making your police calls that the full hearing against the three before the magistrates has been fixed for a certain date and that, depending on the evidence, it is likely that they will be committed to stand trial at the Crown Court.

You attend the hearing. After prosecution evidence has been taken the three are remanded on bail to stand trial at the Crown Court for the area.

TASK 1 *Write an account of the hearing giving what the law allows to be given at this stage of the allegations against the three men and the court's decision.*

TASK 2 *Describe in 300 words the legal reasons why your account is written as it is.*

TASK 3 *There is a good deal of public feeling over the case. The three men are well known in the town and someone, having read the local paper account of the hearing, brings a picture into the office of two of the men taken together. You thank them and accept it but do you use it? Explain the reasons for your decision.*

Notes: Legal restrictions on court reporting might seem onerous but they are aimed at giving the accused person a fair trial. These restrictions must be learned and applied. See Harris and Spark, pages 88–120; Crone: *Law and the Media* 3rd Edition (Focal Press, 1995), chapters 9 and 10; McNae: *Essential Law For Journalists* (Butterworths, 1992), Chapters 2–8. Contempt of Court: Crone, Chapter 10; McNae, Chapter 15.

SET-PIECE INTERVIEWS with people in the news can produce readable and often exclusive material for your readers if you plan the interview properly and research the background of the person. Here, your shorthand needs to be good; better still, use a tape recorder if the person does not object. Try to fix a precise time and, above all, arrive promptly – even if the person chooses to turn up late.

Assignment 12

Your interview with a locally born but nationally known actress who has returned to the town to play in a pre-West End production is not going well. She wants to talk about her big roles and the parts she'd like to play. You are looking for something different that will relate with the readers.

TASK 1   *Creating in your own mind a likely biography for the actress, list six questions you would try to ask her on behalf of your readers.*

TASK 2   *Describe how you would try to lead such an interviewee away from her favourite hobby horses.*

TASK 3   *Describe how and where you would research such a person's background.*

Notes: Interviewing successfully is one of the great arts of reporting and a sure-fire route to a good story. Study techniques all you can as soon as you can. See Harris and Spark, pages 36–48; Hennessy, chapters 9 and 13; Hodgson: *Modern Newspaper Practice* 3rd Edition (Focal Press, 1993), pages 15–16.

OFF-BEAT STORIES: Your contacts with people, including through interviews, can sometimes throw up other ideas for stories as well as on the subject you had in mind. Be on the lookout out for them.

Magistrates, councillors and leading business and professional people are often well-known faces in a community. Your contact with them will mostly be on an official level, yet some of their activities can provide offbeat stories outside their official roles which could well fascinate the readers and set them talking.

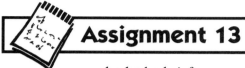

Assignment 13

You go to talk to the new chairman of the magistrates and in the course of the conversation he mentions that in his younger days he had a brief career as a professional music hall comedian.

You ask if he would mind you using this interesting fact and he replies, 'Well, I don't mind really but it's not exactly news, is it?' to which your reply is, 'Well what about a few details for a piece in our People in the News column?'

TASK 1 *Write a 250-word 'diary' piece based on the sort of information the the new chairman of the magistrates might give you on such an occasion.*

TASK 2 *Discuss in 500 words the place of Personal Profiles and Gossip Columns as back-ups to the news and the likely sources of such material.*

Notes: A tuned ear can pick up gems like this from the most unlikely places. Some national papers and magazines pay well for 'gossip' items. See Hennessy, pages 162–76, 213.

READING YOUR OWN NEWSPAPER should be an essential part of your daily routine as a reporter. It gives you the 'feel' of the community it serves; it spells out the style and sort of stories in which your newspaper specializes; it shows the editing and presentation that have been given to your own stories – and it can give you ideas for new stories to follow, or even ideas for new angles on old stories.

Do not forget to include the advertisements when you read your newspaper.

Assignment 14

An advertisement is placed in your newspaper by a local firm for forty machine operatives for their kitchen furniture factory.

With the recession only recently 'bottoming out' you spot the significance of this at once and draw the advertisement to the news editor's attention. Though you are still fairly junior you are rewarded for your sharpness by being sent to cover what looks like a promising news story.

First you check the cuttings files and discover that a year ago the factory was on the point of closing through lack of work. You telephone the manager and he invites you to visit the factory. You find him very willing to talk to you and to let you wander around, and so at the factory you talk to:

1   The factory manager.
2   The shift foreman.
3   A long-serving employee.
4   The newest member of the staff.

To give the story balance you also talk to:

5   The local union secretary.
6   The secretary of the area Chamber of Commerce.
7   The local employment office.

At the latter you find further evidence locally of a rise in job offers. You have taken some useful shorthand notes and are ready to key your story in.

TASK 1   *Creating in your own mind the situation you have uncovered, write a 600-word news story for your evening paper potentially earmarked as a page lead.*

TASK 2   *Explain what pictures you would try to set up to go with the story.*

TASK 3   *Explain briefly any pitfalls you would try to avoid in writing a story of this sort.*

Notes: Spare no effort, in the time you have got, to sew up all the ends in a story of this sort. You do not want to raise false hopes by overstating your case. (Harris and Spark, pages 9–11 news gathering, 15–19 sources, 143–51 industrial reporting).

Assignment 15

You have become an inveterate reader of your own paper. You notice in a routine column of Church Notes that the Rev P. W.

Smith has been inducted into the living of St Jude's, Old Town, in place of the Rev Arthur Jones, who has taken early retirement from the church.

Why does one retire early from a comfortable living like St Jude's? What is the Rev Arthur Jones going to do with his time now that he no longer has the care of the souls of this populous parish to occupy him?

There could be a story here. You find the retiring vicar in the telephone book and ask him if you can have a chat about his plans. He talks freely. There is nothing sinister about his leave-taking – nothing even exciting in the view of the reverend gentleman. He wants more time to work on his great project which is a county history based on a wealth of Saxon and medieval documents that have been lying for centuries in the church archives awaiting scholarly evaluation. He will do part-time parochial duties but, as an expert medievalist, he has been given the church's blessing to bury himself in the manuscripts like the monks of old. Who knows what he will find?

Well, perhaps it is not a great news story, but it is interesting .... Perhaps something else that would make useful material for the paper's People in the News column.

TASK 1 *Write a four-paragraph 'diary' piece about the scholar cleric of Old Town.*

TASK 2 *Discuss briefly what sort of style is needed by a diary or gossip column. Use references to well-known diary columns.*

Notes: Having made friendly contact with the person there is bound to be some circumstance or reference of local interest in the work he is doing that you can discuss and on which you can 'peg' your diary piece – little known facts about the area's history, or connections with characters in history, for example. See Hennessy, chapter 14.

PERIODICALS AND MAGAZINES: The above tasks are based mainly on assignments that reporters are likely to get on weekly and evening papers. Periodicals and some magazines, especially specialist ones, also carry news items. The techniques of news gathering and news writing still apply although the definitions of what is news will vary according to the readership market of each periodical or magazine.

In some cases the range of news carried will be very restricted. A food processing magazine will carry news items to do with food processing, a car magazine items to do with new cars, accessories or methods of maintenance, and so on. The reporter's role, however, is still to examine the new facts and situations that have come to light, to verify them and check the details and to write them up for whatever market is being targeted.

Special aspects will be the amount and depth of detail, often technical detail, that is given, and the degree of technical vocabulary that is acceptable to the reader. These are things that can only be learned by experience and by close study of the magazine or periodical.

 **Assignment 16**

You write a weekly column of news for a car mechanics magazine. This week you have the choice of three items with which to lead the column:

1 A new method of engine tuning.
2 A report on new types of car polishes that have become available.
3 Report on new methods for trapping speeding drivers being tried by police in Somerset or a similarly remote county.

TASK   *Choose from the list a subject you feel you can manage, or on which you feel you have some knowledge, and write a 400-word lead story to your magazine's news section.*

Notes: Handouts and press release material are often the source of this sort of news, but remember that interviews both with experts and users go well alongside information and can bring solid description alive.

 **Assignment 17**

Using knowledge or material from a hobby or favourite subject of your own, imagine a magazine that caters for it and plan the sort of news coverage you would expect it to have.

TASK I   *Write a column of six one-paragaph news-in-briefs ('nibs') likely to be of interest to the magazine's readers.*

TASK 2   *Write a 500-word main news page story for the magazine on a topic of your choice.*

Notes: However technical a news story, as with any other form of reporting, it is essential to apply correct news writing techniques. Give the main fact or facts in the first paragraph, explain and qualify the intro material in the next few paragraphs and thereafter build up the story with quotations and information in descending order of importance.

One paragraph 'briefs', on the other hand, are a tight exercise in which every word counts. Some periodicals and newspapers specify a maximum word or line count, forcing the writer to polish the item word by word to gain the best value from the space and length available.

CHECKLIST FOR REPORTERS

News gathering

Did you:

- Check the cuttings files before leaving for your assignment.
- Double check your briefing from the news editor.
- Arrange check calls with the office while out.
- Arrange appointments in advance by telephone where possible.
- Check that you have with you a notebook, shorthand pencils, tape recorder etc.
- Check your copy deadlines for the various editions.
- Alert the copytakers (if using the telephone) when you expect to come through with copy?

In interviews, did you

- Dress properly.
- Make your credentials properly known to your interviewee.
- Remain courteous even when provoked.
- Take an adequate shorthand note or taped record of the material you want to use (bearing mind that it could be queried)?

News writing

Did you:

- Verify the number of words or column length required.
- Leave a 'correct' note in text for any unusual name spellings.
- Leave a note on screen for the subeditor of anything which you think requires further checking.
- Use the dictionary when in doubt about a spelling.
- Read through your text to spot any ambiguity or lack of clarity.

- Re-read your text against your notes for quotes and names before consigning it to the computer.
- Leave a message of where you can be contacted in the event of copy queries.
- Check the editions in which your story appeared to see what treatment it was given?

REFERENCES AND FURTHER READING:

Bagnall, N: *Newspaper Language* (Focal Press, 1994)

Crone, T: *Law and the Media,* 3rd Edition (Focal Press, 1995).

Dobson, C: *The Freelance Journalist* (Focal Press, 1994)

Harris, G and Spark, D: *Practical Newspaper Reporting,* 2nd Edition (Focal Press, 1993).

Hennessy, B: *Writing Feature Articles,* 2nd Edition (Focal Press, 1993).

Hodgson, FW: *Modern Newspaper Practice,* 3rd Edition (Focal Press,1993).

McNae, LC: *Essential Law for Journalists* (Butterworths, 1992).

2

Feature writing (general)

SINCE features tend to have greater length and complexity, more time needs to be allowed for gathering the material and writing it up than in news reports. The required skills are also more varied. The work is often specialized both in subject and market; feature writers, on top of reporting ability, have to be versed in finding ideas and fitting them to markets, in researching at greater depth, in planning an effective structure and evolving a style for articles that analyse, explain and argue with conviction and readability, and do these things in terms of a targeted readership. (See notes on style and structure on pages 61–3.)

Some young writers find they are better at originating ideas than in building on them, or better at accumulating material than in communicating it effectively. Your first attempts at feature writing will reveal which areas need to be given extra attention.

You will need from the start to adopt a professional attitude: write articles that are aimed at real readers; market study your targets, be they newspapers or magazines, to make sure your topic has not been covered there recently.

Record how long it takes to research and get an article together and compare the work hours with the fee you would expect. Find ways of speeding up tasks that are taking too long. It is a myth to assume that feature writers, with their looser rein, have all the time in the world compared to reporters. Timeliness is of the essence; deadlines must be kept.

The labels given in this book to the various kinds of feature writing assignments are for convenience of presentation. Some will overlap; a particular article may have the elements of several kinds.

```
SUMMARY SHEET FOR ARTICLES

GENERAL

Ref. no./invoice. no.
Author
Title
Number of words
Deadline
Date submitted
Publication aimed at
Published in (with date)


BACKGROUND

Lead
Briefing


RESEARCH

(With addresses, telephone numbers and dates)

Primary sources
Legwork
Interviews by telephone
Interviews (face to face)
Interviews (correspondence)
Original correspondence
Number of questionnaires sent
Number of questionnaires returned
Printed sources

Secondary sources (printed)
Books consulted in libraries
Press cuttings from libraries
Own library and press cuttings
Current newspaper/magazine articles
Campaign literature from organisations
Other publicity materials

Illustrations
Ref. no.
Content/caption
Copyright
Source (if different: e.g. picture agency or publication)
```

Figure 4 Planning that can help – a specimen summary
sheet to go with longer feature articles

Whether you work on the staff of a publication or are being taught feature writing on a course, however, it is the briefing for the feature in hand that counts, be it from your editor or your college tutor. From this must stem your approach and handling of the subject.

An important note on purely writing exercises: students rehashing stories from newspapers or magazines or from press releases as pieces of work for tutors should attach cuttings and relevant sources so that a writing exercise is not made to look like original investigative work. It is a good idea also to include, with any work, a cover sheet listing useful background information such as the source of the idea, the briefing (even if it is your own), research sources and contacts with names and telephone numbers. These are useful for a subeditor trying to settle queries on a feature or for tutors assessing the work.

The summary sheet format on page 26 is somewhat fuller than that recommended by the Royal Society of Arts for NVQs in Journalism but it can be modifed for less complex pieces of work.

BACKGROUNDERS

BACKGROUNDERS or 'current situation' articles are timely features pegged closely to a current event that bear with them something of the urgency of a news report. They may explain the causes of the news event, analyse its implications, predict its consequences. They may go alongside the news item on the page or appear on another page, perhaps with a cross-reference, or they may follow in the next issue.

On local newspapers or in periodicals a backgrounder may follow up a news item on an accident, a disaster, an unusual crime or perhaps some Government legislation that impinges on the community. It might even take the form of a personality piece following the advancement or retirement of an important local figure and will thus qualify under two headings in the assignments that follow.

Assignment 1   A train crashes in your area leaving several people dead and many injured. The reporters have ascertained the main facts and interviewed people on the scene.

TASK   *Provide a 250-word background piece by visiting some of the houses overlooking the track to see what effect the disaster has had on their lives, what impressions they can give of events leading up to the* *disaster, and to what extent the crash has disrupted the lives of the people involved in it.*

Notes: Disasters do not happen to meet your requirements as a student or trainee journalist and so this has to be a simulated 'event' in which your colleagues and fellow students have to do some role-playing. In talking to the 'people' you are probing beyond actualities; looking for opinions, worries, speculation even. For interviewing techniques see Hennessy: *Writing Feature Articles* 2nd Edition (Focal Press, 1993), chapters 9 and 13 and 162–76, and Harris and Spark: *Practical Newspaper Reporting* (Focal Press), pages 36–48.

Assignment 2

A new garden tool factory opens on the outskirts of your town. Your paper has reported the main facts including what it is likely to do for employment in the area.

TASK   *Provide a 350-word follow-up feature for the paper's next issue based on an interview with the managing director giving his/her impressions of the area, his/her own view of the factory's potential and items of general and local interest about their products.*

Notes: Very much a personality piece in which atmosphere and description can interlace with information. As a student, you need a good 'simulated' managing director for this one. See Hennessy and Harris and Spark (as above) on interviewing.

Assignment 3

Backgrounders in consumer magazines and the national tabloids will sometimes present complex national issues in human terms by looking at the effects of legislation through interviews, examples and anecdotes. An article in the magazine *Time Out*, for example, looked at the way, in its view, Londoners were suffering from the effects of the Government's health reforms. Borrow this idea and set it in the context of the readers of your local paper.

TASK 1   *After checking carefully through newspaper cuttings files, or the files maintained by your course, on the Government's recent health reforms, set up local interviews with, say, two doctors and two nurses, or other knowledgeable medical personnel (explaining that* *you are carrying out a student exercise) and write a 600-word backgrounder on the way reforms in the health service have affected your local area.*

TASK 2 *Alternatively (or as well as), check through recent newspaper cuttings on any controversial local council decision reported in the press, set up interviews with people involved or affected by it, and write a 600-word backgrounder on local reaction to the decision.*

Notes: The idea of this assignment is to produce a follow-up backgrounder by gathering information and interviewing people involved in an actual rather than a simulated event until you have enough material to produce a feature which will cast light on or demonstrate reaction to a situation. Task 2 might be easier to set up.

Points to watch:

1 Beware of drawing weighty conclusions from too little evidence.
2 Be prepared to admit that on the basis of what you have found opinion appears to be divided.
3 Let the evidence you gather form the basis of the conclusion (rather than bend the conclusion to support a preconceived idea).

Assignment 4

Several policemen were charged during 1994 with assaulting members of the public. Among them was a widely covered case of a constable who slapped the face of a 14-year-old boy who tormented old people by ringing doorbells. The constable was fined £100 and ordered to pay the teenager £50 compensation. Find similar cases from files and cuttings noting both the official police view and public reaction. Talk to at least two interviewees, including a senior police officer, to get opposing viewpoints.

TASK *Write a 1000-word article aimed at a broadsheet Sunday feature page considering whether the police code of conduct in these matters needs to be relaxed.*

Notes: Avoid oversimplifying this complex question. Explain clearly where the limits are drawn in police behaviour and the reasoning behind them. Help readers to see all sides of the argument, but help them also to make up their own minds.

SPIN-OFFS/FOLLOW-UPS

WHETHER you are a staff or freelance journalist, you should be on the lookout for spin-off or follow-up features from material you have gathered and used as a feature writer. Some specific aspect might warrant being developed for an entirely different market.

For students and trainee journalists it is difficult to exploit this side of feature writing but it is useful, as an exercise, to take a published feature and inject new material into it to re-angle it as for a different publication – provided that it remains a student exercise and that your source material is clearly identified.

Assignment 5

Take a published feature from your local paper which you think could be adapted or developed for a consumer magazine, and:

TASK 1 *Write a 500-word article for the publication you have in mind incorporating suitable new material.*

TASK 2 *Explain in 200 words why you think your idea is suitable for the market chosen.*

TASK 3 *List the sources you have used to rework the feature, including legwork and interviewing.*

Notes: This could be a model for a variety of spin-off and follow-up feature exercises and is useful marketing practice for intending freelances.

Assignment 6

A reverse form of spin-off is one that has its origins in a more general article, perhaps in a national paper or magazine. Assume you have seen a piece in *The Guardian* of the causes on truancy. You decide to look into truancy in your local paper's area.

TASK 1 *Explain in 200 words how you would go about creating such a feature, the sources you would use and the angles you would look for, and also ideas for illustration.*

TASK 2   *Write a 600-word feature using the material you have turned up, aimed for use in your local paper.*

Notes: Again, a useful model and one easy to set up for those on courses since there is no need for simulation. Provided your approach is right most organizations are sympathetic to students working on projects for the class or college magazine. See Hennessy, pages on marketing, chapters 2 and 13; also Davis: *Magazine Journalism Today* (Focal Press, 1992) pages 44–5.

INTERVIEW FEATURES AND PROFILES

UNLIKE reporting in which interest in an interviewee is usually short-lived, the feature interview in its various forms requires a good deal of planning and concentration.

A news angle on which an interview is pegged – the opening of a play, publication of a book, escape from death, release from prison, etc. – will give a good start but even in these areas people come in all sorts and types. There are the rude and difficult, the ebullient talkers, the publicity seekers, the shrinking violets, the suspicious of the press.

Different people – and indeed different purposes – require different text formats. Most common is quotes embedded in a descriptive/expository text with parts summarized in indirect speech. This is the normal format for the rounded portrait or profile.

Some feature interviews are edited into one long quote with a stand-first giving the main facts about the interviewee and setting the scene. The more formal questions-and-answers format is suitable for interviews focusing on argument rather than personality.

Whatever the format, the questions should reflect what the reader of that particular publication will want to know. It is best for interviewers to see themselves as being there on the readers' behalf. And it is the subject's views that are wanted, not the interviewer's.

It is important to research the interviewee's background thoroughly before the interview and to plan at least the main questions, mixing leading questions with open-ended ones such as, 'What do you think of...?'

Some interviewers prefer to let the subject talk away with just a few signposts on the route. This can produce unexpected gems but can land the journalist with a mountain of tape to edit. The best advice is for the interviewer to be prepared to be flexible to suit the occasion and the time available. It is also important to agree at the interview which answers are to be off the record.

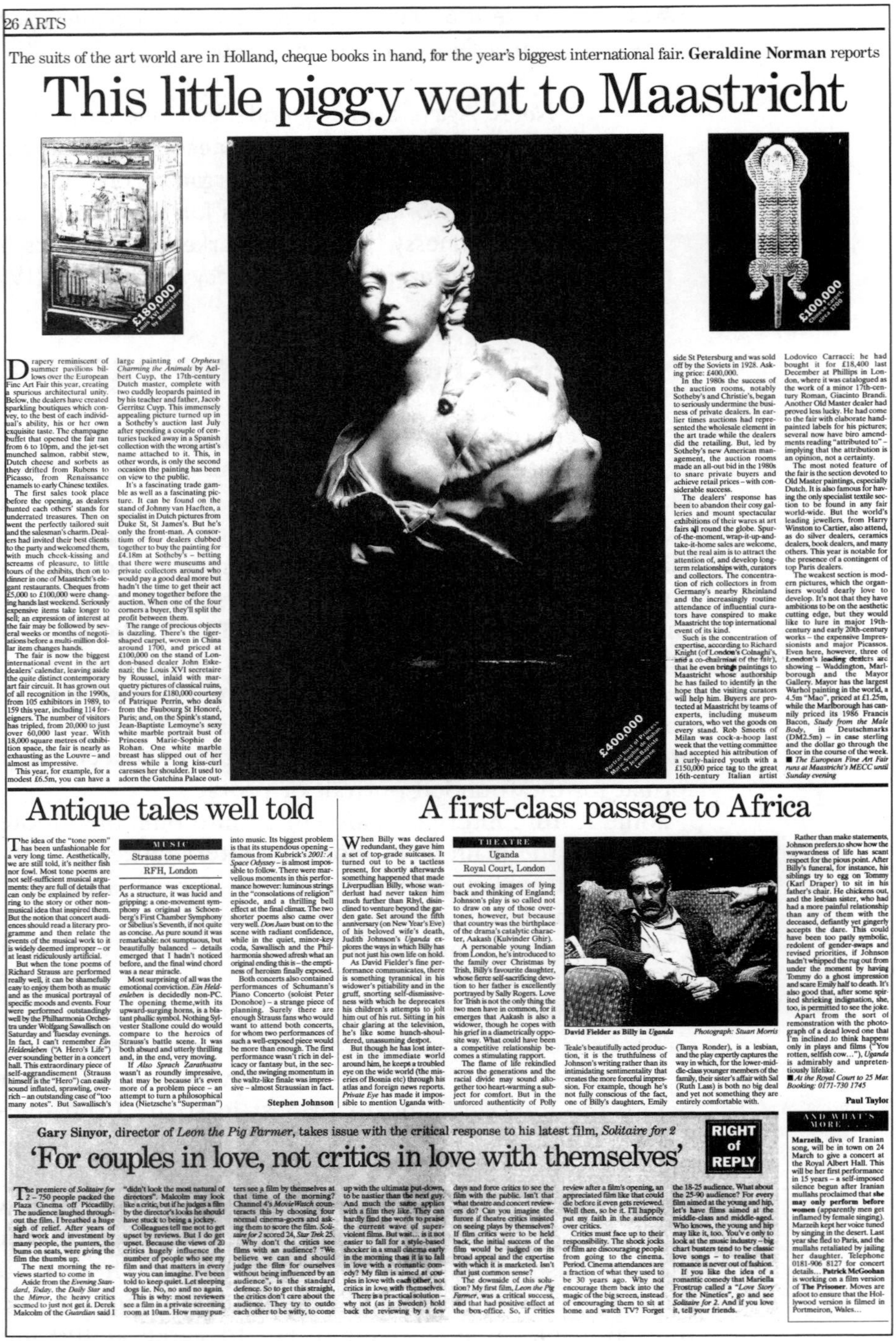

26 ARTS

The suits of the art world are in Holland, cheque books in hand, for the year's biggest international fair. **Geraldine Norman** reports

This little piggy went to Maastricht

£180,000 Louis XVI secretaire by Roussel

£400,000

£100,000 Chinese carpet, circa 1700

Drapery reminiscent of summer pavilions billows over the European Fine Art Fair this year, creating a spurious architectural unity. Below, the dealers have created sparkling boutiques which convey, to the best of each individual's ability, his or her own exquisite taste. The champagne buffet that opened the fair ran from 6 to 10pm, and the jet-set munched salmon, rabbit stew, Dutch cheese and sorbets as they drifted from Rubens to Picasso, from Renaissance enamels to early Chinese textiles.

The first sales took place before the opening, as dealers hunted each others' stands for underrated treasures. Then on went the perfectly tailored suit and the salesman's charm. Dealers had invited their best clients to the party and welcomed them, with much cheek-kissing and screams of pleasure, to little tours of the exhibits, then on to dinner in one of Maastricht's elegant restaurants. Cheques from £5,000 to £100,000 were changing hands last weekend. Seriously expensive items take longer to sell; an expression of interest at the fair may be followed by several weeks or months of negotiations before a multi-million dollar item changes hands.

The fair is now the biggest international event in the art dealers' calendar, leaving aside the quite distinct contemporary art fair circuit. It has grown out of all recognition in the 1990s, from 105 exhibitors in 1989, to 159 this year, including 114 foreigners. The number of visitors has tripled, from 20,000 to just over 60,000 last year. With 18,000 square metres of exhibition space, the fair is nearly as exhausting as the Louvre – and almost as impressive.

This year, for example, for a modest £6.5m, you can have a large painting of *Orpheus Charming the Animals* by Aelbert Cuyp, the 17th-century Dutch master, complete with two cuddly leopards painted in by his teacher and father, Jacob Gerritsz Cuyp. This immensely appealing picture turned up in a Sotheby's auction last July after spending a couple of centuries tucked away in a Spanish collection with the wrong artist's name attached to it. This, in other words, is only the second occasion the painting has been on view to the public.

It's a fascinating trade gamble as well as a fascinating picture. It can be found on the stand of Johnny van Haeften, a specialist in Dutch pictures from Duke St, St James's. But he's only the front-man. A consortium of four dealers clubbed together to buy the painting for £4.18m at Sotheby's – betting that there were museums and private collectors around who would pay a good deal more but hadn't the time to get their act and money together before the auction. When one of the four corners a buyer, they'll split the profit between them.

The range of precious objects is dazzling. There's the tiger-shaped carpet, woven in China around 1700, and priced at £100,000 on the stand of London-based dealer John Eskenazi; the Louis XVI secretaire by Roussel, inlaid with marquetry pictures of classical ruins, and yours for £180,000 courtesy of Patrique Perrin, who deals from the Faubourg St Honoré, Paris; and, on the Spink's stand, Jean-Baptiste Lemoyne's sexy white marble portrait bust of Princess Marie-Sophie de Rohan. One white marble breast has slipped out of her dress while a long kiss-curl caresses her shoulder. It used to adorn the Gatchina Palace outside St Petersburg and was sold off by the Soviets in 1928. Asking price: £400,000.

In the 1980s the success of the auction rooms, notably Sotheby's and Christie's, began to seriously undermine the business of private dealers. In earlier times auctions had represented the wholesale element in the art trade while the dealers did the retailing. But, led by Sotheby's new American management, the auction rooms made an all-out bid in the 1980s to snare private buyers and achieve retail prices – with considerable success.

The dealers' response has been to abandon their cosy galleries and mount spectacular exhibitions of their wares at art fairs all round the globe. Spur-of-the-moment, wrap-it-up-and-take-it-home sales are welcome, but the real aim is to attract the attention of, and develop long-term relationships with, curators and collectors. The concentration of rich collectors in from Germany's nearby Rheinland and the increasingly routine attendance of influential curators have conspired to make Maastricht the top international event of its kind.

Such is the concentration of expertise, according to Richard Knight (of London's Colnaghi's, and a co-chairman of the fair), that he even brings paintings to Maastricht whose authorship he has failed to identify in the hope that the visiting curators will help him. Buyers are protected at Maastricht by teams of experts, including museum curators, who vet the goods on every stand. Rob Smeets of Milan was cock-a-hoop last week that the vetting committee had accepted his attribution of a curly-haired youth with a £150,000 price tag to the great 16th-century Italian artist Lodovico Carracci: he had bought it for £18,400 last December at Phillips in London, where it was catalogued as the work of a minor 17th-century Roman, Giacinto Brandi. Another Old Master dealer had proved less lucky. He had come to the fair with elaborate hand-painted labels for his pictures; several now have biro amendments reading "attributed to" – implying that the attribution is an opinion, not a certainty.

The most noted feature of the fair is the section devoted to Old Master paintings, especially Dutch. It is also famous for having the only specialist textile section to be found in any fair world-wide. But the world's leading jewellers, from Harry Winston to Cartier, also attend, as do silver dealers, ceramics dealers, book dealers, and many others. This year is notable for the presence of a contingent of top Paris dealers.

The weakest section is modern pictures, which the organisers would dearly love to develop. It's not that they have ambitions to be on the aesthetic cutting edge, but they would like to lure in major 19th-century and early 20th-century works – the expensive Impressionists and major Picassos. Even here, however, three of London's leading dealers are showing – Waddington, Marlborough and the Mayor Gallery. Mayor has the largest Warhol painting in the world, a 4.5m "Mao", priced at £1.25m, while the Marlborough has cannily priced its 1986 Francis Bacon, *Study from the Male Body*, in Deutschmarks (DM2.5m) – in case sterling and the dollar go through the floor in the course of the week.

■ *The European Fine Art Fair runs at Maastricht's MECC until Sunday evening*

Antique tales well told

MUSIC

Strauss tone poems

RFH, London

The idea of the "tone poem" has been unfashionable for a very long time. Aesthetically, we are still told, it's neither fish nor fowl. Most tone poems are not self-sufficient musical arguments: they are full of details that can only be explained by referring to the story or other non-musical idea that inspired them. But the notion that concert audiences should read a literary programme and then relate the events of the musical work to it is widely deemed improper – or at least ridiculously artificial.

But when the tone poems of Richard Strauss are performed really well, it can be shamefully easy to enjoy them both as music and as the musical portrayal of specific moods and events. Four were performed outstandingly well by the Philharmonia Orchestra under Wolfgang Sawallisch on Saturday and Tuesday evenings. In fact, I can't remember *Ein Heldenleben* ("A Hero's Life") ever sounding better in a concert hall. This extraordinary piece of self-aggrandisement (Strauss himself is the "Hero") can easily sound inflated, sprawling, over-rich – an outstanding case of "too many notes". But Sawallisch's performance was exceptional. As a structure, it was lucid and gripping: a one-movement symphony as original as Schoenberg's First Chamber Symphony or Sibelius's Seventh, if not quite as concise. As pure sound it was remarkable: not sumptuous, but beautifully balanced – details emerged that I hadn't noticed before, and the final wind chord was a near miracle.

Most surprising of all was the emotional conviction. *Ein Heldenleben* is decidedly non-PC. The opening theme,with its upward-surging horns, is a blatant phallic symbol. Nothing Sylvester Stallone could do would compare to the heroics of Strauss's battle scene. It was both absurd and utterly thrilling and, in the end, very moving.

If *Also Sprach Zarathustra* wasn't as roundly impressive, that may be because it's even more of a problem piece – an attempt to turn a philosophical idea (Nietzsche's "Superman") into music. Its biggest problem is that its stupendous opening – famous from Kubrick's *2001: A Space Odyssey* – is almost impossible to follow. There were marvellous moments in this performance however: luminous strings in the "consolations of religion" episode, and a thrilling bell effect at the final climax. The two shorter poems also came over very well. *Don Juan* bust on to the scene with radiant confidence, while in the quiet, minor-key coda, Sawallisch and the Philharmonia showed afresh what an original ending this is – the emptiness of heroism finally exposed.

Both concerts also contained performances of Schumann's Piano Concerto (soloist Peter Donohoe) – a strange piece of planning. Surely there are enough Strauss fans who would want to attend both concerts, for whom two performances of such a well-exposed piece would be more than enough. The first performance wasn't rich in delicacy or fantasy but, in the second, the swinging momentum in the waltz-like finale was impressive – almost Straussian in fact.

Stephen Johnson

A first-class passage to Africa

THEATRE

Uganda

Royal Court, London

When Billy was declared redundant, they gave him a set of top-grade suitcases. It turned out to be a tactless present, for shortly afterwards something happened that made Liverpudlian Billy, whose wanderlust had never taken him much further than Rhyl, disinclined to venture beyond the garden gate. Set around the fifth anniversary (on New Year's Eve) of his beloved wife's death, Judith Johnson's *Uganda* explores the ways in which Billy has put not just his own life on hold.

As David Fielder's fine performance communicates, there is something tyrannical in his widower's pitiability and in the gruff, snorting self-dismissiveness with which he deprecates his children's attempts to jolt him out of his rut. Sitting in his chair glaring at the television, he's like some hunch-shouldered, unassuming despot.

But though he has lost interest in the immediate world around him, he keeps a troubled eye on the wide world (the miseries of Bosnia etc) through his atlas and foreign news reports. *Private Eye* has made it impossible to mention Uganda without evoking images of lying back and thinking of England; Johnson's play is so called not to draw on any of those overtones, however, but because that country was the birthplace of the drama's catalytic character, Aakash (Kulvinder Ghir).

A personable young Indian from London, he's introduced to the family over Christmas by Trish, Billy's favourite daughter, whose fierce self-sacrificing devotion to her father is excellently portrayed by Sally Rogers. Love for Trish is not the only thing the two men have in common, for it emerges that Aakash is also a widower, though he copes with his grief in a diametrically opposite way. What could have been a competitive relationship becomes a stimulating rapport.

The flame of life rekindled across the generations and the racial divide may sound altogether too heart-warming a subject for comfort. But in the unforced authenticity of Polly

David Fielder as Billy in *Uganda* *Photograph: Stuart Morris*

Teale's beautifully acted production, it is the truthfulness of Johnson's writing rather than its intimidating sentimentality that creates the more forceful impression. For example, though he's not fully conscious of the fact, one of Billy's daughters, Emily (Tanya Ronder), is a lesbian, and the play expertly captures the way in which, for the lower-middle-class younger members of the family, their sister's affair with Sal (Ruth Lass) is both no big deal and yet not something they are entirely comfortable with.

Rather than make statements, Johnson prefers to show how the waywardness of life has scant respect for the pious point. After Billy's funeral, for instance, his siblings try to egg on Tommy (Karl Draper) to sit in his father's chair. He chickens out, and the lesbian sister, who had had a more painful relationship than any of them with the deceased, defiantly yet gingerly accepts the dare. This could have been too patly symbolic, redolent of gender-swaps and revised priorities, if Johnson hadn't whipped the rug out from under the moment by having Tommy do a ghost impression and scare Emily half to death. It's also good that, after some spirited shrieking indignation, she, too, is permitted to see the joke.

Apart from the sort of remonstration with the photograph of a dead loved one that I'm inclined to think happens only in plays and films ("You rotten, selfish cow…"), *Uganda* is admirably and unpretentiously lifelike.

■ *At the Royal Court to 25 Mar. Booking: 0171-730 1745*

Paul Taylor

Gary Sinyor, director of *Leon the Pig Farmer*, takes issue with the critical response to his latest film, *Solitaire for 2*

'For couples in love, not critics in love with themselves'

RIGHT of REPLY

The premiere of *Solitaire for 2* – 750 people packed the Plaza Cinema off Piccadilly. The audience laughed throughout the film. I breathed a huge sigh of relief. After years of hard work and investment by many people, the punters, the bums on seats, were giving the film the thumbs up.

The next morning the reviews started to come in

Aside from the *Evening Standard*, *Today*, the *Daily Star* and the *Mirror*, the heavy critics seemed to just not get it. Derek Malcolm of the *Guardian* said I "didn't look the most natural of directors". Malcolm may look like a critic, but if he judges a film by the director's looks he should have stuck to being a jockey.

Colleagues tell me not to get upset by reviews. But I do get upset. Because the views of 20 critics hugely influence the number of people who see my film and that matters in every way you can imagine. I've been told to keep quiet. Let sleeping dogs lie. No, no and no again.

This is why: most reviewers see a film in a private screening room at 10am. How many punters see a film by themselves at that time of the morning? Channel 4's *MovieWatch* counteracts this by choosing four normal cinema-goers and asking them to score the film. *Solitaire for 2* scored 24, *Star Trek* 25.

Why don't the critics see films with an audience? "We believe we can and should judge the film for ourselves without being influenced by an audience", is the standard defence. So to get this straight, the critics don't care about the audience. They try to outdo each other to be witty, to come up with the ultimate put-down, to be nastier than the next guy. And much the same applies with a film they like. They can hardly find the words to praise the current wave of super-violent films. But wait… is it not easier to fall for a style-based shocker in a small cinema early in the morning than it is to fall in love with a romantic comedy? My film is aimed at couples in love with each other, not critics in love with themselves.

There is a practical solution – why not (as in Sweden) hold back the reviewing by a few days and force critics to see the film with the public. Isn't that what theatre and concert reviewers do? Can you imagine the furore if theatre critics insisted on seeing plays by themselves? If film critics were to be held back, the initial success of the film would be judged on its broad appeal and the expertise with which it is marketed. Isn't that just common sense?

The downside of this solution? My first film, *Leon the Pig Farmer*, was a critical success, and that had positive effect at the box-office. So, if critics review after a film's opening, an appreciated film like that could die before it even gets reviewed. Well then, so be it. I'll happily put my faith in the audience over critics.

Critics must face up to their responsibility. The shock jocks of film are discouraging people from going to the cinema. Period. Cinema attendances are a fraction of what they used to be 30 years ago. Why not encourage them back into the magic of the big screen, instead of encouraging them to sit at home and watch TV? Forget the 18-25 audience. What about the 25-90 audience? For every film aimed at the young and hip, let's have films aimed at the middle-class and middle-aged. Who knows, the young and hip may like it, too. You've only to look at the music industry – big chart busters tend to be classic love songs – to realise that romance is never out of fashion.

If you like the idea of a romantic comedy that Mariella Frostrup called a "*Love Story* for the Nineties", go and see *Solitaire for 2*. And if you love it, tell your friends.

AND WHAT'S MORE . . .

Marzeih, diva of Iranian song, will be in town on 24 March to give a concert at the Royal Albert Hall. This will be her first performance in 15 years – a self-imposed silence begun after Iranian mullahs proclaimed that **she may only perform before women** (apparently men get inflamed by female singing). Marzeih kept her voice tuned by singing in the desert. Last year she fled to Paris, and the mullahs retaliated by jailing her daughter. Telephone 0181-906 8127 for concert details… **Patrick McGoohan** is working on a film version of **The Prisoner**. Moves are afoot to ensure that the Hollywood version is filmed in Portmeiron, Wales…

Figure 5 Up-market features page style – an example from *The Independent*

CELEBRITIES, whether national or local, provide plum material for journalist interviewers but celebrities are hard to come by for student or trainee journalists.

Here is one way in which the handling of celebrity material can be tried.

Assignment 7

Collect and file over a given period of newspaper and magazine interviews with a number of celebrities – Richard Branson, Sir John Gielgud, Salman Rushdie and Elton John are examples, but choose your own. Consult the *British Humanities Index* or similar and collect and file cuttings of your own about your chosen names. Note the questions asked in interviews and the sort of information revealed. Note interviewers who seem to bring out the boring and the stereotyped and those who bring out new or interesting material. Where possible seek material from agents and publicists, mentioning that you are engaged on a student project.

TASK 1   *Write a 600-word scissors-and-paste story, based on published interviews, about one of the celebrities you have chosen aimed at the readers of a popular magazine.*

TASK 2   *Take three of the celebrities you have chosen and list the contacts (agents, press officers, film companies, etc.) you would use to try to obtain an interview in each case. List ten questions you would ask each of the celebrities.*

Notes: By this means you at least get some way inside their lives and can formulate the approach you would take if you were conducting an actual interview. But beware of stealing other writers' work; such projects are strictly for student use only.

Assignment 8

Showbusiness people and authors are good subjects but they plan their publicity carefully and are fussy about which publication an interview appears in. For the purposes of these assignments they are on the whole unapproachable, but it is quite possible that a student or trainee journalist, combing through the people they have met or are connected with, will find they know someone who acts, sings or writes books, or has celebrity status of some sort.

It is possible that such a person will be happy to be chosen as a subject and will be pleased to oblige if they know it is a student project. It is worth a try.

TASK 1   *Write a 600-word interview with a celebrity you know as if it were to appear in The Guardian newspaper.*

TASK 2   *Write up the interview at the same length as if it were to appear in The Sun.*

TASK 3   *Write up your material a third time and aim it for use in your college magazine.*

Notes: It is a good idea to look at several issues of each publication chosen to study the style, the sort of slant usually taken and to try to assess the readership market. The arts section in *The Guardian* and the showbiz pages in *The Sun* are two different worlds, while a college magazine with a different readership again, might provide some useful local leads and angles, not to say 'in' references.

Assignment 9

As a likely route to interviews with real persons, choose one of the following five people in your area (i.e., the one to whom you can most likely gain access) as an interview subject:

1   A Church of England minister who is against women clergy.
2   An AIDS patient who has contracted the disease from a lover.
3   A GP who has views on the over-prescription of tranquillizers by the profession.
4   A geriatric nurse willing to talk about mistreatment of elderly patients in homes.
5   A school teacher willing to talk about how the National Curriculum could be improved.

TASK 1   *Conduct an interview with your chosen person and write a 500-word feature module aimed at forming part of a larger investigation into the subject.*

TASK 2   *List ten questions you have asked your interviewee on the chosen subject.*

TASK 3   *Explain in about 600 words the sort of questions you would expect to have asked the other four interviewees.*

Notes: This assignment contains both the possibility of an actual interview (those on courses would have to stress it is for a student project) and the opportunity of planning questions for interviews dealing with specific subjects — i.e., rather than personal profiles.

Assignment 10

A useful **personal profile** interview could be set up like this: Choose someone you know only as a colleague or classmate but who is willing to be a subject. Formulate questions that go further than the obvious and build up from the answers a picture of the real person within. Supplement your questions and answers with some discreet inquiries among friends and colleagues of your subject.

TASK 1   *Using selected interview material and supplementary sources, write a 600-word personal profile aimed at a college or course magazine.*

TASK 2   *Go through the same process in reverse with yourself as the subject.*

Notes: This sort of interview could be duplicated endlessly with each student or trainee in turn becoming a guinea pig, spreading around the experience. A useful spin-off result could be the publication of a selection of the profiles in the college magazine or student newspaper.

Assignment 11

Choose as an interview subject an expert practitioner of one of the less common sports such as archery, croquet, royal tennis, hang gliding or snorkelling and fortify yourself with a book on the sport.

TASK 1   *Write a 500-word 'what makes them tick' piece based on your interview material and aimed at a local paper's sports page.*

TASK 2   *Explain briefly any special points you would have to keep in mind in interviewing for the sports page and the sort of information you would try to bring out from your practitioner.*

Notes: Another interview project that can be done with real subjects. It would be worth seeking the co-operation of the local paper's editor to try to get an arrangement for the best to be published.

Assignment 12

The comic and the odd can be exploited in an interview feature if you have the right sort of person. Such interviews are easier than most to set up since those doing out-of-the ordinary things are often quite happy to talk about themselves. Select one (or two) of the following, if they are willing:

◊   A much tattooed person.
◊   An ageing punk rocker.
◊   A steeplejack.
◊   A collector of garden gnomes.
◊   A snake lover.
◊   A dude cowboy.

TASK 1   *Write a 600-word interview feature on one (or two) of the above characters aimed at a popular magazine.*

TASK 2   *Explain in 300 words the approach you would take and the sort of questions you would ask of the person(s) you have chosen.*

Notes: With such characters avoid at all costs making fun of them. Your aim is to get the person's confidence in the hope that an unusual interview will result.

SEASONAL FEATURES

FEATURES pegged to the season or time of the year, including anniversaries, are always in demand and are a lucrative source of income for freelances. Dates of murders, disasters, inventions, births, deaths... the list is endless, as is the parade of activities and events through spring, summer, autumn and winter that give timeliness to many a features page.

The trick for the young freelance is to come up with something new, or with a new angle on the familiar. Remember, however, to come up with your idea in good time. Newspapers might work a few days ahead on their features pages but with magazines you have to suit the gestation period of the one you choose. There is many a Christmas number that has been set up in September.

Good tip: the active freelance keeps a folder of cuttings and other materials supporting seasonal ideas – perhaps a concertina file with a pocket for each month.

Assignment 13

School, university and careers provide landmarks in young lives. Select one of the following subjects and work out ideas for a seasonal feature:

◇ Starting primary school.
◇ Starting secondary school.
◇ Starting university.
◇ Starting work.

TASK 1   *Write a 600-word feature aimed at your local evening paper.*

TASK 2   *Write a 1,000-word feature aimed at a general interest magazine.*

TASK 3   *Select a second subject from the four and repeat tasks 1 and 2.*

Notes: Back to school/university articles, as well as a number of other seasonal subjects, have an added draw for editors in that they encourage seasonal advertising – not a thing to be sneezed at if you are trying to sell an article. Remember, however, that writing an independent feature is quite a different thing from writing, or contributing to, an advertising feature in which you might be expected to mention certain merchandise.

Assignment 14

File and study cuttings of seasonal features in a variety of publications on the following subjects: seasonal shop sales, the summer holidays, Easter and Christmas.

TASK 1   *Write 800 words on how you would go about finding something new to say, and ideas you would want to try, if asked to write on these subjects.*

TASK 2   *Think up an idea on a seasonal theme – as original as you can make it – and write a 700-word piece aimed at the week-end magazine page of your local evening paper.*

Notes: This can be the fun side of earning a living for a freelance but real ingenuity is called for. It is too easy to look at Christmas and spring-cleaning through jaded eyes. Find some fresh information or a new way of approaching the familar, although solid information needs to be given to the reader, too.

Assignment 15

Bank Holiday Monday is the occasion for some dotty, publicity-seeking and sometimes dangerous events. You see an advert: 'Wakehurst Gliding Club is holding its annual charity day for Mencap. There will be trial flights for £20 – free if you raise £50 in sponsorship...'

TASK   *Find out what odd or unusual events are being arranged for May or August Bank Holiday in your area and write a 600-word 'silly season' feature about them aimed at your local paper.*

Notes: Light-hearted or fun pieces are welcome at holiday times – known in newspaper offices as the silly season – and here is a subject you could really stretch yourself on. But beware again of making fun of people who are genuinely doing their bit for a needy charity. Let the bizarre or the unusual speak for itself.

Assignment 16

The following anniversaries have been selected from *Chambers Dictionary of Dates*:

28 January, 1596: Death of Sir Francis Drake at sea from dysentery.
15 May, 1895: Death of Joseph Whitaker, founder of *Whitaker's Almanack*.
19 May, 1795: Death of James Boswell, biographer of Dr Johnson.
14 May, 1895: The first stage knighthood conferred on Henry Irving.
24 June, 1895: World heavyweight champion Jack Dempsey born in Manassa, Colorado.
11 September, 1895: The original FA Cup stolen from the window display of a shop in Newton Row, Birmingham.

TASK 1   *Suggest in 200 words for each date your idea for a 600-word feature targeted at a particular publication. Say what research you would do. Include one person you would try to interview by telephone. Say why you have chosen the particular publication.*

TASK 2   *Select one date and write a 600-word feature as targeted.*

Notes: You need more than just history and anecdotes for this sort of feature article. The best idea is to link the anniversary to a contemporary topic or event or to find some means of casting new light on the original event. Such features are often much used in mass-circulation publications so if your feature is aimed at one of these be sure your style and content are correctly geared.

OPINION PIECES

OPINION and comment can be found in most newspaper and magazine features but there are specific types of features – the leader or editorial opinion is one – in which the writer's main aim is to promote or support an idea or to build the whole text round an opinion.

The writer has perhaps been given rein to be controversial, or is noted for his/her forthright views. A 'think piece' in a contrasting voice can boost a publication's claim to be independent. Often, the idea is to set people talking and create feedback in the form of readers' letters. See Hennessy, chapter 5 on themes and chapter 11 on writing techniques.

 **Assignment 17**

The following leader appears in your local paper:

'Collective worship should be carried out daily in schools. That was given the force of law by the 1944 Education Act. Yet head teachers are almost unanimously of the opinion that morning assembly should be a matter for the discretion of individual schools.

Religious education teaching, they argue, including study of the world's major faiths, ensures that Christianity continues to enjoy a dominant role. But we believe that assemblies are the only way children will experience the benefits of worship, and that they are necessary for a full appreciation of Christianity. Parents will keep their right to withdraw their children from such assemblies if they are against their principles. But the Government should be supported in this.'

Read this carefully and tackle the following tasks:

TASK 1   *Describe what inquiries you would make to provide facts and background to help you.*

TASK 2   *Adopting broadly the style of the leader, write one of a similar length taking an alternative view of the subject.*

Notes: With an editorial opinion there is seldom room for sitting on the fence. What the reader expects to see – and what the editor requires – is the newspaper's policy firmly spelt out. You are the persuader, even if the opinions to which you are giving word do not entirely coincide with your own.

Assignment 18

Your weekly paper is running a news story saying that the Tory-run Catewoodham district council, in the wake of increased burglaries and muggings, have decided to establish uniformed community safety patrols in the town. They will be in marked vehicles with radios. Exact powers have yet to be decided but the patrols will probably be able to make citizens' arrests. It is estimated that it will add £25 to each householder's annual tax. Police chiefs are for it but Labour councillors are against it. Your paper supports the idea.

TASK 1   *Write a 200-word leader in favour of the council's proposal. It is needed in 40 minutes for the edition. Try to stick to this deadline; it is how leaders are born.*

TASK 2   *You are appalled at the idea and you also secretly write a 200-word leader opposing it.*

Notes: Either way you need to adopt a punchy approach to what is a controversial scheme. Be prepared to put up good reasons and arguments.

Assignment 19

Consider the following arguments suggesting that the Commonwealth is more important to Britain than is the EEC:

1   We have snubbed the Commonwealth since joining the EEC.

2   There are historic links with Britain that make the Common-
    wealth uniquely strong.
3   The Commonwealth has been turning against us since its
    members have had independence.
4   The Commonwealth countries are now grown up and are no
    longer suspicious of hidden imperialistic motives in our relation-
    ship.
5   The most rapidly growing economies in the Commonwealth are
    its Asian members.
6   'The British Commonwealth, with about a billion and a half
    people largely concentrated in areas of high potential growth, is
    a brilliant twenty-first century concept' – Lord Rees-Mogg.

TASK   *Write a 600-word think piece, aimed at a political weekly, outlining
            the argument either for or against strengthening links with the
            Commonwealth.*

            Notes: The think piece does not need the partisanship and
            verbal punch of a leader but it needs nevertheless to be persua-
            sively argued with opposing views and arguments being noted
            and dealt with. It is often effective to begin by standing up the
            opposing argument and then knocking it down or revealing the
            holes in it.

Assignment 20

The following are some of the points made
at the time of writing by people in favour
of decriminalizing soft drugs:

1   Drug seizures are expensive and raise the price of drugs on the
    streets.
2   The seizures do nothing to reduce demand.
3   More than half British teenagers use cannabis and Ecstasy.
4   Alcohol and tobacco would not be legalized if introduced today.
5   Ecstasy-using teenagers will not listen to smoking-and-drinking
    adults who warn them off it.
6   The law does not deter drug users.
7   A *Sunday Times* survey revealed that four out of five chief
    constables are in favour of decriminalization.
8   In the US it is estimated that more than three-quarters of all crime
    is related to illegal drugs.
9   Legalizing drugs would reduce use and control misuse.

TASK 1   Add to each of the above nine points two further sentences incorporating:
(a) The 'but' of it, or reservation or argument against.
(b) Your own off-the-cuff attitude.

TASK 2   Do some selective research through cuttings and reference sources on the nine points and devise a schematic outline for a feature taking into account the points, or those of them you want to use.

TASK 3   Put together a 1000-word opinion piece aimed at a general-interest magazine on your attitude to decriminalizing soft drugs in Britain, whether for or against.

Notes: Drugs is a subject that has wide exposure in the press so you need more than just a mop-up of the current situation to grab the reader. You need a firm point of view, some potent figures and some persuasive writing. More personalized arguments are dealt with in Chapter 3, pages 45–63.

FORMULA AND HOW-TO ARTICLES

AMONG the general features in demand by popular magazines (and a great incentive to freelance beavering) are formula pieces on the lines of 'The World's Biggest...', 'The Truth About...', 'Where Are They Now?', 'A Day in the Life of...' and similar.

A topical peg is still a useful prop upon which to hang such a feature but it is not essential since the reader's expectations are already whetted by the formula title. The essential thing is to go for the mysterious, the bizarre and the unusual and to keep the writing pithy and well paced.

A rival in courting reader attention in this lighter end of the market is the 'How-to' feature: how to improve your love life, your dinner parties, your health, your popularity, your child's behaviour, even your brain power.

Formulas are covered by Hennessy, chapter 4 and how-to articles in chapter 5.

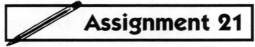
Assignment 21

Consider the title 'Before you Kill Yourself' – once used in a Reader's Digest series – and use it to practise this light-hearted and potentially lucrative side of feature writing.

TASK   *List ten points you want to make under the above title and embody them in a 900-word feature aimed at a popular magazine.*

Notes: See below.

Assignment 22

The 'how to complain' formula has spawned a number of amusing magazine articles and books. Consider the title 'How to Complain about Your Neighbours'.

TASK   *Write a 700-word amusing but slightly barbed feature with this title based on at least one interview and such research as you can carry out.*

Notes: See below.

Assignment 23

'Did You Know?' makes a good potential title for a series of formula features. Some fact in a newspaper or comment in conversation strikes a chord that reminds you of a childhood experience or sets you beavering through reference books for something you half remember. Or it gives you a sudden insight into an aspect of human behaviour. Here is a did-you-know that may do none of these things – but consider it an ingredient of a short formula feature:

'The drumming of the fingers by nervous people boosts blood circulation to the brain by a quarter. This makes for better, more agile minds and improves the memory.'

TASK 1   *Find out more about this assertion and turn it into a 200-word fixed spot magazine feature.*

TASK 2   *Pursuing the medical theme and using the same research sources dig out three more 'did you knows' and write 200 words on each.*

Notes: Formula features like the above ones, often anchored in a fixed regular spot and sometimes accompanied by a line drawing, can make compulsive reading in a popular newspaper or magazine. Whether they are thumbnail ones like Assignment 22 or full length articles they require accurate sourcing, mainly in reference books, and a light compact style.

The writer must be able to pursue ideas through sources, to translate quite technical information into conversational language and to be able to spot oddity and absurdity in unlikely contexts. Above all, where the formula is part of a series the writer must store up ideas or references for future use. A much-liked long-running formula feature can gobble up material.

REFERENCES AND FURTHER READING

Chambers Dictionary of Dates, 2nd Edition (Chambers, 1990).
Davis, A: *Magazine Journalism Today* (Focal Press, 1992)
Harris, G and Spark, D: *Practical Newspaper Reporting*, 2nd Edition (Focal Press, 1994).
Hennessy, B: *Writing Feature Articles*, 2nd Edition (Focal Press, 1993).

3

Feature writing (specialisms)

SPECIALIST writers of one sort or another contribute a large percentage of the features in newspapers and magazines. Many began their careers as reporters or general feature writers and moved for various reasons into writing exclusively on particular subjects – technology, education, politics, aviation, motoring and the like – or particular sorts of features such as arts reviews or specialist columns or the various forms of consumer journalism.

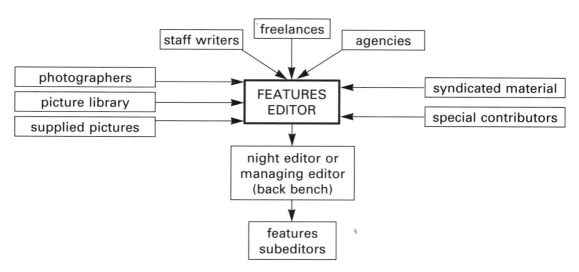

Figure 6 Getting the material together – typical input sources to the features department of a busy newspaper or magazine

Some brought with them into journalism special interests such as cars, sport and the arts; some had already acquired qualifications or had taken a degree in politics or economics or a modern language, or had had previous job experience. In a few cases the writers were already important in such fields as food and drink, astrology and games and hobbies of various sorts and became part-time freelances because their expertise was sought by editors.

Thus one way or another some journalists, often quite early in their careers, become specialists as a result of special interests, qualifications or background. It needs to be said, however, that it is not usually advisable for journalists early in their careers to rely on too narrow a field of interest. See Hennessy, *Writing Feature Articles*, 2nd Edition (Focal Press, 1993), Chapter 18.

The assignments in this chapter look at the world of the specialists and take account of skills and methods of approach in this area of feature writing.

SERVICE COLUMNS

SERVICE columns are reader-based features offering a particular service or information on how to do or buy something, and how to deal with all manner of problems. They can range from buying wine and giving dinner parties to planning holidays, sorting out legal matters and improving one's love life. They cross the board in readership, being found in all types of publications, from the *Financial Times* (investment advice) to popular women's and teenage magazines (fashion advice and 'agony columns').

Many service columns solicit readers' letters, giving advice by post and using some of the letters and answers as themes in the weekly column. Some have legal and medical experts 'sitting in' to provide correct advice to people who are perhaps depending upon the reply they will get and cannot afford to go elsewhere. Name columnists get hundreds of letters a week and might have several secretaries dealing with the mail.

Consumer information features largely in some columns – the best bargains in the sales, the best Christmas presents, things to do for children and seasonal do-it-yourself. Name columnists usually work independently of the advertisers since their 'clout' with their readers depends on their impartiality even though, in merchandising columns, prices, styles and suppliers might be mentioned, and a service column should not be confused with an advertising feature or advertorial in which 'editorial' backing has been guaranteed to advertisers.

Editors generally regard service columns as an important exercise in reader relations and they feature high in sample surveys of most-read newspaper and magazine features. See Hennessy, chapter 5; Davis: *Magazine Journalism Today* (Focal Press, 1992), page 14.

Assignment 24

Imagine you have been asked to contribute a regular weekly eating-out column to a regional paper that serves a wide area including one large town. You are expected to cover three restaurants or other eateries a week, and the editor has said that he does not want 'the usual puffery of local paper restaurant reviews' so you are looking for the unusual and aiming at readability.

TASK 1 *Select for your pilot feature three restaurants or eateries in the circulation area that you think will give you sufficient variety and some good copy and write a 700-word eating-out feature to the above briefing.*

TASK 2 *Explain in 300 words how you would go about selecting restaurants for a regular column and the sort of things you would look for.*

Notes: Food and readability aside, you would need to decide to what extent your choice relates to the readership profile of your nominated paper. Your column is representing the readers' interests. You also need some way in which to rate meals, drinks and service when writing on a regular basis, taking into account the types of eatery chosen.

Assignment 25

Imagine you write a regular weekly consumer column under your name for an evening paper serving a dense conurbation. In response to letters from readers who follow your column you are doing a pre-Christmas issue on the latest video and board games for children.

TASK 1 *Select three of each sort of games and produce an 800-word consumer guide column in the form of a comparative review that will help readers trying to make their choice in this area. Take account of the purpose and price of the games and the target age.*

TASK 2 *Explain in 200 words the sort of precautions and considerations you would take with this sort of column.*

Notes: Remember that in a column like this you are being read because you are the expert. The readers are relying on you and you are representing them, not the retailers. Your comparisons have a critical base.

Students and trainee journalists might find it better to pool setting up the cost of supply in this sort of assignment, unless a friendly store is willing to accept publication of the reviews in a college magazine or newspaper as sufficient recompense for their goods – in which case a sizeable stockist credit would be in order. Some manufacturers might give free samples of products in return for the publicity.

Assignment 26

You are the regular child care writer on a family magazine. This month your theme is travelling with children. In preparing your column you consider the following:

◇   Travelling in taxis and coaches.
◇   Travelling in trains.
◇   Flying with children.
◇   Keeping them amused in the car.
◇   Keeping them amused at airports.
◇   Car picnics.
◇   Books for children.
◇   Games for children.

TASK 1   *Explain in about 400 words the sources you would use for information and guidance.*

TASK 2   *Write an 800-word chatty column aimed at the sort of families who are likely to read your magazine, and include a few 'bewares'.*

Notes: This sort of column must be taken seriously if you are to preserve credibility as an expert, and talks with young mothers with children and with GPs are essential. Make sure you have tested out, or have had tested out, any games you recommend or any medical advice you pass on. Do not forget puzzles, crosswords, I-spy games and quizzes. The simplest ideas are often the most useful.

PERSONAL COLUMNS

THE plum job in the 'writing a column' field is the personal column in which you write because of who you are or because of your individuality of opinion or style rather than because of the subject matter.

Such columns might range from a collection of tart or pertinent comments on current events appended under your by-line in big display type to the 'agony column' liked by teenage magazines and some national tabloids in which advice on love life and teenage spots is doled out to 'Anxious, of Tunbridge Wells' and 'Still Waiting, of Halifax'. Somewhere between the two come the social and occasionally bitchy chit-chat of Messrs Nigel Dempster and Ross Benson, of the *Daily Mail* and *Daily Express* respectively.

'Name' columns might seem a long way ahead for the student or trainee journalist, yet it is always possible that a flair for this sort of writing might come to the notice of your first local editor and you may be allowed to cut your teeth on a trial 'name' column or at least contribute to the sort of diary column some newspapers run under a house name.

Even if you have no intention of becoming a columnist it is a useful art to cultivate and it is a good idea to cut and collect examples of current pundits and practise aiming a column at various markets. The concentration on keeping readers interested and entertained with what you have to say, to put it at its lowest, will develop useful communicating skills.

It could be an earner, too. Some freelances specialize in contributing to various papers' 'diaries' or gossip columns.

There are dangers, of course. Robert Harris, writing in *The Spectator* on 9 April, 1994, said: 'Last week I counted thirty-one regular signed columns in the four broadsheet Sunday newspapers – and that excludes specialist columns on business, sport and the arts... All of them obliged to comment on the same small mound of facts... fewer and fewer journalists discovering facts, more of them passing them back and forth among themselves.'

You can run out of ideas unless you keep a good look-out and a ready-to-hand notebook and keep a lively curiosity about life in many areas. See Hennessy, Chapter 14; Davis, pages 164–5.

 **Assignment 27**

Imagine you write a regular column for your weekly paper and are looking for material for your Wednesday deadline.

TASK 1   *Follow up three subjects that have provoked readers' letters in your local paper in recent weeks (you are The People's Watchdog) and devote about 200 words of pithy, pointed writing to each. Make sure you have something to say.*

TASK 2   *Give yourself a briefing on how you justify to your readers your title of The People's Watchdog, and how you see yourself.*

Notes: This sort of column has to be comment-intensive to attract attention and be quoted while at the same time basing comment on well-researched facts. A reporter who gets a fact wrong might escape attention but not columnists who pride themselves on sticking their necks out.

Assignment 28

You write a monthly Pets Column in a family magazine from the point of view of the countryman who is the animals' friend. You are a well-known lobbyist on behalf of animal rights, though not an aggressive animal libber.

TASK   *Write a 900-word column on the subject of dog behaviour, especially potentially dangerous dogs and our general attitude to dogs. Do some research into the way Kenneth Baker's Dangerous Dogs Act of 1991 is operating, including cases where owners have appealed to the European Court of Human Rights. Be provocative.*

Notes: As with other specialist columns do not underestimate the need to keep your facts and information up to date. Writing regularly on the same subject is the best means of doing this. Cuttings and specialist sources should be carefully monitored. Do not be taken unawares by smart-alec readers. You are only as good as your credibility allows you to be.

Assignment 29

Put yourself in the place of the People in the News columnist of a national quality paper. You monitor the doings and sayings of the famous and comment on them in a column which has become noted for its bite and satire. Your weekly deadline is approaching.

TASK 1   *Scrutinize three quality national papers on a particular day and make notes on four people, in any celebrity field, whose deeds and* *words lend themselves to your special sort of column. Check recent cuttings on each, either through your course cuttings programme or by accessing a cuttings library. Failing either facility, use the newspaper shelves in a good reference library. To go further back you might need to resort to an index, i.e. the British Humanities Index.*

TASK 2 *Select three of the personalities for whom you have material and write an 800-word column on them for your slot.*

Notes: This is a column which must have style and shrewd observation. The famous can expect to have the attention of satirists, but you must not as a columnist go over the top and suggest they are incompetent at what they do. See Crone: *Law and the Media,* 3rd Edition (Focal Press, 1995), Chapters 1 to 4 on libel.

ARTS REVIEWS

ARTS reviewing is perhaps the most subjective of all feature writing. Even at the simplest level you must have a passion for the subject and the kinds of work you are reviewing. You are engaging with the work, trying to fathom the author's or composer's intentions, assessing the actor's/musician's interpretation, determining the likely effect on the readers/audience.

If you think the work is good you will be burning to communicate your response. If you think it is bad you will want to help your readers find and demand better things. This sounds pretentious until you recognize that, of course, you are one of the readers – in fact you are to some extent writing for yourself as a representative reader.

Reviewing plays, films, TV, art and music tends to be a full-time and all-absorbing task for a writer. Reviewing books is more often a part-time occupation; writers, academics and a variety of specialists, including journalists, turn up in the pages of newspapers and magazines reviewing books on their specialism. It helps keep them up to date in their subject and to remind editors that they are around.

Deadlines are vital in reviews (except with certain books). Last night's film premiere or theatre first night or concert needs to be written up in an hour or so for dailies. For weekly newspapers or magazines you might have a day or two. Practise working to these deadlines. It concentrates the mind wonderfully.

Collect cuttings of various types of reviews in different markets to compare and analyse. You will soon discover which arts you would prefer to review and which markets you would prefer to write for.

See Hennessy, chapter 15, and also Hodgson, *Modern Newspaper Practice*, 3rd Edition (Focal Press), pages 40–2 for techniques in arts reviewing.

Assignment 30

Study the spring or autumn number of *The Bookseller* and select a fiction and a non-fiction work to review. Order from the publisher or from a bookshop so that you get them on the day they are published.

TASK 1   *Write a 300-word review of each work for a nominated newspaper or magazine after first studying the book's page for the sort of style and approach used by the reviewers.*

TASK 2   *Compare what you have written with any published reviews of the two books and write a 200-word account on the similarities and differences.*

TASK 3   *Buy or borrow a recently published novel and non-fiction work and review as above.*

TASK 4   *Dig out the reviews of the two works in a good reference library and compare with yours.*

Notes: There is no standard way to review fiction. You certainly need an angle – a comparison with the author's previous work or a close examination of the style or story line, or the place of the book in contemporary fiction or in a particular genre of fiction such as sci-fi or black comedy. Or you might concentrate simply on the book's credibility in the world in which it is located. Whichever way you need to have some previous knowledge of the author and genre.

With non-fiction, such as biography, history or travel, the reviewer's path is usually easier. You tend to look at the author's approach to the subject and the view taken, and the book's strengths and weaknesses and comparisons with others in the field. On a local paper, of course, a good angle might be the book's or author's local connections.

Assignment 31

Try a night at the cinema, making sure a recently released film is showing. Take a notebook.

TASK I *Write a 300-word review, as if on first release, taking note of the film's aim and the extent to which it achieves it. Comment on the acting, camera work and direction, and any special aspects that strike you. Try to have your review ready within an hour of seeing the film.*

TASK 2 *Dig out reviews of the film from cuttings files or newspaper files in a good reference library and compare them with yours. Write 200 words on the comparison.*

Notes: You will notice a difference in objectives between book and film reviewing. With a book it is between you and the author and perhaps the potential reader. With a film you have not only the performers to take account of but also the direction, the camera work and even the scriptwriter (for dialogue). Lighting and soundtrack can count high in some films, as can fidelity to the book where the film script has been derived from one.

Assignment 32

Watch an important TV documentary and make notes.

TASK I *Immediately the programme has finished roughly edit your notes and draft out and dictate a 300-word review aimed at a nominated paper on to a tape recorder. Try to complete the task within 45 minutes of the end of the programme.*

TASK 2 *Transcribe the review and compare it with any account in the next morning's papers and write down a summary of your comments.*

Notes: TV reviewing is the odd one out in the arts in that you cannot recommend a programme to your readers' attention – unless you have been allowed to attend a preview, which many critics do for important programmes. Points to note are the aim of the documentary, the extent to which it achieves its aim, the direction and camera work and any indications of its impartiality or bias or prejudice.

Assignment 33

Visit a performance of a play by an amateur theatre group in your town and make careful notes about the acting and production.

TASK 1   *From your notes and impressions of the production write a 400-word review aimed at your local paper.*

TASK 2   *Compare your review of the production with the one that appears in your local paper, and note down the differences in assessment of the quality and effect of the performance.*

TASK 3   *Write 500 words about any differences in approach and assessment you think should be taken into account in writing about an amateur theatre or musical production compared with a professional one.*

Notes: Reviewing amateur arts productions is a job that commonly falls to young journalists on a local paper and it has many pitfalls. While the standards of the best amateur group might approach and match some professional ones, there can be a great variety in standards and ability and even in aims. It is hard to establish criteria in reviewing such productions but public performers should remember that when an entry ticket is paid for the public is entitled to expect to be reasonably entertained. See Hennessy, chapter 15; and Harris and Spark, *Practical Newspaper Reporting,* 2nd Edition (Focal Press, 1993) pages 192–212 for guidance in this field.

Assignment 34   Visit a new art exhibition in your area as near to its opening as possible and make a note of your impressions both of the works exhibited and of the aims of the exhibition as you see them.

TASK 1   *From the notes you have taken and your visual impressions write a 500-word feature about the exhibition, aimed at your local paper, and choosing, if you can, a particular angle that has struck you. Include some guidance and advice for the readers and (if you feel you can) reasons why they ought to go to see it.*

TASK 2   *Compare your feature with the one about the exhibition that appears in your local paper and write 200 words on the comparison.*

Notes: With art – that is to say paintings, drawings and sculpture – unlike the performing arts you are back to a situation similar to books. It is between you and the artist; it is about the artist's technique and intentions and to what extent they are successful. Art critics need to have special knowledge of the subject if they are to write meaningfully for their readers.

Assignment 35

Zlata's Diary, A Child's Life in Sarajevo, published in the UK in 1994 by Viking Press, quickly became a world best-seller. Comparison with *The Diary of Anne Frank*, written in wartime Holland, which has sold 20 million copies in many languages, was inevitable. Zlata Filipovic started her book just before her eleventh birthday and had read Anne Frank.

Reviews of the book ranged widely from the soppy to the dismissive with comments such as 'a fresh and innocent perspective to the relentless miseries of existence in the Bosnian capital,' and 'banal...boring.' Read both these books with a reviewer's eye in order to carry out the following task.

TASK   *Write an 800-word comparison of the two diaries entitled Zlata's Diary in Retrospect and give your assessment of the Bosnian girl's book. Is it on the whole underrated or overrated or have you a new view to offer? Try to dig out some sales figures. Aim your work at a literary magazine.*

Notes: Points to examine in each work include: overall structure, types of incident, phrasing, convincing use of quoted speech, convincing insights into a child's mind, vocabulary (as far as you can judge this in translation).

'OUR SPECIAL CORRESPONDENT'

OUTSIDE such defined areas as the arts and personal columns there exist a host of specialisms in newspapers and periodicals in which feature writers dedicate their skill and energy to a chosen subject on which they write under their own name and title as the resident expert. Many, depending on the size of the staff, are staff writers; others are freelances called in on a regular basis.

Technology, education, aviation, motoring, diplomacy, medicine, religious affairs, computers, travel, the environment...the list is as long as the editor's requirements, for the readership market of the newspaper or periodical dictates the areas in which a writer's expertise is required.

Specialist journalists who establish themselves – through background, qualifications or experience – as skilled interpreters in their field are highly regarded by editors. Writing for the popular market can offer the greatest challenge where a complex subject might have to be rendered into simple terms for the busy reader.

Although many writers develop their own style, and even become noted for it, specialist features demand substance more than style; valuable information clearly and accurately presented; arguments cogently worked out; purposeful rather than elegant prose. Above all, specialist writers must keep up to date in their subject, which means wide reading of books, reports and specialist journals, attendance at press conferences and membership of the right professional organizations. Subject cuttings files should be relentlessly updated if they are to keep abreast of what has been written.

The following assignments offer a selection of the sort of contribution made by specialist writers in newspapers and periodicals. Some of the specialisms make useful subjects for group discussion on matters of content, approach and reader influence.

CONSUMER journalism covers a wide area of specialist writing in newspapers and magazines and reaches out, in one way or another, to almost every type of reader. The following assignment is an example.

Assignment 36

Consider the store Marks & Spencer and what makes it different from other large retailers. Visit several stores and talk to some sales assistants and a manager or two. Try to find out the following statistics for the last complete year of the company's operation:

◇ World-wide number of stores.
◇ Stores in UK and Ireland.
◇ Operating profits in UK and Ireland.
◇ Operating profits in Continental Europe.
◇ Operating profits in the rest of the world.

Check company view on:

1 Environmental responsibility.
2 Recycling of materials.
3 Service to the community.
4 Sponsorship.
5 Attention to customer complaints.

Check also on the company's origins.

TASK 1   *Write 300 words on special aspects you would seek to bring out and on comparisons you would make with other large retailers.*

TASK 2   *In your role as consumer correspondent of a women's magazine, write a 1000-word readable profile of Marks & Spencer from the research and legwork you have carried out.*

Notes: Given the right approach and careful planning there is no reason why this sort of project could not be set up as a student exercise. It could equally be the model for other similar projects in the consumer and business field. Facts and figures should be carefully checked, however, and your intention to use interview quotes in the project should be made known to your interviewees.

EDUCATION correspondents have a fruitful field to work over. A good academic background is essential to understand the nuances of curriculum manoeuvring, funding, student grants, management changes and political in-fighting in which schools and higher education have to operate.

 **Assignment 37**

What with the National Curriculum, the emergence of GNVQs as an alternative route to A-levels to universities, and endless changes in syllabuses and marking parameters, the debate on standards in sixth forms has never been livelier. Consider a mop-up of the current debate as the basis of a feature. Consider also the following two points of view about students:

1   'Students going up to university are taking jobs because the grant does not even cover the cost of rent for one financial year.'
2   'If students stopped drinking and living it up they would be better off.'

TASK 1   *Explain in 250 words the sort of sources and interviews you would use for such a feature.*

TASK 2   *Taking account of the above, write a 1200-word feature aimed at a quality morning paper under the heading, 'What next for sixth formers?'*

Notes: This could serve as a model for a number of student-originated features dealing with aspects of education, both in practice and theory.

Assignment 38

Dyslexia, in various degrees, is more common than was once thought and can have sad effects on some young people's education. Research a feature by getting both the professionals' views and the sufferers', including the views of relatives of the sufferers. Mention the aids that can now be used, including computers.

TASK 1   *Give yourself a briefing and list of sources and ideas upon which to base your feature.*

TASK 2   *Write a 1500-word feature on dyslexia aimed at a family magazine, covering the misconceptions and any sad or hopeful examples from sufferers.*

Notes: Give some attention to the law that says dyslexic pupils have a right to help from their local authorities and find if in practice the law is operating effectively in the area. Addresses and telephone numbers that will guide readers to special needs education, plus a selected book list, could be included. As with medical conditions it is important in such a feature not to hold out any false hope to sufferers but to concentrate on what can be done and what is being done.

MEDICAL subjects and in particular the National Health Service are regularly covered by writers who specialize in these matters and, as with education, such coverage extends to most newspapers and family magazines. The constant news pegs that arise about Health Service change and renewal ensure that controversy is never far away.

Assignment 39

According to newspaper reports about a dozen NHS patient hotels are currently being built in different parts of the country. They are intended as halfway houses between hospital and home for people, especially those living alone, who have gone through day surgery and are not fit for final discharge. The NHS pays part of the cost of an in-patient bed. Figures and information can be found in a study from the NHS Management Executive's Value for Money Unit issued in 1992: *Patient Hotels: A Quality Alternative to Ward Care*.

Check through recent cuttings and newspaper files for details, and set up interviews with patients and professionals to obtain their views.

TASK *Write an 800-word article aimed at a quality national newspaper assessing the usefulness of the new system, offering praise or criticism as you see it. Try to find out about the systems of patient hotels in use in the US and Scandinavia and compare.*

Notes: As with many medical features this assignment requires some serious research and should not be attempted by students without it.

SOCIAL PROBLEMS of varying sorts are covered by some newspaper specialists and more generally by a number of specialist magazines. The field – which is really the whole of human behaviour – produces some of the most challenging journalism of our time. It requires a good deal of commitment on the part of writers, some being identified with crusades on particular issues.

The three examples that follow are intended as models for assignments in this field that could be set up by students and trainee journalists on courses.

Assignment 40

A motor vehicle project in the London borough of Lewisham has trained, in the past seventeen years, around 2000 young people aged between 12 and 25, half of them young offenders, in motorcycle maintenance and off-road motorcycle and car driving. In the past two years, it was reported by the directors of the scheme, only three of the 200 young offenders who went through training re-offended after leaving it.

Make a study of similar schemes to help young offenders in your area, including their results and such figures as are available.

TASK *Write a 1000-word feature, aimed at your local paper readership, on a local young offender scheme and its effectiveness.*

Notes: This sort of feature is basically a research job; you need to know where to look and who to ask. Interviews help in supplying colour, but your result is only as good as its research and the comparisons and conclusions it enables you to make.

Assignment 41

You are either a house-husband caring for two children at home while your wife or partner works, or you are that wife or partner. You have collected together some material from various publications on the subject of role reversal and feel that some aspects of it have not been properly examined. You are concerned about attitudes to house husbands from neighbours, playgroups, women's organizations, the press and other bodies. Also of concern is your relationship with your partner and your views on things like child-rearing and decision-making in the home. You decide to try to get your views published.

TASK 1   *Prepare an outline scheme for the things you want to say in a feature article, listing points, giving them an order, and setting out a structure for your article.*

TASK 2   *Write a 1200-word feature aimed at a family magazine.*

Notes: It is useful in an exercise like this if, as a student or trainee journalist, you can use the circumstances of someone you know. Likewise the same method could be applied in writing about any other relationship problem of which an example can be found among your circle of friends or colleagues. Alternatively, you can put your article together in the third person through interviewing the friend or colleague. Either way, it is essential to do some research into the organizations that can offer help or advice in such circumstances.

Assignment 42

The following facts appeared in *Home Alone*, a report of the Alzheimer's Disease Society, Gordon House, 10 Greencoat Place, London SW1P 1PH (£2.95):

- 154,000 people with dementia now live alone in Britain.
- By the year 2011 there will be a million pensioners with dementia.
- 36% of those with dementia living in the community live on their own.

Add to this information by means of interviews and inquiries, including talking to experts, local authorities and relatives of sufferers, until you have enough material for a feature on the problem as you see it.

TASK   *Write a 1000-word article on the problems of sufferers from Alzheimer's Disease living in the community and aim it at a weekly paper in a large conurbation. Include some suggestions for future care.*

Notes: Reports and publications from the many societies dealing with social and medical problems are worth combing for ideas in this field of feature writing – particularly those likely to be relevant to your subject or the geographical area you cover as a journalist. Such sources offer useful models for research-based feature articles.

STRUCTURE AND STYLE IN FEATURE WRITING

IT IS difficult to teach firm principles in structure and style in feature writing since the aims in different sorts of features can vary so much.

Skill in structuring an article can be developed by analysing the structures of published articles and, in comparison, by devising plans and detailed outlines for various kinds and lengths of features on given subjects. Even so, there is likely to be some trial and error before trainees confidently adopt the principles that work for them.

How a writer's style develops is even more individual and inscrutable. The crucial advice is to read published work of the sort and quality you are aiming for and to analyse what makes it effective, if necessary drafting and redrafting your work until you (and your editor) are satisfied.

A study of models is necessary to make you conscious of the need to be versatile and to adapt style to the audience, content and aim.

The following assignments are offered as models for exercises that could be put together in this field.

Assignment 43   Cut a printed feature article (any paper – try different ones) into separate paragraphs, jumble them together and paste them on to an A4 sheet. Number each paragraph.

TASK   *Students, each with a copy of the sheet of jumbled paragraphs, must number them back into the correct order.*

Assignment 44

Take four feature articles from each of four varied newspapers or magazines – sixteen in all – and circulate copies to each student.

TASK   *Rewrite the headlines, intros and conclusions found in the feature from one publication in the style of another dissimilar one, i.e., from* The Sun *to* The Times, *for example, or from* The Independent *to the* Daily Mirror, *from* Vogue *to* Women's Own, *or from a popular Sunday magazine supplement to* The Economist.

Assignment 45

In style there are four kinds of writing: description, narration, exposition and argument. Because they are often combined in pieces of journalism to produce a unified effect they are not often separated and considered separately. It is a useful exercise to remind ourselves what the main purposes and techniques of the four kinds are.

For the following task select any place you know well and can evoke vividly in your mind (a building, a disused warehouse, a schoolroom, a patch of wasteland, a river bank...anything).

TASK I   *Write four separate paragraphs under the following headings:*

Description: Describe the place and the atmosphere without story or explanation. Show the danger (or loneliness, happiness, etc.) through physical details. Use all the senses. Find some imagery.

Narration: Tell a story related to the place. Use effective verbs to carry the action forward.

Exposition: Give factual evidence that explains why the place is as it is (isolated, remote, friendly, tantalizing?)

Argument: The owners, or those in charge of it, have decided to demolish/alter/rebuild/change the use of/extend the place. Put up a convincing argument for or against whichever it is that is being considered.

Notes: For guidance on structure see Hennessy, Chapter 7; and on style, Chapters 11 and 12.

REFERENCES AND FURTHER READING

Crone, T: *Law and the Media*, 3rd Edition (Focal Press, 1995).

Davis, A: *Magazine Journalism Today* (Focal Press, 1992)

Harris, G and Spark, D: *Practical Newspaper Reporting*, 2nd Edition (Focal Press, 1993).

Hennessy, B: *Writing Feature Articles*, 2nd Edition (Focal Press, 1993).

Hodgson, FW: *Modern Newspaper Practice*, 3rd Edition (Focal Press, 1993).

4

Photojournalism

IT IS not possible to teach press photography exlusively in the class-room; there comes a time when the student photographer has to be allowed out into the real world and let loose on real people and on situations which, if simulated, should be as near to real news or features situations as possible.

How much can be achieved depends on the size of the class and on the relationship between course instructors and whatever facilities are available locally.

For example, the police would not be too pleased to find a dozen budding press photographers arriving at the scene of the first murder to occur in the area since the local course in press photography started. On the other hand the police district's press officer would probably be willing to come to talk with students about the relationship between the press and the police, and they might be able to offer the course occasional special facilities – for instance photographing public order demonstrations or firearms training for officers.

For many assignments a little role-playing will have to be used with other students or lecturers as guinea pigs acting out the parts of authors, inventors and grieving relatives. On some assignments – of which examples follow in this chapter – students will be working along-side one another in a competitive environment, vying to produce the best picture of an event that has been set up. In others they will be working one-to-one with their subject to get the best result out of their equipment and their briefing.

Taking pictures, of course, is not the end of the job. Students need to be attuned to the technical side of photography – the skills of developing and printing in black and white and in colour, and in the transmission, storage and retrieval of their work and the procedures of picture editing for the page.

They have to develop the organizational skills of liaising with writers, meeting deadlines and anticipating the needs of the subeditors and production journalists who plan and lay out the pages. Very important: they have to remember to check and verify the contents of their pictures so that they can deliver up accurate captions in which people are correctly identified and named. These are journalistic skills without which they cannot do their job properly.

Depending on the course timetable some aspects of press photography may have to be introduced into the classroom environment artificially. For example, a practical assignment might be photographed in one session and processed, captioned and offered to a notional 'picture editor' in a subsequent one.

As well as producing their finished printed work, students should present a full set of contact prints and their notes so that they can be referred to in subsequent discussion about their train of thought during their picture-taking session. Such things can show to what degree a student or trainee photographer is learning correct methods and they can be valuable at the assessment stage.

The assignments that follow are intended to help in the training of press photographers by setting up models of the sort of jobs a young practitioner might be called upon to do.

 **Assignment 1**

Your paper has received an embargoed press release from the local council that the public conveniences in the town's market place have been made a 'listed building'. They are believed to be the first loos in the country to have been granted this status. The press release gives a telephone number for the council's head of environmental services. The picture editor is asked by the editor to arrange suitable coverage.

TASK 1   *Provide two suitable pictures and a short caption that will comply with the picture editor's briefing: 'It may be just a loo but you have got to make it look interesting.' A reporter has already written a full story, which includes quotes from the attendant of the public conveniences, and you have a copy of this.*

TASK 2   *Describe in 300 words what preparations you would expect to have to make to set up your pictures.*

Notes: Having agreed upon a building – preferably a loo – with which to simulate this assignment, a good deal of imagination is needed to carry it through. Obviously you will take as many pictures as you feel you need, but of the two offered one should feature the attendant, big and bold in front of the picture, carrying a mop and bucket. This will back up the reporter's quotes. You can have fun with this assignment.

Points to check:

1   That you have taken pictures in both horizontal and verti-
    cal format.
2   That you have checked your caption names with those in
    the story.
3   That the embargo time/date is clearly marked on your caption.

See Keene: *Practical Photojournalism* (Focal Press, 1993), pages 139–40.

Not all assignments are as straightforward as the above. You might be asked to find pictures to accompany an idea for a **FEATURE** in which a good deal of research will have to be carried out and work done at a variety of locations. The following is an example.

After meeting the Chairman of the local branch of the Royal National Institute for the Blind at a Rotary Club lunch, your editor decides to run a double-page spread of pictures on the problems facing disabled (not just blind) people in the circulation area. You are assigned to the story by the picture editor and briefed on what is needed. You are asked to liaise with a reporter who is setting up the text, but are told the choice of pictures is down to you.

TASK 1   *Provide six pictures that will illustrate the problems of the disabled for a double-page spread that will have some text but which will rely heavily on its illustrations.*

TASK 2   *Describe in 500 words the problems and possibilities in this sort of assignment.*

Notes: This assignment sounds a good idea when first mooted but it can create enormous work and complications for the photographer. The fact that it is being done as a student exercise does not make it any easier. Strictly it is a feature and the trainee on this and similar assignments needs time both during class and on their own for research – instructors please note.

There are various routes to pictures. The local chairman of the RNIB will be able to offer some ideas. The names of other local organizations for the disabled will be be available from the public library and, with some reservations, are usually willing to take part in projects that publicize their cause.

As a student, you may choose to highlight problems faced by people with a wide range of disabilities, or you could work with a few subjects and concentrate on the size of the problems facing them. Aspects could include dangers in the streets to the visually handicapped and problems of access to buildings and public facilities to people in wheelchairs. In either case it might be necessary to use stand-ins as subjects.

Points to check:

1   That you have submitted complete contact sheets to show how you have gone about taking the pictures.
2   That your have shot the pictures in a variety of shapes from which to select your six best.
3   That you have used a selection of lenses.

PERSON SHOTS are one of the less complicated jobs. Given that the person is agreeable and that a proper arrangement has been made, a photographer – even a trainee photographer – working on their own should need just one roll of film to come away with a selection of good pictures

 **Assignment 3**   A professor of astronomy at a nearby university has a star named after her in honour of her work on Black Holes. You are asked to produce pictures to accompany a story that a reporter on your evening paper is writing about her.

TASK 1   *Set up a photo session at an agreed time and take enough shots to produce two good pictures for the early afternoon edition.*

TASK 2   *Explain in 300 words your method for going about this sort of assignment and any particular preparation you would need to make.*

Notes: Bearing in mind your readership market you would need some device to bring your picture alive on the page – something more than just the head and shoulders of a middle-aged lady academic. If she will co-operate, try one of her at her telescope and perhaps one at a blackboard covered in complex formulae. Since, for a student exercise, you are going to have to use a stand-in for this sort of assignment anyway this would not be difficult. More taxing on the imagination would be finding the props for the technical background.

The **ORGANISING** of camera work is one thing a press photographer has to learn to cope with. Photo sessions have to be set up, appointments made, equipment checked, photo files kept, photo libraries searched for stock pictures and work co-ordinated with reporters on many of the stories. A spell of work on the picture desk will give a young press photographer a timely reminder of this aspect, as the following assignment demonstrates.

Assignment 4

Your local league football club is travelling to a club 200 miles away in four days' time to take part in a play-off which will decide if they are to be promoted to a higher league. You regularly cover the team and on this occasion you have been asked to produce six pictures of the game, but since they are needed in your office two hours after the final whistle for your evening paper's late edition there is not enough time to bring the films back to the office for processing.

TASK 1   *Explain how you would ensure that your picture desk gets its pictures on time.*

TASK 2   *At the picture editor's request, prepare a memo outlining a contingency plan, should the team win promotion, for picture coverage of them riding in an open-topped coach through the town to a civic reception at the town hall.*

TASK 3   *From the picture files and the pictures you have taken of the team prepare a memo for the editor listing the picture material you would recommend be used in a special souvenir edition of the paper to sell at the ground at the big match.*

Notes: A hypothetical bit of picture desk work, this one. Every staff photographer can expect sooner or later to do a spell on the desk and can expect to have their brains picked and their time and experience used. See Keene, pages 177–88.

SHOPPING is part of the lives of a family readership on a local evening paper – and part of the advertising manager's plans for revenue – and it inevitably provides subjects for pictures.

Assignment 5

It is the first day of the January sales at Dumbles, the town's largest department store and one of the paper's biggest advertisers, and the editor and the advertising manager want to run a picture on the front of tonight's edition and two more in the early edition tomorrow. The store opens at 9 am and the editor needs today's picture by 10.30 am.

TASK 1   *Take a selection of pictures typifying bargain-hunters or any odd aspect of the sales from which the best three will make the paper.*

TASK 2   *List the sort of ideas for pictures you will be on the look-out for.*

Notes: This is an old chestnut for local papers but nearly every year something new will crop up. Some amazing object someone has longed for and has got at a knockdown price...someone who has camped outside the store all night in a shelter made of copies of the local paper...a bride-to-be rushing home on the bus wearing a wedding dress she has just bought.

It is also a picture assignment actuality that is available to student photographers without recourse to stand-ins. Store managers are always glad of the publicity, and you might even be able to sell a good picture to the local paper – or its rival. Getting the picture taken and printed for the 10.30 am deadline is a good exercise. It is better to have an acceptable picture delivered on time than a brilliant one a student photographer has waited all day for that is too late. There is always the following day's edition for the others.

Once you have most of the routine assignments safely under your belt you might find yourself lined up for one of the plum jobs - particularly if holidays and illness have produced a dearth of photographers in the picture department. It helps if the potential picture is an exclusive that you have uncovered yourself.

Figure 7 How to do it 1: the bride who got a £1,450 wedding dress for £150 on the first day of Liberty's sale in Regent Street, London, pictured by Press Association's Martin Keene (see assignment on page 69)

Figure 8 How to do it 2: attendant John Dervan outside the public toilet in Westbourne Grove, West London, named a Building of the Year by the Royal Fine Arts Commission, pictured by Martin Keene (see assignment on page 65)

Figure 9   Pictures that win awards 1: this dramatic boxing shot at Elland Road Stadium, Leeds, was taken by 23-year-old Justin Lloyd of the *Yorkshire Evening Post* using a Nikon F4 on flash with a 50 mm lens on 250 seconds at aperture F4. It is from a portfolio of four that won for him the £1,000 British Telecom award for the best all-round achievement in the NCTJ's 1994 Spring National Certificate examinations

Figure 10   Pictures that win awards 2: this shot of greyhounds at Owlerton Stadium, Sheffield, was taken by 24-year-old *Bristol Evening Post* photographer Toby Melville using a Canon T.90 with a 300 mm lens at 1500th of a second at aperture F5.6. It was one of two pictures that won for him the David Worthy Award for the best pre-entry student at the Sheffield-based NCTJ press photography course in 1994

Assignment 6

Through a local newsagent contact of yours you learn that Oleg Propov, a former KGB agent who defected to Britain and worked for five years as a double agent, is living in a secluded house in your area. His front door is some hundred yards from the nearest road but the newsagent tells you that the ex-double agent and his wife enjoy an occasional cycle ride in the countryside. You are asked by the picture editor to go along and get a picture to go with a reporter's story.

TASK 1   *What would be your reaction if on making yourself known to Oleg Propov he told you that:*

(a) *He was covered by a D-Notice (under the Official Secrets Act).*

(b) *That by taking his picture you were invading his privacy and that he would report you to the Press Complaints Commission?*

TASK 2   *Do you think a 'snatch' picture in the street taken without the subject's permission would be a better idea and how would you go about getting this?*

TASK 3   *Simulating the circumstances with your stand-in (making sure you can recognize him in public), take a one-off shot without letting your subject realize what is being done.*

Notes: Obviously an assignment of this sort can only be set up with a co-operative stand-in. Having set it up the student photographer has important problems to solve. If he/she knocks on the person's door the person is alerted to the interest in him. If the photographer decides to 'snatch' him in the street the person might be helpful and agree to publication, but the photographer could have a long wait for such a picture.

A decision has to be taken on which way to do it. On balance, the photographer would be probably best to wait, 'snatch' the person in the street so discreetly that he is not aware of it and then approach the person later in the street to tell him that the picture has been taken. By this ruse, the door cannot be slammed, literally or metaphorically, in the face.

The man's claim that he is covered by a D-notice would probably be wishful thinking but could be checked with the Secretary of the D-Notice Committee on D-notices (see Keene, page 173). If the photographer were on the person's property or using a long lens from outside it then the Press Complaints Commission's guidelines would have been broken.

However, once the person is in the public highway then he can be photographed – but not 'harassed'.

Important question for students: how can they be sure they have identified the ex-agent correctly?

FASHION PHOTOGRAPHY is a specialism that may lie some time in the future for the ambitious student photographer but the seeds can be sown by an assignment on your first local paper.

Despite the 'liberating' of the traditional women's pages in many newspapers, fashion in clothes, jewellery, etc. remains an ingredient that not only, according to surveys, has a significant reader interest but can provide attractive pictures for pages on an otherwise flat day.

Fashion pictures need to be eye-catching. The settings can add as much to the pictures as the clothes. Evening wear would look ideal shot at the local five-star hotel, but daring outdoor shots can look good provided the light is right. Denim 'working clothes' could be photographed in a breaker's yard.

The local high street multiple stores are less likely to help in student set-ups than the smaller boutiques who may not only lend clothes for the session but also a member of the staff as a model. Do not ignore ideas from college students on the local fashion or design course. Theirs may be very innovative.

Assignment 7

The women's editor of a magazine wants to brighten up the pages with some fashion pictures showing trends in spring casual wear. You are given wide scope in interpreting the brief.

TASK 1   *Produce a set of pictures with a number of backgrounds from which four could be used as the basis of an informative caption story.*

TASK 2   *Assuming that an interpretative caption is going to be written by an informed fashion writer, list the sort of information you, as the photographer, would expect to have to supply with the pictures.*

Notes: Fashion pictures should, in the first instance, be technically perfect. Focus must be spot on, with distracting backgrounds subdued with a longer lens set at a wide aperture to give a shallow depth of field. See Keene, pages 111–12, on fashion work.

Points to remember:

1 If a particular boutique has helped you, give them a printed credit, even though the pictures are for a student publication; they have earned it.

2 Likewise, readers may want to buy the clothes worn so give 'merchandising' information about prices and outlets.

A ROYAL VISIT to the area would be covered under the watchful eye of the Central Office of Information both for the Rota party (those with special passes), who move with the visitors, and for journalists operating independently at fixed points along the route. The latter tend to be photographing arrivals and departures at each end of an engagement – at airports or railway stations for example – or taking shots during a walkabout.

Access to students for Rota passes is impossible for such occasions but if there is a good relationship between the course authorities and the CoI the office may make available some fixed point passes for a visit.

 **Assignment 8**

You are lucky enough to have been given a fixed point pass at the local sports ground where Princess Margaret is arriving by helicopter for the first of two local functions and your pictures are intended for page one of your student magazine or newspaper.

TASK 1 *Making sure that you have a good viewpoint, produce the best set of pictures you can in the time available.*

TASK 2 *Describe what camera and lens you would equip yourself with for this sort of assignment.*

Notes: Student photographers and experienced press photographers will have to watch out for the unexpected during a Royal visit. Although most go like clockwork and although the photographer can plan the position they will stand in and the sort of pictures they hope to take (for example, close-ups, full lengths showing Royal fashion and meeting well-wishers) an unexpected incident might occur, be it light-hearted or serious.

Royal visits (and sometimes the visits of other important dignitaries) are invariably covered in detail in all the papers circulating in the area so photographers at the event will be expected to produce as wide a range of pictures as possible in the hope that among them will be one or two 'exclusive' to their paper. Student photographers should take the same competitive approach, even though for the purposes of your student assignment the Royal Visitor might have to be a stand-in (Keene, pages 115–25).

COURT COVERAGE is just as much a legal minefield for the photographer as it is for the reporter and a close study of the relevant parts of McNae (*Essential Law For Journalists*) and Crone (*Law and the Media*) on reporting restrictions, contempt of court, libel and confidentiality (see page 80) is recommended before embarking on any assignments to do with court appearances.

 **Assignment 9**

Baron Oldchester, owner of the local stately home, who leads a lifestyle described by some as controversial, is to appear tomorrow at the borough magistrates' court to answer drugs charges and the editor of your evening paper is keen to have a picture of him on the day for the main edition. The Baron is currently on bail after pleading not guilty at a previous hearing.

TASK   *You have been briefed to obtain a photograph of the Baron either arriving for the hearing or leaving afterwards to go with a reporter's story on the case. Describe briefly the legal difficulties of your assignment and how you would go about getting the required picture.*

Notes: This is not an assignment that can be easily simulated by a student photographer so what we are looking for is not a picture but an explanation. Points to note are: since the Baron is on bail he can be expected to walk into court; if the case is proceeded with and he is sentenced then he may leave in a prison van. Therefore it is better to go for a picture on his arrival – which will also be more helpful for the edition deadline.

Questions the student must deal with:

1   How will the photographer be certain that the man photographed arriving at the court is in fact the Baron?
2   What steps will the photographer take to interpret and comply with the law forbidding photographs being taken

within the 'precincts of the court'. What is meant by 'precincts of the court'? (Keene, pages 104–9.)

PICTURE EDITING

EDITING pictures is strictly a task that falls to the subeditor or production journalist in charge of the page who must decide how to obtain the maximum effect from the pictures chosen within the space made available for them, while at the same time taking into account the purpose for which they were selected. The title picture editor is usually given to the person who runs the picture desk, organizes the picture service for the paper and briefs the photographers.

Planning the pages and choosing their contents is a function that the editor delegates to a top executive such as the night editor or the chief subeditor.

As far as the picture content goes, the main one might be chosen for the page in its own right as a piece of picture news – a Royal portrait, a seasonal or Christmas scene, an ususual activity, a weather picture or a pretty girl modelling topical clothes. Or a picture might be of someone mentioned in the story alongside. Within these parameters the photographer's print might turn up as a five column by 20 centimetres deep or as a single column head or 'mug' shot.

Perhaps only part of a picture is wanted for the purpose of the page, or a particular section of a picture needs to be enlarged or 'blown up' because of something it shows, or someone or something in the background of a picture needs to be excluded because it is not relevant to the editorial purpose. All these requirements are met by the various processes of picture editing carried out by the person in charge of the page. Unwanted or intrusive background can be 'blown back' to instructions by an artist retoucher using an air brush on the emulsion or, with electronic page make-up when the picture is being 'scanned'.

The wanted part of a picture (and its shape) is selected for enlarging by a process known as 'cropping' in which usually pencil lines are drawn on the back of a print boxing in the required part (see Figure 11).

The size of picture required for the page is indicated by a process known as scaling in which measurements based on the square of the diagonal of the cropped area on the back of the print take the picture either up or down in size proportionately.

In screen make-up systems in which a good deal of colour is used pictures are stored digitally and are colour-balanced and 'imaged' directly into on-screen pages, the same editing processes being achieved electronically by keyboard and 'mouse' controls.

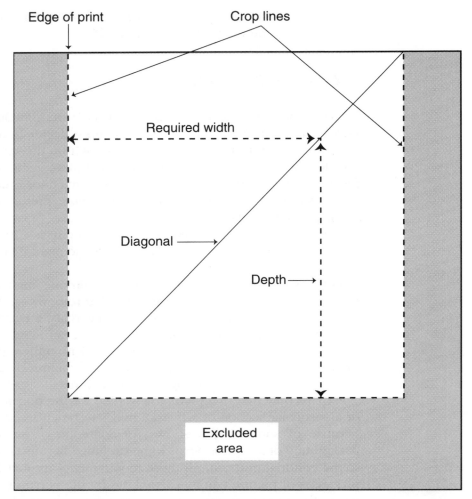

Figure 11   Editing a picture – when working on photographic prints reverse the picture on to a light source and crop the area required by drawing a pencil line on the back to exclude the unwanted part. To work out the size of picture required, draw a diagonal line bottom left to top right of the cropped area and measure across from the left the width available for the picture. Measure from the diagonal to the bottom of the cropped area to obtain the depth

Useful insights can be obtained by photographers, however, by a close study of picture use in their paper and of the mechanics and purposes of picture editing.

See Hodgson: *Subediting*, 2nd Edition (Focal Press, 1993) pages 56-74 for more on picture editing techniques.

Take a set of one day's national daily papers and use them for the following tasks:

TASK I   *Work out (by the way the same picture recurs, for example) which are taken by the paper's own staff photographers, which are distributed to all papers by 'wire' services (Reuter and PA) , which are stock (old) pictures and which have come free from public relations firms and press officers.*

TASK 2   *Select those pictures which are common to, or similar in, a number of the papers, consider the differences in cropping, scaling and projection, and say why you think these differences have occurred (editorial purpose, readership influence, etc.).*

Notes: Student photographers can learn from a close study of the use of pictures in a variety of newspapers, identifying both common factors that apply to many papers, and oddities and idiosyncrasies that apply to the few. They will also learn that editorial purpose is the extra dimension that even the most skilled and experienced photographers have to cope with — that, for example, there is no greater source of conflict than the reasons for cropping a picture. See Giles and Hodgson: *Creative Newspaper Design* (Heinemann Professional Publishing, 1990), pages 75–99 for picture use in newspaper design.

Examine a complete set of one day's editions (check the number first) of your nearest evening paper and use them for the following tasks.

TASK I   *List the the proportion of news pictures against that of features pictures; identify which are the day's input as against stock, or old, pictures; identify which are staff and which (in your view) are from agencies or from readers. Summarize your conclusions about the picture content.*

TASK 2   *Examine the shifts in picture content as editions progress, noting changes in the handling, positioning and cropping of pictures and the changes in page content as news develops and new pictures become available. Summarize, in your view, the reasons for the various changes. Do not be afraid to be critical.*

Notes: This could be a useful recurring exercise in which students on photography and other journalism courses could note the methods and characteristics of the editorial use of pictures of a given newspaper. A critical examination could be made of practices, and comparisons made between different papers. It might also be possible to get the art editor or picture editor of the local, or even a national, paper or magazine to participate in this workshop project. (See also Workshop projects in chapter 7, pages 129–39.)

REFERENCES AND FURTHER READING

Crone, T: *Law and the Media*, 3rd Edition (Focal Press, 1995).

Giles, V and Hodgson, FW: *Creative Newspaper Design* (Heinemann Professional Publishing, 1990).

Hodgson, FW: *Subediting*, 2nd Edition (Focal Press, 1993).

Keene, M: *Practical Photojournalism* (Focal Press, 1993).

McNae, LCJ: *Essential Law For Journalism* (Butterworths, 1992).

5

Subediting

HOWEVER good a reporter is at news gathering and news writing the subeditor remains the necessary mediator between the writer's text, or copy, and the finished newspaper.

The subeditor – who has usually been a reporter beforehand – has the important function of making a story the right size for the space allocated to it on the page, either by cutting it to fit or by collating several copy sources, checking the accuracy of the text and improving its balance and readability as necessary. This can entail 're-nosing' the story to bring the news point to the reader's attention, rewriting part of it in the light of later instructions or changing availability of space, or simply updating the text to take in 'add' matter sent in by the reporter or news agency.

The subeditor also has to write a headline in an appropriate type and size to draw the reader's attention to the story on the page and, if it is so decided, write a 'bill' heading to draw potential buyers' attention to the story at newsagents and points of sale.

Most important from the paper's point of view is the subeditor's role in checking the accuracy of the story and its grammar and watching out for any legal problems it might contain. However experienced the reporter, they might have some blindspots in spelling or language use, or might have had insufficient time to check essential background information.

The subeditor, operating always inside the office (see Figure 12), has easier access to reference books and cuttings files. Working often at speed and away from base, the reporter knows that the text will go through the vetting eye of the subeditor, although it is a good idea to

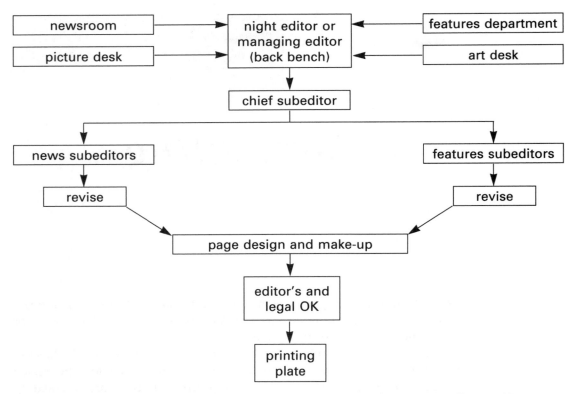

Figure 12 A typical editorial production set-up on an evening or morning newspaper. On a weekly paper, magazine or periodical where staffs are smaller the chief subeditor will probably combine the role of night or duty editor, with layouts being drawn on the subs' table when there is no art desk. Features and news subs' roles might also be combined

leave a note on text of any particular point that the reporter is worried about, with maybe a note of sources that can be referred back to. Some aspect of the copy – names, quotes, figures etc. – might be suspect, which is why it is necessary for the reporter to leave a note of where he or she can be contacted.

The assignments that follow are intended to demonstrate the multifarious jobs and duties that fall to subeditors in the handling of editorial text.

Assignment 1

A reporter, one of a group team serving several papers, files the following story at 3 pm about an inquest. It is just in time to make the late afternoon edition of the group's evening paper:

THE BROTHER of a youth who was found dead near his crashed machine in Long Lane, New Town in the early hours said at the inquest at New Town today that 18-year-old Thomas Jackson 'worshipped speed' .

'He remarked to me during breakfast a few days before the accident that riding his motorcycle fast gave him a "buzz" ', James Jackson, aged 27, who lived with his brother at 42 Kimbolton Street, Old Town, told the Coronor, Mr J W Wilson, 'He seemed to worship speed.'

Jackson's body was found by a constable who had parked his patrol car to watch the behaviour of two dogs at the roadside.

'The dogs kept rushing up and down the grassy bank near a gap in the hedge at a slight bend in the road. I proceeded to the spot on foot and found the deceased's body lying just inside the field a few yards away from his bike,' Pc Charles Peel said in evidence. 'There was no sign of injury. The deceased did not smell of alchohol.'

The officer added that it had been raining and the roads were still wet. There were no skid marks.

Dennis Potts, aged 17, of Beer Street, Old Town, said he and Jackson had spent the evening together at the Golden Dragon Coffee Bar in New Town where they had chatted to some girls. Jackson had a row with one of the girls and left on his own about 11.30 pm.

'He offered me a lift but I declined. He seemed a bit upset,' said Potts. 'I think he wanted to give the girl, who he fancied a bit, a ride on his pillion and she made some sort of joke about his bike.'

Questioned by the Coroner, Potts said from his experience Jackson was a good rider and did not normally take risks. 'He did say to me on one occasion that he would like to find somewhere where he could "open up" his bike, but I think this was just a dream,' Potts added.

Jane Wibbly, aged 16, of Cardigan Road, New Town, said she saw Jackson, whom she knew slightly, riding past her towards Long Lane some time before midnight. 'He seemed to be having trouble with his lights,' she told the Coroner. 'His bike was wobbling about a bit. Then he increased speed and went out of sight.' She turned into her own road and did not see him again.

The Coroner said a post-mortem examination had shown that Jackson had died from a broken neck. It was clear from the evidence that the youth had crashed his motorcycle while riding home in wet conditions from the Golden Dragon Coffee Bar. While it was possible to conjecture why this happened, the precise cause

of him parting from his machine at the point he did would probably never be known.

The problem with his lights could have been a contributory
factor although, when examined, they were found to be service-
able and the machine to be in reasonable condition apart from
slight damage caused by the crash. The slippery surface could have
been a cause, or his attention could have been distracted while
negotiating the bend.

'I am certain from the evidence,' said the Coroner, 'that no-one
else was involved in this tragic circumstance.'

He returned a verdict on Jackson of 'accidental death.'

(Approximately 725 words)

TASK 1   *Sub the report down to 500 words for the group's evening paper.*

TASK 2   *Write a double column headline in capitals with a character count
              of seventeen in each line.*

TASK 3   *Write a two-line caption for a single-column head shot of the dead
              youth portrayed with his bike to go with the story. The picture has
              been supplied by his brother.*

              *Time is short and the chief subeditor wants the story, headline and
              caption, in 25 minutes.*

              *Notes: Points to watch: check that in your view the story has
              the best possible intro in terms of news value. Try to keep in
              any actual quotes. Beware of any police jargon the reporter
              may have allowed to creep in. For caption-writing see Hodgson:
              Subediting, 2nd Edition (Focal Press, 1993) pages 182–5.*

As part of a team serving several newspapers, not all with the same
circulation area, the reporter leaves a copy of the story on screen for the
group's morning paper whose chief sub is grateful to have something for
the early pages. The chief sub instructs a subeditor:

TASK 4   *Sub a 200-word account for the morning paper's edition area page.*

TASK 5   *Write a single-column upper and lower-case headline of three lines
              with a count of nine characters per line.*

              *Being for a morning paper, the sub has a little more time –
              perhaps forty minutes – to check the cuttings and polish the story.
              But there is still time for one more task:*

TASK 6   *Write two area contents bills for points of sale bringing in the geography of the story.*

Notes: Subs should remember to change time references in stories edited for different publication days. Look for tighter style requirements in stories run at shorter length for different circulation areas. Contents bills have a particular style and requirement. The idea is to say enough to persuade the potential reader to buy the paper but not to use too many words; you might get only a brief glimpse of the bill as you drive by. See Hodgson: *Subediting,* pages 185–6; also Sellers: *The Simple Subs Book* (Pergamon Press, 1985).

Assignment 2

A reporter walking home late at night comes across a tobacconist's that has just been broken into. A plate glass window is shattered, stock is strewn around and the police have arrived to take measurements and question the owner, who has been called to the scene. The reporter gets what information he can, returns to the office and keys in the following story:

> THIEVES threw a brick through the window of Bewley's tobacconists in High Street, Old Town, late last night and got away with nearly £500 worth of cigarettes and cigars. They upended a window display and left stock scattered on the pavement.
>
> A passer-by, Hugh Cupps, of Dram Street, Old Town, said he saw two youths about 20 yards in front of him rush from the shop and jump on to a motor bike. One was carrying a bag and got on to the pillion seat. They roared off before he could get the number.
>
> The police later arrested Thomas Chance, aged 19, who lives in New Town, and a 16-year-old youth on suspicion of involvement in the break-in.

An enterprising little story but...beware!...problems for the subeditor.

TASK 1   *Present the story as a two-paragraph filler for a news page.*

TASK 2   *Write a one-line stock filler heading of fifteen upper and lower case characters.*

TASK 3   *Explain in a hundred words the legal aspects that have to be taken into account by the subeditor in handling this story.*

Notes: Where arrests have been made, or people charged, the regulations governing the reporting of crime must be adhered to. Check McNae: *Essential Law for Journalists* (Butterworth, 1992); and Crone: *Law and the Media*, 3rd Edition (Focal Press, 1995) for legal aspects.

Assignment 3

The following report is sent in by a local correspondent living in an edition area. It is from a part-time journalist but he is an alert local 'watcher' and the chief sub likes to use his copy to give him encouragement.

WHILE on her way to school in Green Lane, Blacktown, this morning eight-year-old Clara Bow was knocked down by a fishmonger's mobile shop which had been selling fish in the road. She was rushed to hospital where she was found to have a fractured skull.

Fishmonger Charlie Finn told the Gazette: 'She seemed to appear from nowhere as I began to pull away.'

Police called and told her mother, Mrs Harriet Bow, of Green Close, Blacktown, just as she was leaving to go shopping with Clara's sister Jane, aged two.

Inspector John Giles, who is in charge of Green Lane police station, has asked for any witnesses who were in Green Lane at about a quarter to nine in the morning to come forward.

TASK 1   *Rewrite the report as a three-paragraph news story in a style acceptable to your local evening paper.*

TASK 2   *Write a two-line single-column headline of nine upper and lower-case characters to the line.*

TASK 3   *Write a local area bill.*

TASK 4   *Discuss in 300 words the faults in the correspondent's copy as a piece of news writing.*

TASK 5   *What checks, if any, would you, as a subeditor, make with the newsroom about the contents of the story?*

Notes: There are both structural and factual faults in this story although on the face of it it seems to have been faithfully reported. The intro, for example, cannot be left as it is. See Hodgson: *Subediting*, pages 77–87, and Sellers, page 17.

Assignment 4

A young reporter making night calls on her morning paper – her first job – hears about a fire at a large detached house in the town's suburbs. Enterprisingly, she quickly takes a taxi to the spot, gets what information she can, and rushes back to the office and files the following story in time for the area edition:

A MYSTERY fire caused £150,000 worth of damage to a four-bedroomed period house in Low Lane, Blacktown, last night. Valuable paintings damaged by water were among the main items lost.

The fire is thought by a neighbour to have started in the garage. The owners, Mr and Mrs Charles Padgett, were abroad at the time and police are trying to contact them.

Four appliances attended the outbreak and at the height of the blaze the flames reached forty feet high and could be seen for three miles. Firemen using oxygen masks searched the rooms to make sure no one was trapped inside.

The neighbour, Mrs Leila Gossipp, said that the owner, Mr Padgett, stored chemicals for his photographic business in the garage.

A police spokesman said it was not known what caused the fire.

TASK 1   *Rewrite the story as it stands making it legally safe and acceptable.*

TASK 2   *Explain briefly what further inquiries you, as the subeditor, would make of the newsroom or elsewhere to harden and improve the story.*

Notes: Where an insurance claim is likely it is unwise for the reporter to speculate, except in the most general terms, about liability or the loss from damage. The neighbour in this case could have been completely wrong in her supposition about the origin of the fire. It is unlikely that anyone except the owners would know the value of the paintings in relation to the whole. In rewriting this kind of story great care has to be exercised by the subeditor.

Assignment 5

The chief reporter of the area's evening paper is short of staff and sends the newest trainee reporter to cover the local comprehensive school sports day. The lad diligently sets about getting all the results of the events accurately plus a bit of the opening speech by the chairman of the governors. The copy is needed for the late afternoon edition so he phones it in in two long takes, starting with a few platitudes from the chairman, Colonel Wacker, and then running into the tabulated results:

'VALOUR on the sports field is necessary to complement achievement in the classroom,' Colonel Walter Wacker, the new chairman of the governors, told the packed sports day crowd on the playing field of St Hilda's Comprehensive School in Newtown today.

The Colonel, himself a former Cambridge rugby blue, said playing fields inculcated the right competitive spirit that would be needed through life...etc.

After the second take of telephoned results, the subeditor handling the copy, notices that a girl of the same name, N. Jackson, has come first in three races and second in another and asks the newsroom to find out something about her. It turns out that she is Norma Jackson and that she has had polio as a child.

TASK 1   *Imagining the circumstances of the sports day, and taking into account the new information, re-nose the story on the girl winner, giving the first four paragraphs as you would want them to read.*

TASK 2   *Explain what steps you would take to build up the story of the girl and obtain a picture in time for the late edition.*

Notes: A good deal can be done by the subeditor in setting up this sort of story, especially where the reporter on the spot is a novice or is feeling pushed for time. With the flow of copy into the system at peak times it is the subeditor handling the story for the page – especially a running story like this – who is closest to it and can alert the newsroom to certain angles.

Assignment 6

A mother and her teenage daughter have been killed crossing the road near a busy roundabout on the edge of the town. The reporter covering the story interviews the husband and turns in the following copy:

GRIEVING husband Archie Rice told this afternoon how he waved goodbye to his wife Helen and 14-year-old daughter Tracy minutes before they were killed crossing Outer Road, New Town, to buy pet food for their new kitten. 'We had just been given the kitten and they were happy and excited,' he said.

'I left them to go to a newsagent's and when I came out I saw a crowd on the pedestrian crossing just beyond the roundabout. It was them. They had never even reached the shop they had set out for.'

Mr Rice said he blamed himself for not going with them across the busy road: 'The traffic on this stretch goes too fast,' he said. 'The driver who hit them never even stopped. Fortunately someone got a description of the car.'

Mrs Rice and her daughter, who lived at Cornfield Road, Old Town, were regular members of Old Town Baptist Church. 'They were lovely people. It is a great shock,' Pastor James Jones told *The Gazette*.

The police are trying to trace a black A-registration Ford Sierra with a roof rack, rust marks on the boot and possible front-end damage. An inquest is to be opened on Thursday.

It is a fruitful interview and the reporter has made good use of it in her intro, but the subeditor remembers that it is not the first accident in recent months at that particular spot and turns up the cuttings. A previous accident also involved a hit-and-run driver. The subeditor finds a quote from a local councillor who, after a previous death, branded the crossing an 'accident black spot'. The sub draws the new information to the chief subeditor's attention and it is agreed that the story should be 're-nosed.' The chief sub decides that on this basis it also warrants being given a page lead on the first edition which sells in the area.

TASK I   *Prepare a 300-word story from the reporter's copy but re-nosed to bring in the information gleaned from cuttings.*

TASK 2   *Write an inside news page lead headline with a four-column line of twenty-three upper and lower-case characters and a second deck three-line heading in single-column with nine lower case characters per line.*

TASK 3   *Write a one-line caption across three columns for a picture of the mother and daughter, blown up from a picture of a chapel outing, for use alongside the story.*

TASK 4   *Write area bills for all newsagents and public buildings in New Town and Old Town.*

TASK 5   *Write 200 words on the way in which cuttings files can be of use in spot news stories of this sort.*

TASK 6   *Suggest any other reference or use that might be made of the story in the edition in view of the circumstances that have come to light.*

Notes: The circumstances have made this more than just another statistic in local road deaths. It also demonstrates the importance of always checking things in the cuttings files, which subeditors should do even though they might have expected the reporter to have already done so.

IT IS wrong to think that all stories have to be cut by the subeditor to fit. Some have to have text added to take account of further developments, or to bring out aspects of a story that were not at first thought to be important.

Some stories have to be collated from several text sources with the subeditor editing in split-screen mode with stories displayed side by side. Big multi-source stories such as elections or disasters might have reporters and correspondents turning in copy from different parts of the country or even from different countries, and the copy input can run on from edition to edition or even from day to day. These are called **RUNNING STORIES**.

Such stories can be tricky to handle and usually go to senior subeditors, although an apparently simple story can blossom into a complicated one and give the young subeditor handling it a baptism of fire. Here are some examples of the more complicated kind of subbing some stories might require.

Assignment 7

A Government junior minister has resigned over allegations in a national newspaper that he has been having an affair with an Italian actress. The story is broken by the Press Association which runs a bald statement from the Minister himself for evening papers. During the day the story builds up with the following sources filing copy.

Press Association:
Ernest Riskitt, Minister of State for the Arts, handed the following statement to the Press Association at midday today: 'I have

tendered my resignation from office to the Prime Minister at 10.30 this morning following the allegations about my private life published in the *Sunday Watchdog*. The Prime Minister has accepted my resignation with regret. I wish it to be known that I hotly deny the allegations published and have commenced legal proceedings against the newspaper company and its editor. My purpose in resigning from the Government is to minimize embarrassment to the Prime Minister while I fight to establish my honour. My wife is standing by me.'

Correspondent in Rome:
Alicia Beddi, the actress named in the allegations made in the *Sunday Watchdog* last week about British Government Minister Ernest Riskitt, has left her flat in the Via Venuto and is believed to be staying with friends some distance from Rome. A neighbour said Miss Beddi had lived alone in the flat for about 18 months but was a very private person who kept herself to herself. She did not have many visitors and was often away filming.

Staff reporter:
Messages of support for Arts Minister Ernest Riskitt, who has resigned from the Government in the wake of allegations made in last week's *Sunday Watchdog*, and for his wife Sally, began arriving today at his wife's mother's home in Low Lane, Old Town. Mrs Riskitt is a popular figure in Old Town, where she grew up as a child, and she and her husband used to be frequent visitors to area functions.

Mrs Riskitt was captain of the Old Town Girls' Grammar School before it became a comprehensive school and is a former governor. Mr Riskitt is a popular member of Old Town Golf Club though his appearance on the greens since joining the Government two years ago have been rare.

Blanktown correspondent:
In a hurriedly convened press conference at the MP's constituency headquarters in Blanktown today, Mrs Lorna Backup, the Party Chairman, told reporters: 'We are naturally upset at what this newspaper has published about our MP but we are absolutely sure that Ernest Riskitt has a complete answer.

'He need not have resigned but he believed it to be the honourable thing to leave office while he fights this gross calumny. He knows that in doing so he has our full support and backing. He has been a good MP for this consitutuency.'

Asked by one questioner if she had met Miss Beddi, the woman named in the *Sunday Watchdog* article, Mrs Backup said she had not called the press conference to answer scurrilous questions of that sort.

Parliamentary correspondent:
Mr Dennis Scanner MP has put down a Question in the House for Friday asking the Prime Minister 'What steps he proposes to take to put an end to the incessant probing by the national press into the private lives of Members, and what steps he proposes to take to make the use of bugging devices and long-lens cameras by the press an offence punishable by imprisonment.'

TASK 1   *Sub a page one evening paper lead story collating the five sources with no prescribed limit on length.*

TASK 2   *Write a main heading in capitals of two lines across seven columns with sixteen letters in each, and a second deck in upper and lower case of three lines across two columns with fourteen letters in each.*

TASK 3   *Write a single-line caption to go under a three-column picture with the story showing the MP and his wife at his last election poll declaration.*

TASK 4   *Write a general bill and a bill giving the local connection.*

TASK 5   *Explain in about 400 words any dangers in handling and presenting text of this sort.*

Notes: Stick to the known facts in a story like this – make no assumptions about who is right. It is not a newspaper's job to stand in judgement.

You may know something confidential in addition to the copy received – the existence of tapes perhaps. This information should not be used except with good legal reasons and under the advice and guidance of your editorial superior. Keep your paper out of trouble with the law and the Press Complaints Commission.

Remember that, for the moment, litigation is pending even though the threat to sue may turn out to be an empty one when all is revealed.

Assignment 8

The following agency story about an avalanche in the French Alps arrives on screen mid-morning as the local evening paper is working on its early editions:

Two skiers were killed and five were still trapped under a snow avalanche at the resort of St Symphorien, near Chamonix in the French Alps this morning. Four others managed to struggle free and summon help.

The eleven, which are believed to include a party from Manchester, were all experienced skiiers and were thought to have been descending the notorious Montluce slope off-piste when the avalanche struck without warning. Conditions at the resort had been good and most of those involved were nearing the end of their holiday.

The two dead were pulled by guides from a 'snow hole'. Two trapped skiers were found to be still breathing and rescuers were working to release them. The other three were still unaccounted for at 11 am local time.

The names of the dead skiiers have not been released. Police at St Symphorien, who are co-ordinating the rescue work with local guides, said they expected to be able to make a statement soon after midday.

The chief subeditor earmarks the story for page one. As well as being topical for the season, it concerns Manchester which is within the paper's circulation area. Meanwhile the news editor has seen the agency story on screen and has put a reporter on to check the local end. Half an hour later the reporter files the following:

ADD: AVALANCHE. There were fears today that members of Manchester University Ski Club party might be involved in the avalanche tragedy that occurred at St Symphorien in the French Alps this morning.

The party of eight, all experienced skiers, set off last Saturday for what they called an 'adventure' skiing holiday to mark the start of their last term at the university and their finals due in May.

The university authorities confirmed that the ski-club had sent a party to St Symphorien but declined to give the names until more details were available.

'Obviously we are anxious and worried but we have no reason at present to believe that any of our party was among the casualties,' said Wilbur Hackett, secretary of the ski-club, who added that he would have been with the group himself had he not gone down with flu at the last minute.

'We were all looking forward immensely to the trip,' he said.

TASK 1   *Sub a page one 'splash' story from the above two copy sources.*

TASK 2   *Write a banner headline in capitals, two lines across eight columns with a count of fourteen characters to a line, and a second deck of two lines in upper and lower-case across two columns, each with twelve characters.*

TASK 3   *Write a one-line three-column caption for a map of the area of the avalanche for use alongside the story.*

TASK 4   *Discuss in 300 words the policy to adopt in handling a story of this sort where there is a danger of identifying casualties before the next-of-kin have been informed.*

TASK 5   *Write a general bill for all the circulation area.*

At 1.15 pm an agency 'flash' appears on screen:

ADD: AVALANCHE. Three trapped skiers now safe. Third body found by rescuers.

At 2.05 pm the news agency runs a new lead on their AVALANCHE story:

Two Britons were among three skiers killed by an avalanche on the notorious Montluce slope at St Symphorien in the French Alps this morning . Three other Britons were rescued from near death under suffocating snow by guides who worked desperately as the weather deteriorated and further snow slips threatened. One skier is still missing.

Two of the dead were named by the police at St Symphorien as Charles Wackett, aged 22, and Jean Morgan, also 22, both students from Manchester University. The other was Ulrich Gabernock, believed to be an Austrian, who was staying at the resort

Two of the injured, Willy Brand and Clare Rainey, also students from Manchester, were detained in hospital suffering from shock and exposure. The third skier rescued, Walter Mitchell, a middle-aged hotel worker from Bristol, was released after treatment. The

French police have not released the name of the skier still missing.

The party, including the Austrian, who was an off-duty guide, were believed to have been skiing off-piste when the avalanche hit them without warning.

It was at first thought that a twelfth person had been involved but police say that 20-year-old Christopher Robbins, from Manchester, whose parents lived at Long Lane, Bolton, had returned to the hotel with a broken ski just before the incident

Police said next-of-kin of the dead students were expected to arrive at nearby Chamonix this evening. An inquiry had begun into the circumstances of the tragedy.

Pick up earlier story...etc.

TASK 6   *Re-nose and update the splash story and headline for the late edition to take in the new information, above, allowing the story to run to its natural length.*

TASK 7   *Write one line captions for each of three pictures — two two-column pictures of the dead students, and one four-column picture of the ski party taken a week earlier as they boarded their aircraft at the start of their holiday.*

TASK 8   *Write a local area bill to cover the student who escaped the disaster.*

Notes: A running story like this can tie a subeditor down for long periods and is a test of news sense and nerves as changes and new angles present themselves and edition deadlines rush up. Facts have to be updated, rewriting and collating carried out, pictures and maps considered, names and geography checked; matters of taste and legality can crop up. See Hodgson: *Subediting,* on running stories, pages 187–98.

NEWS value, as we have seen, dictates the intro and structure of an edited news story. There is one exception, however. This is the story we call the **SOFT SELL**.

'Soft sell' is the term given to stories in which the interest lies in the telling rather than in the unfolding of facts. They are usually stories that have a touch of humour or oddness, and they often concern children or animals or some extraordinary pattern of events.

Chief subeditors look out for such a story, which might start out as a simply told account of an event, to fill a special place on the page. They are usually given to a subeditor who is known to be good at the sort of creative rewriting such stories demand. Here is an example:

Assignment 9

An evening paper reporter files a story from a reader's tip-off about a bulldog rescued from a rabbit hole into which he had pursued a rabbit and got stuck. There are several interesting facts about this animal. He is called Hector and he is notoriously overweight for a bulldog. In fact he is a glutton and had recently gobbled up a sapphire engagement ring that his mistress had accidentally dropped into his food tray. The reporter writes it as a conventional news story.

An overweight bulldog had a lucky escape after pursuing a rabbit into a rabbit hole in Warren Copse, Old Town, yesterday.

Portly Hector got firmly stuck but fortunately his squeals were heard by two boys who called Mr Charles Brown, of nearby Copse Road, who managed to dig him out after a two-hour struggle.

Nigel Potter, aged 12, of Copse Road, said they were flying kites when they heard Hector's squeals. They traced them to a rabbit hole but could not see any sign of the dog.

Last night Hector was reunited with his mistress, Tracey Dibble, of Warren Road, Old Town.

'He's a naughty dog,' she told a Gazette reporter. 'It's the second incident we've had with him this week. On Wednesday he swallowed my engagement ring which had fallen into his food tray. I suppose that's the last I'll see of that.'

The chief subeditor immediately spots a possible development to the story – the fate of the missing ring. He gets the newsroom to dispatch the reporter back to Warren Road – with a dog laxative from the local vet. Three hours later Hector delivers the ring to its owner! There is just time for the subeditor to rewrite the story as a soft sell 'doggy' piece for the main edition.

TASK 1   *Rewrite the story of Hector, the rabbit and the ring as a humorous 'soft sell' piece for a prime position on page one.*

TASK 2   *Write a free-style headline that will sell the story to the readers on the assumption that an appropriate type will be found for it that will fit it into the page.*

Notes: Think your way well into the facts of this story and consider the humorous side – the valuable ring having vanished into the dog, the dog now vanishes down the rabbit hole. It is a double problem for its owner. Has Hector's gluttony gone too far? Think also of the possibility of a good last sentence, or pay-off line, to round off what is an unusual seqence of events. Consult soft-sell writing in Hodgson: *Subediting,* pages 220–2.

FEATURES SUBBING

ON MOST papers, except the more departmentalized national ones, subeditors will find themselves subbing both news and features copy. The two areas have a good deal in common. Both demand accuracy of fact, quote and language and careful checking for legality, taste and house style; both require headlines to be written in the right type and size and for captions and contents bills to be provided as needed.

But there are some important differences. News writing is, or should be, the objective recording of fact, subject to the selectivity imposed by market and readership. A feature is a subjective piece of writing in which fact, opinion, argument, persuasion and even confession can all form part.

Features tend to be carried on separate pages, to be longer than news stories and to be ordered and written for a pre-allocated space. The page design does not usually allow for fillers on features pages. A sub would not normally be expected to make heavy cuts in the text or collate several copy sources to create one story. In fact, with accepted stylists or important outside contributors cuts without consulting the writer are likely to be frowned on or even banned.

This does not mean that changes are not made. The paper has still to be guarded against nonsenses or lawsuits or breaches of taste, and the subeditor must not be lulled into thinking that everything an expert or top by-liner writes is gospel. Also a feature can still turn out to be too long. The need is for watchfulness tempered with discretion.

There is also a need, in the headlining and captioning and the use of pictures, to identify with the writer's aims and point of view where a major (and perhaps costly) feature is being given a lot of display and even promotion. Such writing has to be sold more deliberately to the readers than news stories.

There can be a blurring of the ground between features and news in some papers where young journalists might find their daily tasks range from reporting courts and councils to writing arts reviews and contributing to shopping and holiday guides. There is no reason why they should not do all these things – the variety provides excellent training – but the definitions given above should be kept in mind in the writing and subbing of the material.

The following exercises are intended to reflect aspects of subbing that are peculiar to the handling of features.

Assignment 10

A reporter is sent to cover the first night of the local amateur dramatic society's annual Shakespearean production, *The Tempest*, and finds on arriving at the theatre that the understudy is playing the part of Prospero. The reporter is told that this is because the actor named in the programme fell and broke his leg at the dress rehearsal the night before. The reporter mentions this in his review and devotes some space to praising the understudy's performance.

The chief subeditor decides that the circumstances of the accident and the task facing the stand-in warrant a separate news story on page one with a cross-reference to the review on the arts page and dispatches the subeditor to question the reporter further about this aspect.

TASK 1   *Using your imagination to simulate the above circumstances, draw from the review awaiting editing on screen and from further material you would expect to get from the reporter and write a 200-word news story for page one with an appropriate one-line cross-reference at the end.*

TASK 2   *Write a three-line single-column headline, with nine upper and lower case characters per line.*

TASK 3   *Write a 300-word account of the way in which page one 'floaters' can be used to draw attention to stories inside a newspaper, both news and features, and of the sort of stories that lend themselves to this treatment. An example would be, say, an octogenarian winning a top prize at the local horticultural show, with a cross reference to the show results inside the paper. Give two other examples.*

   Notes: This is a good example of how the same assignment can produce both a feature – i.e. a review – and a news story. It can have advantages. Some papers try to give an important feature inside the paper a topical news 'peg' on page one in order to draw readers' attention to it.

Assignment 11

The hard-pressed **SHOWBIZ GOSSIP** writer is late with her column of TV programme notes, having attended a number of previews. She takes particular exception at one of them to a well-known actor's portrayal of a cotton mill owner in a new serial, deciding that it shows little feeling for a character typical of an industry once important in the newspaper's circulation area. She writes:

THE PERIOD feeling in sets and dialogue in Down at t' Mill is realistically achieved and Sydney Glover looks well cast as Ackroyd, the mill owner. Yet something assails him. From his first fumbling entry he splutters and stammers as if he has had perhaps a drink too many with his lunch. Why does he have to look so unsteady? Does he really believe that Ackroyd is a blathering idiot? What is he trying to tell us? Perhaps the producer is at fault, but fault there is somewhere in this flawed concept...Compared to which Anne Morris gets every nuance of feeling – and our accolade – in her portrayal of the doomed wife.

Showbiz writers can get carried away, particularly when writing about something of which they feel they have first-hand knowledge. In this case the writer had had a crowded day and perhaps had not enough time to reread her text, otherwise she might have remembered that however much you disagree with an actor's portrayal you must not suggest they are drunk or professionally incompetent for the role. Words similar to these have cost newspapers a lot of money.

With by-line columnists noted for their style it is not a good idea for the subeditor in a case like this, to arbitrarily change the text but potentially libellous wording should be brought to the notice of the writer concerned or of the office legal adviser. Either way, the subeditor is responsible for ensuring that the text is made legally safe.

TASK 1 *Amend the text to make it, in your view, legally safe for publication while preserving the writer's words as far as possible.*

TASK 2 *Write a two-line single-column headline with twelve upper and lower case characters to a line appropriate to a features page.*

TASK 3 *Write 300 words explaining the libel pitfalls in writing about people in showbusiness.*

Notes: Consult McNae and Crone (Chapters 1 to 6) for libel dangers in a text like this.

WITH features subbing we enter the world of **BLURBS** and **STAND-FIRSTS** and promotions. From time to time newspapers that can afford it will spend money to give the readers something special that they hope will get the paper talked about and put on circulation. Such features need to be well laid out in the paper and well displayed in terms of type, pictures and headlines.

Sometimes they will be promoted by advertising on television or in other newspapers. Invariably they will be signposted to the reader by a blurb (i.e. a piece of self-advertisment) on page one, and by a standfirst (an explanation that stands first above the intro) on the page where the special feature appears.

Assignment 12

A Sunday tabloid has bought up the 'confessions' of ageing sex siren Bessie Blott who has decided to tell all now that she is finding work hard to come by. She writes about the men in her life (mostly now dead which enables her to get away with rather colourful statements), and what Mae West called the life in her men; the daring things she did to get herself first talked about, the 'love child' that no one knew she had had, and the famous rows she staged just for the publicity.

TASK 1   *Filling in the fictitious details of her career from the above, write a deep single-column blurb for page one, choosing display types and some illustration, to launch the series on Day One, and cross-referring to a double-page spread inside. Target it on the sort of readers you would expect to want to read the series, which has been chosen as a circulation puller.*

TASK 2   *Write a standfirst, including in it a prominent by-line, to go with the double-page spread.*

TASK 3   *Write (without type restrictions) the sort of headline and supporting line that would make a tabloid reader want to pause and read such a story further.*

TASK 4   *Write two general bills to go with Day One of the series.*

Notes: Nowhere is life in the features department more removed from that of the news desk than in the 'hard sell' world of heavily promoted 'big read' series, whether the paper be a popular tabloid or a quality Sunday broadsheet. The money spent and the potential extra circulation at stake require commitment and special skills in subeditors to promote the paper's top ingredient of the day. It is the point at which print journalism comes closest to publicity and public relations. See Hodgson: *Subediting*, pages 226–52, for techniques in this field.

Assignment 13

Drug-taking among sub-teenagers is being examined in depth in a city's evening paper. The features department has been given a whole page for it and has assembled three separate reports, two of case histories and one based on national and regional statistics; an excellent mood picture taken with models, and another of youngsters with their faces blacked out for identification reasons in a street in a bad area of the city.

TASK I   *Devise one main headline giving emotive force to the city's problem and two subsidiary headlines on the case histories (imagining the circumstances). Do not worry about character count. The page in this case will be built round the headlines and the pictures.*

TASK 2   *Devise a standfirst of about 60 words knitting the elements of the page together.*

TASK 3   *Write two careful captions for the pictures.*

Notes: The facts should be sufficient to energize the headlines in material of this sort. Assume that the standfirst, in special type, will be run close to the main headline. Beware of legal traps in the captions. The blacking out of faces, curiously, will add drama to the street picture. Above all, no identity of the youngsters must be possible. Probably most of them appearing in the picture will not be concerned with drugs anyway; it is the 'street of shame' image that the feature is trying to establish.

READER PARTICIPATION is part of many newspaper features – advice columns, how-to columns, consumer guides to shopping, holidays etc., readers' letters pages. Beware the dangers in readers' letters.

Assignment 14

It is seldom possible to publish readers' letters at length but editing should be with care. Here is a letter chosen as the lead item for the weekly letters column:

Dear Editor – You may think me a carping reader but I have to tell you that a resident's lot in Long Lane, Newtown, is not a happy one. Consider the following: in the past three months two cars have leapt the fence and finished up in my front garden, the second one demolishing my bed of prize leeks; my son's pet kitten was flattened to a wafer a week ago when trying to escape a lorry in the road; a wheel-trim from a Ford Sierra shot like a flying saucer over my hedge and settled near my recently vacated deckchair on my own lawn last week. I could have been too dead to write this letter!

Newtown Council do not seem to care. My neighbours and I have complained in vain about: (a) the speed of traffic in Long Lane; (b) the dangerous bend that makes cars brake like lunatics outside my house, and (c) the use of horns at midnight as homegoing revellers pursue their slalom course from the Dog and Doublet to God knows where.

Have Newtown councillors given up on residents' peace and safety? Has Long Lane become a 'no go' area for the traffic police? Is moving house the only way I can get on with my life with any certainty of living?

Perhaps I am just an old fuddy-duddy and it is cars, not people, that matter in Newtown. It is time we withheld our council tax till something is done – or would a rocket up their collective bum get some results?

Yours etc. – Disgusted (Mr E. Travers), Long Lane, Newtown

TASK 1   *Cut this angry letter to about half of its length, keeping in the reader's main points and something of the style.*

TASK 2   *Write a two-line headline of eighteen and nine characters in capitals.*

Notes: The old Press Council ruled that editing should be done 'solely to qualify a letter for publication. It should never be allowed to defeat or obscure the point or points which the correspondent wanted to make,' and it was 'desirable, where practical, to obtain consent from a correspondent to any substantial alterations to his/her letter.' *The Times*, for instance, never cuts a line of a reader's letter without permission. See Hodgson: *Modern Newspaper Practice*, 3rd Edition (Focal Press, 1993) pages 58–60.

Assignment 15

Gossip columns, local and national, are popular with readers, frequently sharing a features page with the leader, or editorial opinion and the main feature. They can be a trap for the young journalist.

Man in the News is late with his column of topical titbits for his evening paper's Friday edition. He rushes in the following as an 'add column' to fill out the space:

THERE'S trouble at t'mill down in Old Town. The Townshire Arts Association, I am told, has had an avalanche of letters from members accusing it of being disinterested in local writers.

Less than twenty members attended the Association's annual meeting the other week when a request from the Old Town Writers' Guild for space in the Association's Newsletter was rejected. There were weighty arguments supporting the decision but they have cut no ice with the Guild scribes who naturally feel their creative efforts are being slighted – or with the association members who had failed to turn up for the vote.

I hear that some of the dissatisfied letter writers are threatening to join forces with the Guild to launch a rival arts association.

'What we need is a proper concensus of views on the matter. The situation is ridiculous,' Councillor Charlie Todd, former Chairman of the Arts Association – and one of the AGM absentees – told me.

Wounded feelings and righteous indignation are the stuff of gossip columns, but beware! Many of the contestants in this titanic struggle could be better users of the language than our too-hasty columnist. What does the subeditor need to do to save him from his errors?

TASK 1   *In subbing this diary piece, put right any mistakes in spelling or usage.*

TASK 2   *Write a suitable one-line heading in fourteen upper and lower case characters.*

Notes: See Hennessy: *Writing Feature Articles*, 2nd Edition (Focal Press, 1993), chapter 14, and Hodgson: *Subediting*, pages 100–36 on language and word use. Also see Bagnall: *Newspaper Language* (Focal Press, 1993).

Assignment 16

It is a thin day for pictures and the chief sub has decided to liven up page three, a good printing page, with an attractive picture from a news agency of a local girl model riding a penny farthing bicycle at a national exhibition of old-world transport. She is a pretty blonde dressed in the unlikely comination of tutu and crash helmet. Paid onlookers in yokel costume are ooh-ing and ah-ing. The chief subeditor plans it as a deep four-column.

The photographer's caption on the back of the print simply says: 'Sally Wheeler, of Old Town, Lancashire, tries out a penny farthing at the Motor Cycle Exhibition of Transport Through the Ages, at Earl's Court, London, today.'

TASK 1   *Write a hundred-word self-contained display caption, visualizing the picture in your mind as it is described above, using the composition of the picture, the local connection, the photographer's supplied caption and such whimsy as you feel is justified to grab the readers' attention.*

TASK 2   *Write a two-line heading, eight capital characters per line, to go on top of the picture.*

TASK 3   *Write a bill giving the local connection.*

Notes: Writing a caption for a stand-alone picture (as opposed to one that goes with a story) is a creative task that is often assigned to a features subeditor. See caption writing, Hodgson: *Subediting*, pages 182–5.

HEADLINE WRITING

WRITING a good headline, either on a news story or a feature, is an acquired skill. It requires a keen news sense, a knowledge of typography and the ability to render the essence of a story into a few words that will attract the reader's eye without doing damage to the facts. The computer has not made this process any easier. The headline still has to fit its circumscribed space on the page and must have typographical balance and look right; the sub has not only to work at it on screen but to visualize how it will look when it prints. Nor can the sub expect the chief sub to change the type every time he/she cannot think of the right words.

Some subs are good at instant headlines on first reading the story; some stories lend themselves to this. Otherwise a good tip, especially to new subs, is to list the main words in the story on a notepad and juggle them till the right headline with the right balance, width and number of lines emerges.

A police search has been going on in the area for a six-year-old girl who has gone missing. She is found in dramatic circumstances. The following is your first attempt at a headline:

MISSING GIRL JACKIE,
AGED SIX, IS DISCOVERED
HIDING IN
AN EMPTY HOUSE

TASK 1   *A tighter headline is needed. Write down on your pad the essential words you would want to use in the headline.*

TASK 2   *Write a four-line single-column headline of eight capitals to the line.*

TASK 3   *It is given more space: write a two-line headline across two columns with thirteen lower case characters to the line.*

TASK 4   *The story becomes a page lead for the area edition. Write a strapline of twenty-eight lower case characters and a main headline of seventeen capitals across six columns.*

Notes: To save space (always tight in headlines) it is common to miss out articles and auxiliary verbs. Thus, in the above headline 'is' and 'an' could be dropped, still leaving the meaning clear. Beware, however, of leaving out active verbs that energize a headline – goes, falls, criticises, destroys, makes, etc. For general guidance on headline writing, see Hodgson: *Subediting,* pages 137–69.

The following headline on a strike is rejected by the chief sub on the ground that the over-use of abbreviations has made it look like gobbeldygook.

NUM and
EETPU
join forces
to outwit
NCB

TASK 1   *Rewrite the headline to the same count and number of lines in lower case without abbreviations while keeping in the headline facts. (For those who might rightly wonder what the initials stand for, NUM is the National Union of Mineworkers, EETPU the Electrical, Electronic, Telecommunications and Plumbing Union, and NCB the National Coal Board.)*

TASK 2   *Assuming that the headline represents a story of two unions who have taken a united stand against their employers, write another version for a different edition in two lines of capitals with fourteen characters in each line.*

Notes: Some abbreviations that are really well known to all the readers, such as BBC and Nato, are acceptable in headlines but one abbreviation per headline is enough for the reader. They are visually ugly and some may not not be readily known to some readers. Abbreviations such as the NUM will be known in areas where the activity or industry indicated is located, and might therefore be used. Note that abbreviations that produce an acronym, such as Nato, are rendered normally in lower case with an initial capital, otherwise BBC, USA etc. are given in capitals. See abbreviations in Hodgson: *Subediting,* pages 55, 135 and 143–4.

The following headline is written by the subeditor on a 'soft sell' story about a comical mishap that happened to a couple who went for a drive in a horse-drawn equipage they had restored:

THE OLD WAGON WHEEL
WENT
ROLLING...ROLLING...
ROLLING....

TASK 1   *Rearrange the words into a better visual balance, using three lines of capitals taking up to fourteen characters a line. A bit of white space at the ends of each line is acceptable.*

TASK 2   *Enhancing the story with such facts as you feel it might have contained, write an alternative headline of six lines in lower case with a character count per line of eleven.*

Notes: Writing 'soft sell' headlines can be fun since the subeditor is not bound by the need to convey the hard news to the reader. Imagination and a sense of humour can be helpful, but beware of straining the reader's patience with too many puns and lavatorial jokes! See facetiousness in Hodgson: *Subediting,* pages 220–3, also Waterhouse: *Waterhouse on Newspaper Style* (Viking, 1989), pages 94–102.

Assignment 20

Some newspapers centre their headlines on the space available in the case of single, double or three-column headlines (and magazines do, too) while others set them left against the column rule with perhaps an en or an em (pica) of space between the first letter and the rule. Either way, good balance is essential for a smooth read.

TASK 1 *Consider what is wrong visually with the following headlines and adjust the balance so that they look better, keeping the same number of lines. Do not worry about a maximum character count:*

Six
Cabinet
Ministers go
in big re-shuffle

Factory
'leakage' ruins
100 acres
of
farmland

Angola war scare hits
new trade agreement on tea

BBC CONCEDES
NEED
FOR
'NEW LOOK'
CONTRACTS

Notes: Feel free to delete or introduce new words provided the headlines still carry the same message. Note that one headline is in capitals and the others in lower case.

REFERENCES AND FURTHER READING

Bagnall, N: *Newspaper Language* (Focal Press, 1993).
Crone, T: *Law and the Media*, 3rd Edition (Focal Press, 1995).
Hodgson, FW: *Modern Newspaper Practice*, 3rd Edition (Focal Press, 1993).
Hodgson, FW: *Subediting*, 2nd Edition (Focal Press, 1993).
McNae, LCJ: *Essential Law For Journalists* (Butterworths, 1992).
Sellers, L: *The Simple Subs Book* (Pergamon Press, 1985).
Waterhouse, K: *Waterhouse on Newspaper Style* (Viking, 1989).

6

Page planning and design

IF YOU examine closely the pages of your local paper – or any other newspaper – you will become aware that they have focal points, or areas that attract the eye on first turning to them. These focal points are created by the deliberate use of type and pictures to form a kind of pattern, the aim of which is first to grab the reader's attention and then to guide the reader through the contents of the page.

You will notice that one of the stories is given a bigger headline and frequently more space than the other stories on the page, creating an immediate focus for the eye. This story is known as the page lead. The main picture on the page likewise demands the eye's attention. The second most important story, the half-lead, is given the second biggest type headline on the page, creating another focal point.

At the opposite pole of what we might call the display of the material are a number of short one- or two-paragraph items with headlines in small type. These are known as fillers – i.e., they fill the odd corners of space left under or around the bigger items. You would be right in assuming that these are the stories which, in the view of the editor or the page executive, are of least importance on the page. They and the body text are the material that fill the spaces between the focal points we have just described.

In between the main items and the fillers are the rest of the stories, perhaps filling single or double-column spaces and each carrying a headline of maybe three or four lines of type. These are referred to as ops from the fact that in the early newspapers with their simple columnar layout all stories began at the top of the page and ran down on to fillers.

The main picture, as with the page lead story, has been given its space because it is important, either for its news value or its intrinsic value as a picture. Unless a page has been deliberately planned as a picture page it will not usually have more than one big picture. If there are other pictures they are likely to be smaller, perhaps just head shots of persons mentioned in stories. They are of lesser importance to the page.

Thus in the design of the page the various ingredients have been given a value which is reflected in the space and prominence they occupy and the degree to which they catch the eye of the reader on first turning to the page.

This eye-catching is the crux of page design. Newspapers – and nowhere is this more important than on page one on the newstands – commend themselves visually to the eye upon first sight, first of all encouraging the reader to buy and then to turn the pages. The theory is that the eye is led from item to item in order of importance. The fact that some newspaper readers read the smaller items first or even the paper from the back to the front is an aberration that page designers have learned to live with.

There is another factor that should be taken into account in newspaper design: the advertising carried on the pages. Since the editorial material is competing with the advertisements for the reader's eye it is important that it should not appear too visually subservient. It must balance well against the adverts while at the same time not clashing in typography or picture content – or looking the same or very similar.

It is also a good idea for obvious reasons for the editorial content not to be similar to the product content of the advertising, such as an account of insurance frauds alongside an insurance advert or a picture of a sinking ship alongside a cruise line advert.

You could say page design is akin to packaging. There is nothing wrong with this. Early newspapers with no display type or pictures and all their items running up and down the columns starting with column one – and with few readers – would not be liked by the modern reader used to a competitive press and to the display and design on every side which we take for granted in our consumer society.

Allowing that the aim is to attract and guide the reader, you can, nevertheless, over-design. Excessive display can short-change the text. A good balance between visual display and reading text is required, and some regard must be paid to the readership market. For example, in

national papers in Britain tastes are reflected in newspapers catego-
rized, for want of a better description, as popular, middle of the road
and quality – what some irreverently call the 'heavies'. Each has its
design characteristics.

An examination of a range of daily, evening, weekly and Sunday
newspapers, both national and regional, will a reveal a variety of
'weights' and styles in page design, reflecting their market tastes and
purpose. The popular national tabloids, for example, are strong on
pictures and visual appeal while the qualities carry more words in their
news and features than the popular tabloids. All, however, have the
basic design purpose we have defined above.

The following exercises, based on the close reading and examination
of different sorts of newspapers, are aimed at helping students understand the basics of page design and why it is necessary, and to try out
ideas for themselves.

Assignment 1

Cut up four news pages from one issue of
a tabloid-sized evening paper, separate the
items into news stories, pictures and
adverts and set them aside.

TASK 1   *Draw a page outline of the same size, drawing in vertical lines to
provide the same number and width of columns and allow for one
fourteen-centimetre by three-column advert space on the bottom left
and one eleven-centimetre by three-column advert space on the
bottom right. Paste in appropriate advertising material from your
cuttings, trimming to fit as necessary.*

TASK 2   *Using the cut material, irrespective of which page it came from,
choose and paste into the page a page lead, a half lead, a main
picture and such other tops, fillers and pictures as are needed to
give a balanced page which will fit the space available but not clash
visually with the adverts.*

Notes: In this exercise we can forget about the actual content
of the news stories and the pictures, or even what the words
say. What we are looking for is visual balance giving focal points
that attract the eye and guide the reader round the page, and
one that does not clash with, or copy, the advertising on the
page. See Giles and Hodgson: *Creative Newspaper Design*
(Heinemann Professional Publishing, 1990), pages 1–10 on
theory of design and 124–36 on page planning.

Assignment 2

Using the same pile of material you have cut and set aside from your local evening paper, try the following:

TASK 1 *Draw a second page to the same scale as the above, marking in the columns, but allowing this time a horizontal bottom half-page advert. If you do not have such an advert among your cuttings cannibalize a couple together to achieve as realistic an effect as possible. Again we are concerned with the visual effect, not with what the words say.*

TASK 2 *Choose from your cuttings a page lead, a half lead, a main picture and such other tops, fillers and pictures as will fit together to fill the available space effectively to form a typical news page.*

Notes: The problem here is that you have, in effect, a horizontal-shaped page and you are competing with a big advert of the same size and shape which has already been designed, bought and placed on the bottom half of the page. As the page designer, your are faced with a challenge. See Giles and Hodgson as above.

A KNOWLEDGE of **TYPE** is fundamental in page design. Each newspaper has a particular type character in which certain types are used in different sizes and weights to produce a consistent appearance which differentiates the paper from others, even though their market and design philosophy may be similar.

Once you read newspapers professionally, as journalists should, you will be able to tell at a glance the difference between a page, say, from the *Daily Telegraph* and one from *The Times*. In the same way the *Daily Mail*, or *The Sun* – or your local evening paper – will have its recognizable type characteristics with which you will quickly become familiar.

The creative use of type lies at the basis of this. While there is a bigger number of type faces available today than there ever were under the old hot-metal typesetting, a newspaper stocks its system with the range of types it needs to produce the sort of paper it is. Some of these types might be for special occasions only but all are carefully chosen. In no way is type allowed to become a ragbag to be dipped into.

Types, despite their many names and design characteristics, come broadly in two families – serif and sanserif. Serif types are those characterized by a little flourish or serif at the end of each stroke (see Figures 13 and 14) and are the descendants of the early Latin or Roman alphabets that can be still seen carved in stone. Sanserif means simply what it says

abcdefghijklmnopqrstuvwxyz
ABCDEFGHIJKLMNOPQRSTUVWXYZ
abcdefghijklmnopqrstuvwxyz
ABCDEFGHIJKLMNOPQRSTUVWXYZ

Figure 13   A stock serif type used in some of the older country
weeklies – Clearface Heavy with its condensed version

abcdefghijklmnopqrstuvwxyz
ABCDEFGHIJKLMNOPQRSTUVWXYZ
abcdefghijklmnopqrstuvwxyz
ABCDEFGHIJKLMNOPQRSTUVWXYZ

Figure 14   A decorative type face with thick serifs used as a variant on news pages
– Cooper Black (or Ludlow Black), with its Outline version for glossy magazine pages

abcdefghijklmnopqrstuvwxyz
ABCDEFGHIJKLMNOPQRSTUVWXYZ

**abcdefghijklmnopqrstuvwxyz
ABCDEFGHIJKLMNOPQQRSTUVWXYZ**

Figure 15   Take the light or the bold – two much used versions of the popular Futura sans type

– type that has plain strokes without serifs (see Figure 15). Both have spawned many designs and both are still widely used in newspapers.

Newspapers generally opt for one type family or the other, using the occasional sanserif type as a variant in a predominantly serif format, or the occasional serif variant in a sanserif format. The following exercises are intended to make you aware of type use and type formats and how to use the occasional variant in serif and sanserif pages.

For a more detailed account of types and type use, see Giles and Hodgson, pages 11-37 and 178-87 on typography; also Hodgson: *Subediting*, pages 33-55 and 152-69 on page planning and headlines; and Davis: *Magazine Journalism Today* (Focal Press) chapter 7.

Assignment 3

Using the remaining items from the four cut pages from your local paper used in assignments 1 and 2, try the following:

TASK 1 *Draw a page the same size as the ones you have cut, showing the correct number and widths of columns and mark in a vertical half page advert (or vertical three- or four-column advert if it is a seven-column page) on the right, or two same-shaped adverts, one on top of the other.*

TASK 2 *Select a page lead, a half lead, tops, pictures and fillers to paste in to create a satisfactory design, with focal points, in such a way that the editorial part balances and does not clash with the advertising content to the right of it. Pay regard to type balance as referred to above, identifying, if you can, the paper's type format.*

Notes: A vertical half page is harder to fill satisfactorily than a horizontal half page because of the equal amount of space 'below the fold'. Consider running the half lead about the middle of the page and a story in several legs across the bottom to prevent the end of the page degenerating into bittiness. You can cut up a single-column headline and paste the lines together end to end to do this if you have not got one of the correct width. Leave at least one of your pictures for use below the fold. (See book references above.)

Assignment 4

Cut up all the news pages in one issue of *The Sun* and set aside the items in piles – stories (with headlines), pictures and adverts. Imagine that there have been edition advertising changes and that you have to redraw three of the pages to different advertising shapes for the next edition, selecting from the material you have already got.

TASK 1 *Draw a page with the right number and width of columns (simply measure them) and insert a deep five-column display (i.e., type and illustration) advert on the right. It is a right-hand page. Choose a page lead and other such stories and pictures which you consider will make a typical Sun news page, with type size and weight as you would expect to see used, and paste the items in position.*

TASK 2   *Draw a page with the the right number of columns as above but this time paste in a half page horizontal advert, cannibalizing adverts together if need be to fill the space. Choose a page lead and other news stories and pictures and paste them in to produce the sort of editorial top half news page you would expect to find in* The Sun, *playing close attention to the paper's typographical style.*

TASK 3   *Draw a third page as above, paste in a three-column by eleven-centimetre advert on the bottom left and a two-column by eight-centimetre advert on the bottom right, cutting up advertising material to fit if necessary, and select editorial matter from your remaining cut items to turn the available space into a Sun-style news page.*

TASK 4   *Summarize in 500 words the design characteristics and aims of* The Sun *as you see them. Consider its use of serif and sanserif types, its use of headlines and pictures and the general balance of the pages and the number of items carried.*

Notes: As with any other newspaper design tasks, a close reading and examination of the appropriate paper is necessary to do this sort of excercise well. Having read and examined copies of *The Sun*, put them aside so that you are not tempted to copy existing pages. What we want you to do is to choose and manipulate type in the way *The Sun* does it and to show an understanding of the paper's design characteristics. In placing the headlines, text and pictures take care over the size and weight of the type. Beware of making the pages a mish-mash. Behind a brash boldly designed tabloid page there usually lies a good deal of care, typographical skill and reader psychology.

See Giles and Hodgson, pages 137–45 on markets and style.

A simple guide to design in national papers is that the popular tabloids are strong on display and the broadsheet qualities (or heavies) on words. This does not mean that *The Times*, *The Guardian* and the *Daily Telegraph* pay no attention to display. There are themes and subtleties and a great deal of concern about visual balance as well as balance of contents. The following two exercises are intended to make you familiar with the parameters of design in the national **QUALITY NEWSPAPERS**.

Assignment 5

Cut up two news pages and two main features pages of any edition of *The Times* and make separate piles of the items.

TASK 1 *Draw a broadsheet* Times *page with appropriate numbers and widths of columns (you are going to need some pretty large paper for this) and allow for two three-column by fourteen-centimetre adverts, one on either side at the bottom. Select and paste into position your editorial material to produce a typical* Times *news page.*

TASK 2 *Draw another* Times *page, this time without any adverts on it, select appropriate pictures and material and carefully lay out a main* Times *features page as you would expect it to look. Pay attention to balance of display and to type style as used in* The Times.

TASK 3 *Summarize in 500 words how your see the type character of* The Times, *referring to its use of serif and sanserif type, its use of white space and the general page balance and number of items contained in news and features pages.*

Notes: As with *The Sun* exercise, it is necessary to read and examine several editions of *The Times* in order to carry out the above tasks effectively. You should quickly become aware that good visual balance plays its part in a quality daily just as much as in a popular tabloid, although the parameters are different. Look for ways in which type character is imposed on the pages so that a page of *The Times* looks distinctively what it is and is unlikely to be mistaken for a page from any other newspaper. (Giles and Hodgson, pages 137–45).

A FEW years ago *The Guardian* brought in what was then a revolutionary and much debated new type format for its masthead and pages, which has given it a distinctive appearance among British national papers (Figure 16). Try the following exercise.

Assignment 6

Cut up a selection of news and features items, including pictures, from two editions of *The Guardian* and set aside in two separate piles.

TASK 1 *Draw a Guardian-sized page with columns of appropriate width, allowing for two three-column by fourteen-centimetre adverts bottom*

Figure 16 Breaking new ground in type use – a sports page from *The Guardian*
The Guardian ©

left and right, and paste in a page lead and other news items and pictures to form a typical Guardian news page. Take care over the use of white space.

TASK 2   *Draw another page of the same size and number of columns, with no advertising, and select material and pictures to create a* Guardian *main features page. Take great care in the use and placing of pictures and in the use of white space. Try to create eye focus in the way* The Guardian *does it.*

TASK 3   *Summarize in 500 words your views on* The Guardian's *design characteristics and identify its virtues and its difficulties.*

Notes: Close reading and examination of issues of *The Guardian* is needed for this assignment. Despite the controversy at the time surrounding the launch of its new format *The Guardian* has stuck to its guns and has become a highly regarded example of modern typographical style. It is also a reminder that, however good its contributors and its reputation, a quality daily still places importance on its visual presentation, even to the point of changing it drastically if it feels it is to the good of the paper – which is what *The Guardian* did.

COUNTY and suburban **WEEKLY PAPERS** fulfil an important role in the community. They are immensely varied in style and sophistication and also in purpose. The readership market and the sort of community in which they operate has to be taken into account in the presentation of the editorial contents page by page, and there is usually quite a bit to be learned about the sort of paper they are by study of their type character and visual appearance. Here are some assignments that will help to give you insights into this design field.

 **Assignment 7**   Take three editions of a country weekly paper that is accessible to you, read them closely and cut up two news pages and two features pages from each and set the items on one side.

TASK 1   *Draw a page of the appropriate size (tabloid or broadsheet), columns and column widths, paste in a five-column by fifteen-centimetre advert on the bottom right. Select and arrange a news page lead, a main picture and such other items and pictures as will make up a news page of the sort you would expect to find in the paper.*

SUSSEX TODAY — ARGUS, Monday, January 16, 1995 — 5

MP's rail ticket check

SUSSEX MP Jacqui Lait has stepped in over the threat to through tickets in British Rail privatisation plans.

Through tickets may only be offered at certain stations under options being considered by Rail Regulator John Swift.

A leaked list of stations which would offer through ticket services under the plan included Hastings, but not Rye, and Mrs Lait, who represents Rye, has written to Richard Fearn, director of Network South Eastern, to get an assurance that they will continue to be sold at Rye.

● **Crowborough:** Leslie Reeves, 83, who went missing on Friday morning after going out for a stroll, is recovering after being found in a field in Rotherfield, four miles from his home in Southridge Rise, Crowborough. Mr Reeves, who has senile dementia, was flown to Eastbourne District General Hospital in the Sussex police helicopter. He said to be in a comfortable condition.

● **Lewes:** Furniture Now, the Lewes district furniture recycling project, has opened its first shop in Spring Gardens, North Street. It will provide information about the project and sell items of furniture to raise money for collection, renovation and delivery of other items for recycling.

● **Haywards Heath:** The annual meeting of the Mid Sussex Parkinson's Disease Society will be held on Friday at 2.30pm at Clair Hall, Haywards Heath.

● **Sussex:** Four West Sussex ambulance officers who accepted voluntary early retirement in the shake-up of Sussex services, said farewell to colleagues at a party. Supplies officer David Lelliot, from Sompting, fleet manager Allan Ware, from Chichester, major incident planning officer Peter Wells, from Bognor, and control manager Peter Williams, from Chichester, shared 160 years of service. The two Sussex ambulance services merge from April 1.

● **Hove:** Work is to start later this month on replacing the defective roof on the ladies' bowls pavilion at Kingsway.

LUCKY NUMBERS

AS a service to Argus readers we are publishing the bingo numbers from competitions being run by yesterday's national newspapers.

News of the World Tringo: Top Section: 1 42 73 70 19 15 37 38 35 80 52 14 68 13 63 62 24 71 33 83 66. Second Section: 44 8 77 50 87 3 21 55 85 36 51 25 28 11 2 6 56 41 64 48 40 81 88 90 89 10 45 65 47 76 17 26 60 30 59 86 22 67 78 74 29 61 34 20 72 54 7 9 57.

The People (Game 246 Week 2): 4 40 21 67 79 87 31 26 74 10 43 2 57 38 81 12 52 18 86 39 72 16 62 3 60 22 70 7 56 37 76 54 42 71 35 85 1 58 13 68 9 33.

Sunday Mirror (Game 248 Week 1): Top Section: 18 39 57 41 9 4 89 43 36 21 52 73 49 31 7 85 29 70 54 81. Second Section: 22 77 8 60 69 46 3 88 6 74.

Every care is taken to ensure the accuracy of these numbers but the Argus cannot accept responsibility for any errors or omissions.

Death school head praised

HEADMASTER Robert Smith has been officially praised for his actions during the meningitis outbreak which killed two girls at his primary school.

Mr Smith is headmaster of Rottingdean Primary, which suffered the loss of five-year-olds Emma Harris and Alexandra Yates to the disease.

After hearing of the outbreak he worked non-stop to allay parents'

Phil Dennett

fears and advise them on what they should do for their children.

His prompt actions are singled out for special mention in a report by East Sussex Heath Authority, which meets this week.

In the report, Dr Brendan O'Connor, East Sussex director of Public Health, said the speed of response was particularly due to Mr Smith.

Among the steps taken to inform parents was a school open day arranged by Mr Smith on January 7.

This was attended by many experts and allowed parents to understand what happened and what could happen before the children returned to school a few days later.

Dr O'Connor said 150 calls a day were coming in to the authority from anxious parents in the days immediately after Emma's death on Boxing Day.

Letters were also sent to parents,

This is the man who worked non-stop to allay parents' fears

staff and local GPs, as well as a host of advice from other organisations.

The report says the incident was more complicated because of the speed of Emma's death, the intense media interest and the fact that it happened over a bank holiday.

Dr O'Connor said professional

and secretarial staff gave up their holiday to help deal with the inquiries and he praised what he called "the excellent general level of support".

But he picked out Mr Smith, and the authority will be asked on Thursday officially to record a vote of thanks to him and his staff.

ABOVE: How the Argus broke the news

Robert Smith: Prompt action over the death of two of his young pupils

Countdown to tragedy

THE report details the timetable of the crucial first four days of work to contain the tragedy:

● Boxing Day: Emma and Alexandra are both admitted to hospital, and Emma dies. The tracing of all close contacts is ordered for vaccination and antibiotics. A plan to fight the outbreak is formed.

● December 27: The remaining contacts are traced, some by calling at parents' homes and leaving letters. All local GPs are faxed, and letters to 150 parents of children in other classes are also posted.

● December 28: The fatal strain is identified as group C meningococcus and manufacturers are contacted for the vaccine. Letters are sent to everyone needing vaccination asking them to see their GP.

● December 29: Preparations for vaccinating close contacts are completed. The parents of other children at the school are consulted about swabbing sessions to be held on January 11.

A SCOUT group is appealing for help after arsonists wrecked their bus.

The 19th Brighton Scout Group bus was reduced to a burnt-out shell after it was torched on Saturday afternoon.

The 50-seater bus, which was not insured, was parked in front of the Scout hut behind Woodingdean County Primary School in Warren Road.

Scout group helper and Woodingdean School caretaker Paul Gumbrill, pictured at the scene, said the bus was already off the road because it had broken down and was waiting to be repaired.

Now the Scout group is appealing for help to get a new bus.

Mr Gumbrill said: "We used to use the bus to take the boys out. It has been broken down for some time, but now we really need someone to help us move it."

Police are appealing for witnesses who may have seen anyone in the area early on Saturday afternoon.

Allotment soil gets all-clear

MORE tests have been completed on soil at the North Nevill allotments in Hove following fears about high lead levels on some plots.

The fears were raised last year but test results indicate that no particular area of the site was contaminated before it was used as allotments.

A report to the council says:

"The contamination does not appear to follow any pattern and lead must have been introduced by individual plot holders at some stage in the past."

Allotment holders are being told that produce should be all right provided vegetables are washed before use and the outer leaves of cabbages are discarded.

Water leak conmen trick OAP

THREE crooks conned a 92-year-old man into giving them £700 to repair a plumbing leak.

The three confronted the pensioner outside his home in Coombe Lea, Hove, and told him they lived in the flat below him.

They claimed water was leaking down into their flat and

they needed money to pay for a plumber.

They walked with him to the National Westminster bank near Hove town hall where he withdraw the money. After he handed over the cash they disappeared.

One conman is between 40 and 50, 5ft 7in and stocky build. Another is 35 to 40, 5ft 8in and average build.

Figure 17 A busy area page on a local evening paper – the *Brighton Evening Argus*.

Figure 18   A page is born – notice how changes are made in both headlines and positioning between (a) the first rough layout, above, and (b) the finished *News of the World* page, opposite

4 NEWS OF THE WORLD, February 28, 1993

CINEMA GUIDE
by Jo Fletcher
our girl in the stalls

★ WHAT a gem! Lorenzo's Oil (12) is a passionate movie which grabs you by the throat.

It is based on the true story of Augusto and Michaela Odone, whose son Lorenzo, five, is found to have a rare, incurable congenital disease called ALD.

Most sufferers die within two years, so the frantic parents played by Nick Nolte and Susan Sarandon, begin a desperate search for a cure.

Susan Sarandon has justifiably been nomin-

BRILLIANT: Sarandon

ated for an Oscar for this performance, and Nolte is also totally convincing.

It's quite brilliant—despite the choral background music!

★ ACTION fans will certainly get their fill in Under Siege (15), starring martial arts hero Steven Seagal.

The plot, about terrorists hijacking a battleship, is unlikely — but there's loads of excitement to make up.

★ THERE'S also a strange plot to Leon The Pig Farmer (15), but this one is fun.

Leon Geller (Mark Frankel) is a nice Jewish boy who discovers his dad isn't net curtain king Sidney (David Keyser) but Yorkshire pig farmer Brian Glover!

Occasionally hilarious—and always bizarre.

★ RATHER more successful is Honeymoon In Vegas (12), starring Nicholas Cage as a momma's boy.

He's plucking up courage to wed girlfriend Sarah Jessica Parker—but then mobster James Caan moves in. Look out for the Flying Elvises as you soak up this sunny, enjoyable comedy!

TASK 2   *Draw another page of the above size, paste in a half page advert and select features text and pictures from your cut items to make up a features presentation of the sort you would expect to find in the same paper.*

TASK 3   *Summarize in 500 words your impressions of the design characteristics and presentation style of the paper you have chosen.*

TASK 4   *Compare, in 500 words, the presentation and design characteristics of the paper you have chosen for this exercise and those of another weekly paper operating in a similar market. Discuss their ideas as far as you can identify them, and any differences you have noted in approach. Work out the number of stories and the amount of text each carries on:*

   (a) Its news pages.
   (b) Its features pages.

Notes: You may think you can easily improve on the sort of page design you have come across in the paper that you have selected, but beware! Some county and suburban weeklies might leave something to be desired in their display but remember that the element of familiarity is important in such papers, and can account for design characteristics. The appearance and location of items, especially on features pages (regular columns, TV programme notes, etc.) must be allowed for and any violent change in display that will confuse the reader should be avoided.

By all means, if you spot poor visual balance or eye difficulties, try to do better when you carry out tasks 1 and 2, but be sure you have understood what the paper is trying to do for its readers. Also, the recording of the life of a community may be what makes most readers buy such papers. A skilful but over-enthusiastic journalist given his or her head on the pages could well lose such readers.

MAGAZINE AND PERIODICAL DESIGN

MAGAZINE and periodical design is based on the same broad principles as newspaper design in that the aim is to attract readers, hold their attention and render the contents readable, but there are more variables at work. Publications have more but usually much smaller pages. The content is often highly specialized and many are read for what they have to say rather than how they look.

As a result, the method of targeting readers produces every kind of typographical format from the glossy fashion magazines full of colour pictures and expensive artwork printed by gravure, to learned journals which consist almost entirely of reading matter and straightforward informative headlines.

In between is a world of magazines serving a variety of interests in which typography and pictures are still used to create the focal points that drive the reader through the pages, with each product developing its distinctive typographical style. Desktop publishing, running on a modest budget, has spawned a host of titles, some of which show signs that the simple principles of page design have yet to be learned.

The following exercises are intended to give student journalists some insights into this field.

 Assignment 8 You are planning a monthly twelve-page house magazine of approximately foolscap format for a small company serving the building trade with products that include prefabricated windows, doors, sheds, staircases and partitioning and you have got together the following materials:

1 A 1500-word story about a new plastic cladded long-life wooden window suited to office buildings.

2 Three pictures, of which you want to use two; one is a wide shot of the new products being loaded on to a wagon.

3 An 800-word piece of the firm's garden sheds *in situ* based on a tour of customers' sites.

4 Four varied pictures showing the sheds with their owners.

5 A 1000-word story about a London suburban building site where a number of the company products are being used.

6 Two useful general shots of the site showing cranes and activity.

7 A picture of the new deputy managing director and short biography.

8 A picture of the firm's annual dance with a caption story that can be cut or extended as needed.

9 Two wedding pictures and one christening to do with company employees, together with caption material.

10 A 1000 word account of a speech made by the company's chairman at the recent annual meeting.

11 A picture of the chairman making his speech.

campaign

A Haymarket publication — 20 January 1995 — £1.70

ITV pressures Govt over BBC deals

by Tina Mistry

Top ITV sales chiefs have set in motion plans to stop the BBC from striking any more commercial deals such as the recent controversial tie-up with Mirror Group Newspapers (*Campaign*, 6 January).

Senior ITV figures plan to lobby top-ranking cross-party Parliamentary ministers on the issue and are about to embark on a campaign which will focus on encouraging senior industry figures to debate the matter in public.

The aim is to make the Gov-

Bowley... unfair competition

ernment force the BBC to observe its Charter more strictly and keep its public service and commercial activities totally separate.

News of ITV's offensive coincides with leaks suggesting

the BBC has struck a similar deal with News International's *Sunday Times* for the *Antiques Roadshow*. Ads for this promotion break on LWT this weekend, sources say.

The deal between the BBC's Saturday night snooker programme, *Big Break*, and MGN, centres on what the BBC and MGN are calling an "interactive gamecard promotion". But ITV companies are branding it sponsorship, even though MGN is not credited on air.

Martin Bowley, the manag-

ing director of Carlton UK Sales, said: "The BBC is entering a commercial world which is not theirs to compete in. They are entitled to compete with us for audience — but not for revenue."

Bowley and his opposite numbers at other ITV sales houses have been backed by the ITV Network Centre, and, more significantly, David Glencross, the chief executive of the regulatory body, the Independent Television Commission.

The *Big Break*/MGN deal

has also re-ignited ITV's desire to change ITC regulations requiring that they broadcast advertising from rival TV stations. ITV also wants to stop taking advertising from Sky TV, which it is forced to do at the moment by the ITC rules.

One ITV sales chief said: "In the case of the BBC, we can't use it to advertise our programmes so why should we carry its ads? With Sky, the advertising is pushing up dish sales, and that is detrimental to our audience figures."

DBBH braces itself for fight to hold on to Gaymer's ciders

by Tabitha Cole

Matthew Clark Gaymer is understood to be staging a review of its cider brands' advertising in what could signal a rethink of the entire merged £60 million portfolio.

The decision to review the £2 million cider accounts, embracing K and Gaymer's Olde English, comes three months after Matthew Clark took over Gaymer. The accounts are currently held by Butterfield Day Devito Hockney.

Matthew Clark's marketing director, Mike Ader, is understood to be in secret talks with London agencies about drawing up a pitch-list.

Bartle Bogle Hegarty's Gaymer account, Babycham, worth over £3 million, plus Gaymer brands - Warninks, QC and Concorde wine, could also be reviewed.

Sources say Butterfield Day is likely to be included in any shortlist, as well as BBH and Rainey Kelly Campbell Roalfe.

Simon Green, a joint creative director at Butterfield Day, said: "All Matthew Clark's agencies are being asked to review the work they've done for the group."

Maurice lists three networks to handle international tasks

Three networks have been put on a shortlist by Maurice Saatchi to fight for the task of providing the international service for the big clients his new agency is poised to attract.

Sources close to Maurice said this week there had been no shortage of approaches about potential alliances with the agency, but Maurice is said to be considering seriously three offers. However, it is also possible he may yet reject all overtures and build his own international operation.

"It may sound like a cliché, but he really is considering all his options," a source said.

Maurice will shortly move into offices in London's West End, where he can meet potential clients and staff. No name has yet been agreed for the venture, which launches officially in May. The "New Saatchi Agency" was never meant to be more than a working title, but its extensive use has caused Maurice to consider adopting the name permanently.

Whether or not Charles Saatchi will be joining his brother remains unclear. His situation and his contract, which still has four years to run, were discussed at Monday's meeting of the Saatchi group board but no conclusions were reached.

Tories go to law to sever Saatchi ties

by our Parliamentary correspondent

The Conservative Party is taking legal advice on how it can withdraw from a contract committing it to Saatchi and Saatchi at the next general election.

The move has fuelled speculation that the Tories plan to switch their account to the new agency being set up by Maurice Saatchi.

Ministers revealed to *Campaign* this week that the Tory Party made a firm commitment to use Saatchi and Saatchi "up to and including the next general election" as part of an agreement to pay back £3 million the party owed the agency for its work on the 1992 election.

About £600,000 of the debt remains and will continue to be repaid. But Jeremy Hanley, the Tory chairman, has called in lawyers to investigate whether the departure of Maurice Saatchi and other

Saatchi... speculation that the Tories will move its business

key executives will allow the party to pull out of the contract it has with the agency.

Maurice Saatchi would have headed the campaign team at the next election. Day-to-day responsibility until then rested with David Kershaw, another defector who was London chairman of

Saatchi. Others who have departed had key roles at the last election — Bill Muirhead, the former Saatchi chief in North America; Jeremy Sinclair, former acting group chairman, Simon Dicketts, the creative director; and Steve Hilton, who acted as link man between the agency and Con-

servative Central Office.

Tory officials who are keen to move to Maurice Saatchi's new agency believe privately that the legal obstacles will "not be insurmountable".

However, they have been told not to talk publicly about a switch in case the scope of the contract has to be resolved by the courts.

Insiders believe a legal dispute is unlikely since it would be virtually impossible for Saatchi and Saatchi to insist on handling the election advertising if the party did not want to use the agency.

The wrangle could drag on for some months. The Tories have no advertising budget for this year's local elections and could easily contract out its party political broadcasts to another company.

One ministerial source said: "The ball is in Saatchi and Saatchi's court. It is up to the agency to say whether it will fulfil the contract."

THE SIEGE OF SAATCHI

Writs and threats, paranoia and fear, excitement mixed with loathing. It's another week at Charlotte Street. A five-page inside guide. p10

CROSS MEDIA OWNERS

Q: How do you make media owners cross? A: Don't let them become cross-media owners. The issue that isn't going to disappear yet. p17

Saatchi client slams 'ambulance chaser' shops

by John Tylee

A Saatchi and Saatchi client has turned angrily on agencies attempting to take advantage of the Charlotte Street turmoil to seduce its business.

Club 18-30, the holiday company that appointed Saatchi to its £500,000 account two months ago, says it is astounded by the insensitivity shown in the letters it has received from rival shops.

Jeremy Muller, the company's managing director, claimed the agencies' action surpassed even the cut-throat competition of the travel industry. "We at least wait until the body is cold," Muller said.

The company's anger was aroused by mailshots from S. P. Lintas and McCann Erickson.

One, from Lindsey Roberts, SPL's marketing director, expresses sympathy for Saatchi's situation but adds: "We also have to face the harsh commercial reality that

Crozier... rivals are 'pathetic'

these events may destabilise both staff and clients."

The letter from McCanns stresses the agency "will not chase ambulances" but says it would be on hand if the company decided to review its relationship.

But Jane Geraghty, the McCanns new business director, said: "We expressed sadness at the events at Charlotte Street and we have not asked for a response from Club 18-30. We're not ambulance-

chasers because we don't need to be."

Richard Hytner, the SPL chief executive, said: "I'm surprised at the reaction. Our only aim was to raise our awareness with the company in the event of its situation changing."

Adam Crozier, the Saatchi joint chief executive, said: "These calls are backfiring. Our clients think they are pathetic and are telling the agencies so."

Account Reviews 8 Saatchi Q&A 10 Newsmaker 12 Media Forum 17 Letters 22 Private View 30 Moves 31

Figure 19(a) Magazine methods – an early stage page one from *Campaign* shown in computer print-out. Note the windows left for pictures to be scanned in

campaign

A Haymarket publication   20 January 1995   £1.70

ITV pressures Govt over BBC deals

by Tina Mistry

Top ITV sales chiefs have set in motion plans to stop the BBC from striking any more commercial deals such as the recent controversial tie-up with Mirror Group Newspapers (*Campaign*, 6 January).

Senior ITV figures plan to lobby top-ranking cross-party Parliamentary ministers on the issue and are about to embark on a campaign which will focus on encouraging senior industry figures to debate the matter in public.

The aim is to make the Gov-

Bowley...unfair competition

ernment force the BBC to observe its Charter more strictly and keep its public service and commercial activities totally separate.

News of ITV's offensive coincides with leaks suggesting

the BBC has struck a similar deal with News International's *Sunday Times* for the *Antiques Roadshow*. Ads for this promotion break on LWT this weekend, sources say.

The deal between the BBC's Saturday night snooker programme, *Big Break*, and MGN, centres on what the BBC and MGN are calling an "interactive gamecard promotion". But ITV companies are branding it sponsorship, even though MGN is not credited on air.

Martin Bowley, the manag-

ing director of Carlton UK Sales, said: "The BBC is entering a commercial world which is not theirs to compete in. They are entitled to compete with us for audience — but not for revenue."

Bowley and his opposite numbers at other ITV sales houses have been backed by the ITV Network Centre, and, more significantly, David Glencross, the chief executive of the regulatory body, the Independent Television Commission.

The *Big Break*/MGN deal

has also re-ignited ITV's desire to change ITC regulations requiring that they broadcast advertising from rival TV stations. ITV also wants to stop taking advertising from Sky TV, which it is forced to do at the moment by the ITC rules.

One ITV sales chief said: "In the case of the BBC, we can't use it to advertise our programmes so why should we carry its ads? With Sky, the advertising is pushing up dish sales and that is detrimental to our audience figures."

Green...agency review

BDDH braces itself for fight to hold on to Gaymer's ciders

by Tabitha Cole

Matthew Clark Gaymer is understood to be staging a review of its cider brands' advertising in what could signal a rethink of the entire merged £6 million portfolio.

The decision to review the £2 million cider accounts, embracing K and Gaymer's Olde English, comes three months after Matthew Clark took over Gaymer. The accounts are currently held by Butterfield Day Devito Hockney.

Matthew Clark's marketing director, Mike Ader, is understood to be in secret talks with London agencies about drawing up a pitch-list.

Bartle Bogle Hegarty's Gaymer account, Babycham, worth over £3 million, plus the Gaymer brands, Warninks, QC and Concorde wine, could also be reviewed.

Sources say Butterfield Day is likely to be shortlisted, as well as BBH and Rainey Kelly Campbell Roalfe, which handles Stowells of Chelsea.

Simon Green, a joint creative director at Butterfield Day, said: "All Matthew Clark's agencies are being asked to review the work they've done for the group."

Maurice lists three networks to handle international tasks

Three networks have been put on a shortlist by Maurice Saatchi for the task of providing the international service needed by the big clients his new agency is poised to attract.

Sources close to Maurice said this week that there had been no shortage of approaches about potential alliances with the agency, but Maurice is said to be considering three offers seriously. Current speculation centres on D'Arcy Masius Benton and Bowles, Young and Rubicam and the Lowe Group. But all have refused to comment on any tie-up. However, it is also possible he may yet reject the offers and build his own international operation.

"It may sound like a cliché, but he really is considering all his options," a source said.

Maurice will shortly move into offices in London's West End, where he can meet potential clients and staff. No name has yet been agreed for the venture, which launches officially in May. The "New Saatchi Agency" was never meant to be more than a working title, but its extensive use has caused Maurice to consider adopting the name permanently.

Meanwhile, the future of Charles Saatchi, who has four years left on his contract, remains unclear.

Tories go to law to sever Saatchi ties

by our Parliamentary correspondent

The Conservative Party is taking legal advice on how it can withdraw from a contract committing it to Saatchi and Saatchi at the next general election.

The move has fuelled speculation that the Tories plan to switch their account to the new agency being set up by Maurice Saatchi.

Ministers revealed to *Campaign* this week that the Tory Party made a firm commitment to use Saatchi and Saatchi "up to and including the next general election" as part of an agreement to pay back £3 million the party owed the agency for its work on the 1992 election.

About £600,000 of the debt remains and will continue to be repaid. But Jeremy Hanley, the Tory chairman, has called in lawyers to investigate whether the departure of Maurice Saatchi and other

Maurice Saatchi...speculation that the Tories will follow him

key executives will allow the party to pull out of the contract it has with the agency.

Maurice Saatchi would have headed the campaign team at the next election. Day-to-day responsibility until then rested with David Kershaw, another defector who was London chairman of

Saatchi. Others who have departed had key roles at the last election — Bill Muirhead, the former Saatchi chief in North America; Jeremy Sinclair, former acting group chairman; Simon Dicketts, the creative director; and Steve Hilton, the link man with Conservative Central Office.

Tory officials who are keen to move to Maurice Saatchi's new agency believe privately that the legal obstacles will "not be insurmountable".

Insiders believe a legal dispute is unlikely since it would be virtually impossible for Saatchi and Saatchi to insist on handling the election advertising if the party did not want to use the agency.

The wrangle could drag on for some months. The Tories have no advertising budget for this year's local elections and could easily contract out their party political broadcasts to another company.

Another sign that the Tories will eventually switch the account came when Hanley met Maurice Saatchi last week to be briefed on his new agency. Although Hanley made no commitments because of the legal doubts, the talks were described as "warm and positive" by Tory insiders.

Industry reaction, page 2

THIS WEEK

THE SIEGE OF SAATCHI

Writs and threats, paranoia and fear, excitement mixed with loathing. It's another week at Charlotte Street. A five-page inside guide. p10

Saatchi client slams 'ambulance chaser' shops

by John Tylee

A Saatchi and Saatchi client has turned angrily on agencies attempting to take advantage of the Charlotte Street turmoil to steal its business.

Club 18-30, the holiday company that appointed Saatchi to its £500,000 account two months ago, says it is astounded by the insensitivity shown in the letters it has received from rival shops.

Jeremy Muller, the company's managing director,

claimed the agencies' action surpassed even the cut-throat competition of the travel industry. "We at least wait until the body is cold," Muller said.

The company's anger was aroused by mailshots from S. P. Lintas and McCann-Erickson.

One, from Lindsey Roberts, SPL's new-business director, expresses sympathy for Saatchi's situation but adds: "We also have to face the harsh commercial reality that

Crozier...rivals are 'pathetic'

these events may destabilise both staff and clients."

The letter from McCanns stresses the agency "will not chase ambulances" but says it would be on hand if the company decided to review its relationship.

But Jane Geraghty, the McCanns new-business director, said: "We expressed sadness at the events at Charlotte Street and we have not asked for a response from Club 18-30. We're not ambu-

lance-chasers because we don't need to be."

Richard Hytner, the SPL chief executive, said: "I'm surprised at the reaction. Our only aim was to raise our awareness with the company in the event of its situation changing."

Adam Crozier, the Saatchi joint chief executive, said: "These calls are backfiring. Our clients think they are pathetic and are telling the agencies so."

CROSS MEDIA OWNERS

Q: How do you make media owners cross? A: Don't let them become cross-media owners. The issue that isn't going to disappear yet. p17

9 770008 230044   03>

Figure 19(b)   The *Campaign* page one as it appeared with the pictures in place

12 Four stock pictures of 'people in the news' – principally company appointments and awards, along with twelve short items.

You also have three half-page adverts about the company's products:

TASK 1   *Devise twelve simple pages, including a cover page, from the material that you have, using double-page spreads if need be, writing and drawing in notional headlines, and indicating the spaces for pictures, text and adverts.*

TASK 2   *Explain in about 500 words the factors you would take into account in identifying and targeting your readership market and relating it to your page designs.*

Notes: Not easy tasks, these, but they are useful as an exercise in the planning and use of editorial materials. Consult appropriate chapters (above) in Giles and Hodgson.

 Assignment 9   Imagine you are editing a magazine on a subject close to your heart – a hobby, say, such as bird watching, jazz or motorbikes – and you have got together some appropriate pictures and text enough to fill the front page and one inside page.

TASK 1   *Decide on the size and column format for your magazine and draw a front (cover) page, marking in the columns, and showing the following:*

1   *The title, or masthead, you have chosen for your magazine (either across the top of the picture or in a separate box or panel).*
2   *The size and location of a main picture (preferably the most eye-catching you have got).*
3   *A drawn-in headline on your cover story, using a type and size you have chosen, together with a placement for the text at the required length.*
4   *Any other items (blurbs, secondary text, pictures, adverts) that you want to get on to the page.*

TASK 2   *Draw a typical inside page for the magazine you have in mind, of the same size and column format, and showing the following:*

1 *The main story with appropriate headline in your chosen type, and placement of text.*

2 *Such illustrations (pictures or graphics) as you want to get into the page.*

3 *Any adverts or other material you wish to include.*

Notes: This is very much a freestyle exercise but you should aim at typographical unity and the two pages should look like they are for the same magazine. The pages should be drawn in some detail and should contain instructions on type and setting as if intended for use.

It is also an exercise that can be used as a model for other similar projects. (Giles and Hodgson, Chapters 2, 8, 12 and 13; Hodgson: *Subediting,* pages 33–55).

CHECKLIST

Page planning and design assignments

Did you:

☐ Understand what is meant in page design by focal points.

☐ Learn to measure columns and type setting with a print rule.

☐ Understand what picas, ems and ens mean.

☐ Measure and check the column format and column widths of your pages.

☐ Understand the difference between serif and sanserif types.

☐ Check and note the types used in the pages cut for tasks.

☐ Note the use in newspapers of different sizes and 'weights' of the same type

☐ Note the positioning of pictures as design ingredients.

☐ Develop an awareness of what is meant by visual balance on pages.

☐ Study and compare between papers style in by-lines, standfirsts and blurbs.

☐ Identify the type character of the papers with which you were dealing.

☐ Check the the visual balance against adverts in the cut-up pages you have put together.

☐ Note the main visual differences between popular tabloid and the quality papers.

☐ Check the meaning and usage of terms: tabloid, broadsheet, display, strapline, masthead? (See Glossary.)

REFERENCES AND FURTHER READING

Davis, A: *Magazine Journalism Today* (Focal Press, 1988).

Giles, V and Hodgson, FW: *Creative Newspaper Design* (Heinemann Professional Publishing, 1990).

Hodgson, FW: *Subediting*, 2nd Edition (Focal Press, 1993).

7

Workshop projects

GROUP projects run on a workshop basis can form a useful part of journalism training where there is a year of students or entrants under instruction either in-house or pre-house. The trainee can gain insights into newspaper and magazine practice through group activities that would be much harder – even impossible in some cases – to achieve working alone.

Group projects can be used to break away from formal assignments, with tutors concentrating instead on teaching students to read and analyse the contents of newspapers and magazines, to study the methods by which they are put together. They can be used to identify the policy of editors, the social and political stances within the pages, ideas in visual presentation and the targeting of readership – all areas of knowledge that are important in good journalism.

READING AND CUTTING

AN ESSENTIAL basis for group projects is an efficient cuttings library; not the ready-to-use main cuttings libraries that are available in-house but a students-own cuttings library built up systematically day by day and week by week as courses unfold and to which all contribute and which all can use.

For a workable library of cuttings files to be put together time should be allocated on courses and training programmes for the daily examination of a given number of newspapers by a roster of students who take it in turn to cut and file. To save on costs it is a good idea to agree a certain number of publications to be bought in regularly for cutting – say, two popular tabloids, two quality dailies, two Sunday papers and perhaps the two main provincial papers in the area – and always sticking to the same titles. A couple of magazines should also be included.

There needs to be a time span to the collecting of cuttings; ideally it should be the duration of the course or programme. And provision needs to be made for someone to cut papers through holidays so that the record over the nominated period is as complete as possible. The cuttings are best housed in clearly labelled pocket files for which storage space needs to be set aside.

A valuable aspect of cutting for the files regularly, apart from any purpose to which the files might be put, is the enforced systematic reading of newspaper pages that it develops. The close reading of newspapers will form an essential part of the workshop projects in this chapter.

Hints on cutting

Cutting requires two copies of each chosen paper to allow for backing stories to be cut. Choosing file names depends on the thoroughness with which cutting is carried out and the demands likely to be made upon the system. It will soon be apparent that to avoid fat and unwieldy files it is best to break aspects of a subject into separate files. Thus Government might suit general aspects of government, but particular areas such as legislation, privatization, defence projects, etc., will quickly spawn their own collections.

Likewise Royal Family might suit for a while, but separate files will inevitably be needed for Prince Charles, the Yorks, the Princess of Wales, etc. There might be logic in giving some personalities separate files for their public and private lives.

A lot depends upon the topics that are uppermost in press coverage during the duration of the cutting programme – the war in Bosnia and voting rights in the EEC are examples. Those familiar with newspaper cuttings libraries will have come across yellowing files on subjects that were once heavily covered and called for that have had hardly an addition in the past couple of years.

What is important is to annotate file names with short cross-references to related files. Thus, Royal Family might have: *see Prince Charles*. The TUC file will probably require cross-references to separate files for individual trade unions.

CONTENTS ANALYSIS

NEWSPAPERS have a variety of markets. Some might be heavily political or even owned by a political party; some exist to promote religions, such as the *Catholic Herald*, the *Methodist Recorder* and the *Jewish Chronicle*. Many published in the provinces in Britain give almost exclusively local news while others include a good cross-section of national and world news alongside their area coverage. There are also newspapers run by and for ethnic communities

Nationally, newspapers divide roughly into popular and quality, the former concentrating strongly on human interest, celebrities and sport in a tabloid format, and the latter giving a good deal of space to world news and to political, economic and cultural matters in broadsheet format. Even here, slants towards certain types of news can be detected if one reads them carefully. Business and city interests can predominate; concern in the affairs of certain parts of the world can be detected; there can be distinct social attitudes, while some people claim that there are newspapers that target younger readers or women readers.

The following specimen workshop projects are designed to broaden students' and young journalists' awareness of newspaper content and the variety of purpose and attitude to be found in the press. They are based on British newspapers and on the working requirement that there are classes or year-groups of students who can be divided into teams reporting on projects to a tutor.

Project 1

Working as a group under an elected editor, read and measure the columnage of world (i.e., non-UK) coverage in the two dailies *The Guardian* and *The Independent* on a given day and report with comments on the comparison in coverage and on any aspects of it that strike the team.

Notes: Ideally, individuals in the group should undertake comparisons of specific areas of content such as political news, 'spot' news, backgrounders, comment, etc. so as to give the fullest possible account of what the two papers are reporting and saying on the day. Each individual should report on their area with the accounts being collated and introduced by the editor as a basis for class discussion and questions. All the group will be expected to have read the two papers.

Checklist

Did you:

☐ Measure the number of columns and types of coverage against the total columnage of editorial space.
☐ Read the leaders or editorial opinion.

- ☐ Include the features pages.
- ☐ Form any opinions on political attitude.
- ☐ Detect any noticeable gaps in the coverage.
- ☐ Log contributions by own correspondents or reporters.
- ☐ Work out percentage of news agency copy used.

Project 2

Working under an elected editor, measure and compare the features (i.e. non-news) content of the *Daily Mail* and *Daily Express* on a given day and report with comments on the comparison between attitudes, approach, content etc. in the two papers.

Notes: It is a useful exercise to examine two newspapers which might appear to have similarities in market and presentation to detect if there are differences that are not at first apparent. There may not, of course, be pronounced differences. Features pages are a good way of finding out where a paper stands since it is here that opinion, social and political bias and deliberate targeting of readers are more likely to be apparent.

Checklist

Did you:

- ☐ Read the leader or editorial opinion.
- ☐ Detect attitudes implicit in 'women's page' material.
- ☐ Become aware of any social or class bias in the features.
- ☐ Feel there was advertising influence in some of the material.
- ☐ Feel any political leaning towards party or segment of party.
- ☐ Detect any targeting towards women or younger readers.
- ☐ Detect any specifically *Mail* or *Express* attitudes towards certain things.

Project 3

Working under an elected editor, examine and measure the advertising and editorial content, including sport, in a given issue of *The Observer* Sunday newspaper and devise a readership profile based upon what you find.

Notes: The advertising departments of most newspapers work to a readership profile based upon sample surveys carried out by the National Readership Survey, which classify readers into A, B, C1, C2,

D and E categories. These categories are based mainly upon job and spending habits and have been much criticized by journalists for the things they do not tell about readers. *The Observer*, which has a long history (founded in 1791) and has been noted for its quirky and independent outlook, is a good place to start examining readership from the point of view of a newspaper's content and to devise a likely readership profile upon this basis. The method could, of course, be equally applied to devising readership profiles for a variety of newspapers.

Ideally, each person in the team should take an aspect such as news, features, sport, presentation, display advertising, classified advertising, etc. and attempt to draw conclusions from what they find about the sort of readers that are being targeted. Inevitably these will be personalized conclusions to some extent but the discussion arising from the findings – everyone should have read the issue in question – can be a revealing exercise in contents analysis.

Checklist

Did you:

- ☐ Agree as a team on the various types of readers aimed at.
- ☐ Include the pictures and other illustrations in your examination.
- ☐ Look at strengths and weaknesses in the papers's coverage.
- ☐ Detect any social or political bias.
- ☐ Detect whether the views of by-line writers differed from each other or from the paper's.
- ☐ Detect any dominant type of advertising.
- ☐ Arrive at any views about *The Observer* sports pages.

 **Project 4** Working under an elected editor, examine issues of *The Sun* and the *Daily Mirror* on a given day and work out by measurement and analysis of content to what extent, in the team's opinion, they share a common readership market.

Notes: This is a task where individuals should compare like content with like in areas such as politics, non-UK news, human interest, presentation, sport, readership participation, etc., bring to light any similarities or differences, and assess degrees of success in what is being attempted. The fact that some of the findings might be coloured by the personal views of the team's members should lend piquancy to the group discussion that follows.

Checklist

Did you:

☐   Compare typographical style.
☐   Compare editorial opinion.
☐   Examine attitudes to and coverage of showbusiness.
☐   Examine styles of headline writing.
☐   Weigh up the advertising.
☐   Compare presentation in political stories.
☐   Detect targeting of special segments of readership.

Project 5

Working under an elected editor, examine given issues of a leading provincial morning and a provincial evening paper and determine by measurement and analysis of content and style to what extent their market aims are different.

Notes: This is another series of comparisons covering news and features content, sport, presentation, advertising and social and political attitudes in which members of the team compare like for like, with the editor collating and introducing their findings to set off a class discussion. As with other projects of this sort it is essential that all the members of the group should have read the same issues of the two papers.

Checklist

Did you:

☐   Compare circulation catchment areas of the two papers.
☐   Measure the space given in each to non-area news.
☐   Compare page design and visual presentation.
☐   Analyse advertising volume and type.
☐   Consider and compare the features content.
☐   Compare material in readers' letters columns.
☐   Weigh up the sports coverage.

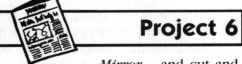

Project 6

Comb, as a class, six Monday-to-Saturday issues of two contrasting national papers – say, the *Daily Telegraph* and the *Daily Mirror* – and cut and read everything to do with wages, salaries and company profits. Make notes and be prepared to contribute to a discussion on the theme: 'The *Mirror* v the *Telegraph*: who cares about the people?'. Choose two students to lead the discussion.

Project 7

Read, as a class, six Monday-to-Saturday issues of your local evening paper, log the range of subjects covered in the news pages, make careful notes and be prepared to contribute, for or against, to a discussion on the theme, 'Our local paper is failing to give a proper news service to our community.' Choose two students to lead the discussion.

Project 8

Comb, as a class, four contrasting national dailies over three days, looking for, and filing, stories that suggest racist, sexist or ageist attitudes (or noting the lack of them). Make careful notes and be prepared to contributed to a discussion on the subject, 'The national press and the three "isms". How much prejudice is there?' Choose two students to lead the discussion.

Notes: There could be endless variations on these three projects. All the class should do the reading, what ever the subject, in order to contribute with facts and opinions. Try projects with four contrasting national magazines.

Checklist

Did you:

- ☐ Study editorial and other opinion pieces to detect attitudes, consistent or otherwise.
- ☐ Study the balance of news content in each paper in your search for material.
- ☐ Study the balance of feature material.
- ☐ Detect in the advertising any significant pointers.
- ☐ Draw any conclusions from headline and display methods.

INVESTIGATIVE PROJECTS

INVESTIGATIVE journalism, of which the Insight investigations carried out by the *Sunday Times* over the last few decades are the most notable example, is a world on its own and calls for developed skills and a great deal of time and planning. Frequently matters of corruption and malpractice are involved and experienced reporter–investigators know how near to the law they can skate to get information for their newspaper for which their justification is that it is for the public good.

Team investigations on this scale are not suitable for use on training courses both on the grounds of the time they take and the experience they call for, yet lower key investigative projects such as the following, provided they can be slotted into the training programme, can provide useful experience.

It is necessary to allocate aspects of the work to the team members to avoid overlap of effort and to fix a deadline for the collated report.

Project 9 Working as a team of five investigators, including a leader/collator, put together a 3000-word news feature aimed at a regional newspaper on street and door-to-door trading in your town, including the working of the council licensing system.

Project 10 Working as a team of five investigators, including a leader/collator, put together a 3000-word news feature aimed at the features page of your local evening paper on the problems of use and abuse of rights of way in the countryside around where you live.

Project 11 Working as a team of five investigators, including a leader/collator, put together a 3000 world news feature aimed at a specialist magazine on the effect of technological advance on farming methods in your area during the past decade.

Notes: Investigative tasks call for a good deal of ingenuity as well as hard slog. The relevant law should be closely studied, interviews carried out with people concerned, organizations and pressure groups, including police and council departments, identified and consulted and personal observation carefully made. Cuttings libraries and reference books should also be consulted.While preconceived ideas can be a burden, there is a need, by the end of the investigation, to draw the threads together and formulate a point of view or conclusion, even though it might seem a negative one or not what you thought it would be when you started.

GROUP PUBLICATIONS

IN ANY sort of journalism course putting together a magazine or newspaper is a good way of tackling for the first time the tasks likely to come the way of a young journalist.

The format can be quite basic – perhaps ten or twelve folded sheets. Fortunately with desktop publishing programmes it is possible to lend quite a high degree of sophistication to the layout and typography, though one should remember that however fascinating the systems are they remain just a tool to help accomplish and polish journalistic tasks that remain as skill-intensive as ever they were.

Ideally, the various jobs should be taken in turn by the members of the group to give everyone some exposure to hands-on journalistic work. Thus, in a group, say, of ten the work could be split up as follows:

Editor: One person in overall control of policy, planning, leading group discussions or conferences on aspects of the work, allocating the work and passing the final pages (plus, of course, being the final carrier of cans!).

Chief subeditor: The only other executive really necessary on such a small-scale publication. He/she would plan the pages in detail from the material submitted (in consultation with the editor), write the main headlines and decide on the allocation of space and length for items, and the placing of pictures and advertisements (if any).

Subeditors: Perhaps one to help with the detailed editing of items, writing headlines and designing pages.

Reporters: At least three to allow for a sufficient variety of copy input.

Feature writers: Two hardworking ones should be able to set up what is needed.

Photographers: At least two. Pictures are hard to come by; old holiday snaps can fill only so much space and good news pictures cost money. Also, encouraging ingenuity in illustration is a good idea in a publication of this sort. PR departments of local companies can be approached for free pictures.

The balance of content of the publication should be set to suit the numbers of personnel and a set of agreed aims, but a variety of work experience should be included. For this reason a newspaper rather than a magazine is the best choice since it would have a wider catchment area of tasks, even though its readership market is its college environment. But check on other student publications before deciding.

Getting in paid advertising is a good way of offsetting running costs but you would need to appoint someone with a persuasive tongue to carry out this rather specialised (and not to be underestimated) task. Equally, if you are ambitious of building up readership, especially if you have a small cover charge, you would need to appoint someone to look after circulation and distribution – and the accounts!

MEDIA DEBATES

THERE are a number of issues of general concern to students of the media and young journalists that are best dealt with by group participation either directly by debate led by chosen class speakers who have been given a brief or by inviting visiting experts to answer questions and lead a discussion.

A weekly debate on a general media topic could be a regular part of group workshop activities and would spin off naturally from the intensive reading of newspapers developed by organized cutting and filing and by the sort of contents analysis projects demonstrated above. The following are specimen subjects that would lend themselves to debate with speakers leading the 'for' and 'against' sides:

◇ That the current system of press regulation is inadequate.
◇ That the law has become a form of creeping censorship.
◇ That the academic discipline of media studies is out of touch with the media.
◇ That political parties are anti-press.
◇ That the national tabloids have done the press a disservice.
◇ That an independent newspaper is an impossibility.
◇ That journalism training should be handed over to the academic establishment.
◇ That press freedom is endangered by the current concentration of newspaper ownership.
◇ That the public do not understand the importance of press freedom.
◇ That advertising influence on editors is impossible to avoid.
◇ That the modern newspaper has become a slave to display.

VISITING EXPERTS

AREAS that are less open to student speakers and course tutors might be usefully introduced to the group by visiting experts – perhaps one such speaker a month during the course – with a set time for exposition followed by questions and discussion.

Such areas might include: newspaper management, press advertising practice, influences on the press, the working of news agencies, recent advances in computerized technology, press room and publishing practice, media law, political journalism, the press and local government, the function of press officers, the practice of colour printing, the role of press freedom in a democracy, public relations and the press, the future of broadcasting, and relations between the press and broadcasting.

8

Study programmes

MANY journalism courses run individual study programmes alongside lectures, assignments and workshop projects. Ideally, each student or trainee journalist selects a subject relating to the media and accumulates material on it for use in a long paper to be delivered towards the end of the course.

An example of this type of programme is the preparation of a situationer based upon a news subject that is currently being covered in newspapers.

SITUATIONERS

A SITUATIONER is a background feature outlining a news situation in a given area or country which sums up progress made over a period and gives the position reached at the time of writing. It is a device frequently used by quality Sunday papers and news magazines which aim to give a briefing from time to time on world or contemporary news situations.

Preparing a situationer gives the student an opportunity of presenting a piece of news-based written work rooted in the close reading of newspapers over a period, as required by the group activities outlined in the previous chapter, and which also contains the elements of a news feature. Such a piece of work thus extends the student's involvement in two directions and ideally should count as a percentage of marks for the course year.

The mechanics of such a project for those on journalism or media studies courses are as follows. The student, having selected a news subject – say, drug abuse in sub-teenagers, suburban loneliness or mercenary warfare – monitors it for a nominated period in successive issues of a number of chosen newspapers and magazines, cutting and date-filing material, until an agreed cut-off date which needs to allow time for the file to be digested and the piece of work to be pegged out, written and handed in. As with all journalistic exercises, deadlines should be firmly adhered to, with marking penalties for lateness.

The resources of the newspapers and magazines chosen – at least four suitable publications and preferably five – should be augmented by additional background research carried out in reference books and any other sources or publications relevant to the subject chosen. With some subjects pre-period research might be necessary to set a context.

While the structure of the situationer should not be formula-ized too much, since the text is aimed with newspaper readers in mind rather than academic marking boards, it is necessary to show where things stand at the beginning of the chosen period, the progress made during the period covered, and how things are at the time of writing. Within these general guidelines a convincing narrative and argument should be developed.

As with the group work described in the previous chapter the specimen study programmes that follow will be referred to as projects. As with the assignments in previous chapters they are intended as models for similar projects

Project 1

Prepare a 4000-word situationer on hard drug law enforcement in Britain, cutting and filing material for a six-month period from the *Daily Telegraph*, *The Guardian*, *The Observer* and the *New Scientist* and checking on any figures or material published during the period by official bodies concerned with the problem.

Include, for submission with the work, a summary page (see page 206) and list of contents giving the main headings and parts for the work and a list of sources and file of cuttings.

Notes: A file should be kept of editorial comment and feature articles in your chosen newspapers and periodicals as well as news stories. Where possible, obtain and use official statistics.

Project 2

Prepare a 4000-word situationer on child abuse in Britain, cutting and filing material for a six-month period from the *Daily Mail*, *Daily Mirror*, *Sunday Telegraph* and *Nursing World*. As with Project 1, above, seek out and use material from official sources as well. If relevant, use interviews. Include a summary page giving the main headings and parts for the work and a list of sources.

Notes: It is useful for this project and for Project 1 to monitor any television or radio programmes that are relevant, if necessary asking for transcripts.

Project 3

Prepare a 4000-word situationer on the Ulster problem, cutting and filing material for a six-month period from the *Belfast Telegraph*, the *Irish Independent*, the *Sunday Times* and the *New Statesman and Society*, and taking in any other sources that are relevant.

Include, for submission with the work, a summary page giving the main headings and parts for the work and list of sources.

Notes: The attempt by Britain and Eire, successful or otherwise, to achieve a political solution would have to loom large in this situationer and some cuttings research on the Anglo-Irish initiative in the run-up to the period would have to be carried out.

Project 4

Prepare a 4000-word situationer on 'political correctness' and attitudes to it, cutting and filing material for a six-month period from *The Guardian*, *The Times*, the *Daily Telegraph* and the *New Statesman*. Use any other references or broadcasting sources that you consider relevant.

Include, as above, a summary page giving the main headings and parts for the work, a list of sources and a file of cuttings.

Notes: Here is a situationer where a clear definition of terms would need to be discreetly introduced at an early stage to avoid any uncertainty among readers. It is a subject that could allow for humour in the exposition. Features sources should be well combed and the use of book references and quoted opinions could be useful.

Project 5

Prepare a 4000-word situationer on crime and social problems in high-rise urban estates, cutting and filing material for a six-month period from the *Daily Mirror*, *The Guardian*, the London *Evening Standard* and *The Observer*. Look out, in HMSO Stationery Office and Government press offices, for any official publications that touch on this issue.

Include a summary page giving the main headings and parts for the work, a list of sources and a file of cuttings. Personal interviews could form an important part of this project.

Notes: Official statistics as well as interviews are needed to bring this situationer alive. Use libraries.

Project 6

Prepare a 4000-word situationer on the state of the British aircraft industry, cutting and filing material over a six-month period from the *Financial Times*, *Daily Telegraph*, *Daily Express* and the *Economist*.

Include a summary page giving the main headings and parts of the work, a list of sources and a file of cuttings. Include statistics.

Notes: There will be many strands here but look for a topical news peg towards the end of the period to hang the text on. It is a perennial newspaper subject. Check the press offices of companies and organizations for handouts and official statistics.

MEDIA RESEARCH PAPERS

ASPECTS of the media, its practice and its relations with its readers/viewers and the community are an important part of training in journalism. With the power of the media as it is, and no shortage of vocal critics, it is not sufficient for a responsible journalist simply to be able to produce work in the practitioner world without regard to reasons or consequences.

The following specimen projects define areas in which research is needed to broaden knowledge of the media environment and prepare journalists for professional life. They are intended to slot in alongside training programmes to provide material for a long paper, either in place of or in addition to situationer projects, depending on the course.

Project 7

'There can be no absolutes in news value.' To what extent is this statement true for the newspaper editor? Can it be shown to be true in terms of specimen newspaper content? Discuss in 4000 words.

Notes: The kernel of the journalists's job, 'What is news?' needs to be probed in very close detail to answer the question posed. Consider both the media sociologists' view (Boorstin, Galtung and Ruge, McQuail, Seymour-Ure, and others) and the journalists' view (Evans, Hodgson, Harris and Spark). See Bibliography on pages 197–206.

Project 8

Is bias a serious fault in the British press? Discuss in 4000 words.

Notes: Two things need looking at very closely here: the nature of bias as it affects newspapers, and any dangerous consequences of bias. Consider among other things where the line is between unconscious, avoidable bias and the imposed bias of an editorial policy. One could add a third consideration: to what extent bias in newspapers can be deemed a fault.

Project 9

Distortion, or misrepresentation, in presenting or disseminating news is something a reporter is taught to avoid. When and how does distortion happen in the news pages of newspapers? How can it be avoided? Discuss in 4000 words.

Notes: One should be looking here for two sorts of distortion: deliberate and unintentional. Find examples. Make sure you define distortion in news terms and show how it differs from bias. Show how, in your opinion, it can happen and the precise steps that should be taken to avoid it.

Project 10

Few reporters avoid being accused of intrusion in the course of their job. Using the guidelines issued by the National Union of Journalists and the Press Complaints Commission's Code of Practice (both given in the Appendix, on pages 207–11), discuss in 4000 words the practical problems and definitions of intrusion from the reporter's point of view.

Notes: You will need, among other things, to define the circumstances in which legitimate pursuit of the facts becomes intrusion; also to what extent individuals, especially public figures, can claim right of privacy in matters being investigated by the reporter that are of public concern.

Project 11

Is it a newspaper's fault if readers are confused about what, in its pages, is objective news and what is comment and opinion? Discuss in 4000 words, giving examples.

Notes: Planning, presentation, typography all help to point a newspaper's many functions, but is enough being done to preserve for the reader the sacredness of the facts when there is more to the modern newspaper than news alone? An important part of this task will be to note how the language of opinion encroaches upon the language of fact in places where it should not

Project 12

'Attempts at news management by outside sources is a serious problem for editors, especially of national newspapers', Discuss in 4000 words to what extent this contention is true. How can news management be recognized and countered?

Notes: Information coming to newspapers, especially via specialist writers, can have strings attached. Correspondents can, if they are not careful, be used by people; press officers can insert their own bias into their information; Government ministers can be floating political kites; hidden bribery can lurk in an innocent-sounding proposal. Press and PR people can conceal as well as present information. Look for examples and spell out the dangers of news management.

Project 13

'The press's role as watchdog of democracy has been overtaken by its role as a consumer watchdog'. Discuss in 4000 words to what extent this is true.

Notes: Examine service columns and reader participation in a selection of newspapers and measure and map out the area it covers. Look also at coverage of national and local government activities.

Project 14

How important is the freedom of the press? Discuss in 4000 words.

Notes: Examine the various aspects of a newspaper's role in the community and the ways in which its attempts to tell the truth are hamstrung by legal and other restrictions. Try to imagine society with only Government-controlled newspapers. Contrast with restrictions in other countries. To what extent does the need for press freedom demand public support?

Project 15

Britain is said to have an unfettered press. But has the law become a form of creeping censorship? Discuss in 4000 words.

Notes: See notes on Project 14. Examine the various aspects of the law of libel, contempt of court, Official Secrets Act, confidentiality and the restrictions on reporting. Use McNae's *Essential Law for Journalists* (Butterworths, 1992) and Crone's *Law and the Media* (Focal Press, 1995).

Project 16

Try to anwer, in 4000 words, the question: Why bother with newspapers?

Notes: Consider what life, in your view, would be like without newspapers and the various roles they perform and the convenience they offer, and whether these roles could be adequately fulfilled by the other media. Consider, for example, a world in which all news information and comment came via radio and television and what would be lacking.

SEMINARS

AN INTERMEDIATE stage between the formal debate with a motion (see Chapter 7) and the individual research paper is the group seminar in which members contribute short study papers on aspects of a chosen media topic, which topic is then thrown open for discussion by the whole group.

It is usual for the course tutor or instructor to nominate the topic and to allocate who does what, making sure that all members of the group get their turn at presenting a paper. It is a good idea to base papers – say, three or four of them at a time – on controversial or comparative coverage of some current issue or on the views or book of some controversial media writer, the idea being to encourage group discussion and feedback.

While discussion can be open-ended and perhaps, in the end, inconclusive a seminar gives everyone the opportunity to express their views, and the beavering required to put a paper together can bring interesting and often little known facts and views before the group. It also reminds students and trainee journalists of the variety of purpose and content of different kinds of newspapers and periodicals.

The work need not be very time-consuming; about 800 words is usually enough for each when several papers are being read and time needs to be left for discussion. A close study is required of a topic, however, for a seminar to be worth setting up, and it is useful for students to have had some exposure to group projects in contents analysis of the kind outlined in Chapter 7.

Seminars offer a great field for ideas. The role of the press in society can be broken down into many individual topics covering social and political attitudes and the aims and readership markets of differing newspapers and periodicals. The effect of advertising on editorial content; comparisons between the different media – between TV and newspapers in their content and coverage, for example; class attitudes, concentration of ownership, cross-media ownership...the list is almost endless. There is also some merit in looking at the writings of critics of the press (see Bibliography, pages 197–205) and considering where, in the opinion of members of a seminar, criticism is justified or where it is wrong-headed.

Here, to start things off, are a few suggested seminar topics:

1   Consider what disadvantages television works under in its news coverage compared to the national dailies.
2   *The Times* was once described as a caste newspaper. Is it one today?
3   Has the *Daily Express* got a social axe to grind?
4   What does the advertising in *The Guardian* tell you about its readers?
5   'Television has more political influence than newspapers these days.' Is this true?
6   Do the popular tabloids have more influence on their readers than do the qualities?
7   Analyse the current political stance of the *Daily Mirror*.
8   Contrast and discuss the attitudes to women found (in your view) in the *Daily Mail* with those in *The Guardian*.
9   Select three local weeklies in your area and consider to what extent they are fulfilling a worthwhile role in the community in which they circulate.
10 How relevant is radio to today's needs in Britain?

11 Have newspaper editors something to learn from the writings of media sociologists?

12 Has the academic discipline of media studies lost touch with the role of the press?

REFERENCES AND FURTHER READING

Boyd, A: *Broadcast Journalism*, 2nd Edition (Focal Press 1993).
Crone, T: *Law and the Media*, 3rd Edition (Focal Press, 1995).
Hodgson, FW: *Modern Newspaper Practice*, 3rd Edition (Focal Press, 1993).
McNae, LCJ: *Essential Law for Journalists* (Butterworths, 1992).
See also Bibliography, pages 197–205.

9

Marking and assessment

MARKING and assessment systems are not only difficult to establish in journalism training – there are probably as many of them, both in style and method, as there are courses.

The following guidance is not intended to replace systems already in use but rather to give help with marking and assessment to those using the exercises in this book, whether they be tutors or students on courses, trainee journalists working in-house, or students with self-learning packs. The guidance is also offered as a supplement to the guidelines spelt out for instructors and assessors serving NVQ courses.

For the purposes of this chapter, marking is regarded as the overall or total mark or grade applied to a piece of work; assessment is the level of achievement reached in individual skills relating to the work.

To arrive at an overall mark for a piece of work–journalism being what it is – three aspects need to be taken into account:

1   The degree to which the piece of work fulfils its brief.
2   The success, in the judgement of the tutor, of the work as a finished piece of written journalism.
3   The level of journalistic skill reached based on the list of criteria applicable to the piece of work.

The first two are qualitative judgements on the part of the tutor based on the tutor's professional experience and the requirements of the course. They could be said to show to what extent the student's or trainee's finished work would warrant being published. A sliding scale of percentages is usually used on courses to denote the level of achievement in this area.

The third aspect can be arrived at with some degree of accuracy by reference to the tables of criteria listed below for the various types of task.

The amount of weighting given in an overall mark to its components is a matter for the tutor and accepted practice on taught courses. For the purpose of the tasks in this book it is felt that assessment based on the tables of criteria for the different types of work should form at least half the overall mark, with the other two aspects referred to above, either combined or separate, forming the remaining half.

By this means the cultivation of precise skills in journalism receives its proper weighting.

Self-assessment offers greater difficulties, especially in judging the success of work as pieces of journalism, but those attempting to measure the success of their own efforts are commended to apply the criteria in the tables below to determine how far they are learning and applying the various skills.

In using the tables it is suggested that the skill level in completing the assignments, either real or simulated, in this book be measured by ticking or crossing or marking n/a (not applicable) against the numbered items. A percentage mark, if required, could be calculated from the number of criteria ticked. The assessment could be further refined by giving each item a grading from 1 to 10.

REPORTING

REPORTING can be divided for assessment purposes into news gathering and news writing.

The two do not always sit happily together. There are born news gatherers full of initiative and natural curiosity (and the right sort of educational background) who leave no stone unturned in their hunger for the facts but who struggle when it comes to pen and keyboard.

There are born communicators who can size up a readership's requirements, put in order their material and have a natural touch with words but who are clumsy and ill at ease when faced with the hurly-burly of officialdom and awkward people.

There are, of course, the gifted ones who excel naturally in both areas. For the majority, however, there is a good deal that has to be learned. In fact for all journalists there is a huge area of expertise that can be acquired only by instruction, example and hard graft.

NEWS GATHERING

CRITERIA for assessing news gathering skills in **SPOT NEWS** stories.

Have the essential facts been established by:

1 Observation.
2 Interviewing those involved.
3 Getting corroborative quotes.
4 Getting the official view from police, council, fire brigade, organizations.
5 Double-checking figures.
6 Giving both (or more) sides to a situation where there are two (or more) sides.
7 Checking with people any information you have been given about them by a third party.
8 Checking the names, addresses, titles, etc. of people interviewed or involved, including those not present.
9 Checking the names of streets, buildings, places, etc.
10 Checking technical matters and terms with appropriate sources/ organizations.
11 Noting (if relevant) the weather, traffic, temperature, season.
12 Examining the area, background, setting, etc.

Have the facts obtained at the scene been supplemented (as necessary) by means of:

1 The office press cuttings library.
2 Appropriate reference books.
3 Further inquiries by telephone to press officers, organizations, etc.
4 Checks, using other sources, of any statements or denials made to you by press officers.
5 Inquiries from contacts.

Many 'diary' jobs consist of covering **MEETINGS** that are known about in advance such as council and council committee meetings by which local government operates, organization meetings at which speeches and reports might be given, party election and campaign meetings, speech days and prize givings and ad hoc public meetings. The following criteria should be applied.

Have the essential facts been established by:

1 Checking the names of the chairman and other officers who spoke.
2 Taking a note of (or checking against a handout) those parts of the speeches that you considered to be newsworthy.
3 Noting any decisions taken by vote, and by what majority.
4 Reporting parts of any debate that you considered to be newsworthy.
5 Checking the names and credentials of anyone who spoke from the body of the meeting.
6 Reading the minutes of the previous meeting.
7 Checking the names and details of any special speakers or invited guests.
8 Checking, or seeking explanation for, material in balance sheets that you considered to be newsworthy.
9 Checking the attendance at the meeting and its behaviour (if relevant).
10 Checking 'any other business' for future plans, meetings etc.

Have the facts of your assignment been further supported by:

1 Comparing reports of previous meetings in the office press cuttings files.
2 Checking names and references in appropriate reference books.
3 Researching background material to stand up references made at the meeting.

Some important assignments rest almost entirely on **INTERVIEWING** one person (or occasionally two or three). The following criteria should be applied.

Have the essential facts been established by:

1 Researching (or at least checking) the background of the person you are going to interview.
2 Preparing a list of questions you want to ask.
3 Arranging an acceptable time and place.
4 Dressing correctly for the interview, taking into account your interviewee.
5 Agreeing with the subject whether to use shorthand note or tape.
6 Putting the person at ease in opening the interview.
7 Allowing the person to do the talking.
8 Not putting answers into the person's mouth.
9 Agreeing what is on and what is off the record.

10 Pursuing any useful points that crop up outside the expected brief.

Have the facts of the interview been further supported by:

1   Reference to cuttings files on the the person or subject discussed.
2   Checking through telephone inquiries statements made and facts or figures given by the person.
3   Making legal checks on any statements or information that may be of dubious legality.

COURTS, PUBLIC INQUIRIES and **TRIBUNALS** can be a minefield for the young or trainee reporter and the basics of the law on libel, contempt of court, confidentiality, the Official Secrets Act and on reporting restrictions must be learned before tackling such assignments. The following criteria should be applied to the coverage of stories at magistrates' courts.

Have the essential (and publishable) facts of the story been established by:

1   Checking the names and addresses of accused persons in the court sheet supplied by the police.
2   Checking whether the accused is being dealt with summarily or is being committed for trial to another court.
3   Applying the rules of what can be published contained in the restrictions on reporting where the accused person is committed for trial.
4   Reporting fairly the case given by the prosecution and defence, the comments of the magistrate and the verdict and sentence in cases dealt with summarily (i.e., not writing in other known information).
5   Giving a fair balance to prosecution and defence whether the plea is guilty or not guilty.
6   Checking the spelling of names of the magistrate(s) and the prosecuting and defending solicitors.
7   Checking with the magistrates' clerk or the police any parts of the case or evidence you are not clear about.
8   Checking and confirming with the magistrates' clerk the amount of any costs awarded against the accused.
9   Checking with the police any future dates for cases that have been adjourned or committed for trial and noting whether or not bail has been granted by the magistrates.
10 Taking care that any pictures of an accused person are not used with a story before evidence of identification has been given.

WRITTEN SOURCES, whether they be press handouts, Government reports, newly published books or offbeat articles found in abstruse publications can spark off important news stories in the hands of a perceptive reader-conscious young journalist thumbing through them. The possibility of follow-ups should be considered. The following criteria should be applied to such stories:

Have the essential facts been uncovered and established by:

1 Thorough skim-reading (i.e., every other paragraph or the first few words of each paragraph) of the document.
2 Checking with the document source – publisher, Government office, etc. – to build on any promising reference.
3 Checking related material and references, including to people mentioned, in cuttings files and reference books.
4 Making telephone inquiries to establish confirmation and back-up for the material.
5 Making clear in writing and targeting your story why what you have found is relevant to the reader.
6 Ordering and researching file pictures to go with material.
7 Checking on copyright, and obtaining permissions where necessary (important with books and authors) for any verbatim text you want to use.
8 Checking any technical terms or technical concepts that are part of the material you want to use.
9 Deciding whether the material, as a result of what you have found, merits a further follow-up story.
10 Alerting the newsroom to the likely significance and estimated column space required for the material you have brought to light and checking the edition times.

LOCAL ISSUES – matters that are being talked about or are the subject of public debate in the area – can make important stories in provincial evening and weekly papers. They might be contentious matters in which tempers have run high, or to which there are several sides, such as a dangerous road or a contested development or the threatened destruction of a local amenity. Such investigative stories might take a reporter several days. The following criteria should be applied to such an assignment.

Has a balanced story been uncovered by:

1 Identifying the crux of the matter that is bothering people, be it for different reasons.
2 Finding out if there is more than one issue involved.
3 Talking to a balanced cross-section of the people involved.

4   Talking to the leaders of any pressure groups or representative bodies concerned.

5   Talking to the owners or people responsible (such as the council) for the building/road/monument/amenity that is the subject of the debate.

6   Observing personally the activity/nuisance/development, etc. that is the source of the trouble.

7   Searching cuttings files, council minutes and reference books for anything that casts light on the history of the dispute.

8   Examining any legal or planning aspects.

9   Checking with any other relevant organizations (English Heritage, National Trust, etc.) that might have something useful or interesting to say about the matter.

10 Organizing appropriate picture coverage from staff photographers, archives, etc. to go with your text.

NEWS WRITING

NEWS WRITING is the presentation to the reader of the fruits of your news gathering put into readable form. Where your story appears on the page depends on the judgement of the page executive – the chief subeditor or night editor – but wherever it appears and at whatever its length it should be written in such a way that:

◇   It captures the reader's attention in the first paragraph.
◇   It encourages the reader to read on.

We have examined the requirements of news writing in Chapter 1 on reporting in this book. They can be found in greater detail in Harris and Spark's *Practical Newspaper Reporting*, 2nd Edition (Focal Press, 1993), pages 49–73. For the purposes of the exercises in Chapter 1 assessment should be based on the following parameters.

Has your news story got:

1   A first paragraph (intro) that gives clearly the main facts of the story.

2   An intro that is also succinct, easy to read and eye-catching.

3   Sufficient explanation in the next few paragraphs to justify and (if need be) qualify your intro.

4   Facts thereafter in order of importance.

5   A clear indication in the story of the where, how, when and (if possible) the why of the matter.

6 A clear identity of the people involved (Harold Evans: 'People make news.').

7 Relevant and properly attributed quotations, where possible, from people involved.

8 A fair representation of what the person (or persons) has said in an interview-based story.

9 A reasonable hearing to both sides in a dispute-based story.

10 Any useful background infirmation that will give the story context.

11 Correct usage in titles, ranks, abbreviation etc. in accordance with the office style book.

12 A style that is concise, objective and free of comment.

FEATURE WRITING

FEATURE WRITING, like reporting, involves two main activities: information gathering and writing. The recommended criteria are in six sections:

1 Briefing – includes purpose and objectives; implicit or explicit thesis; point of view.

2 Information gathering (news).

3 Information gathering (wider ranging research).

4 Content – use made of material.

5 Structure – generally more complex than in news report.

6 Style – generally greater language skill than in in reporting.

Features cover such a variety of fields, structures and styles that criteria have to be put in general terms. Tutors will see how to extend the following for differing kinds of features. Use the index to Hennessy's *Writing Feature Articles*, 2nd Edition (Focal Press, 1993) to point you to any aspects requiring information or discussion in greater depth.

Assessing the briefing

1 Is the briefing, if given by an instructor or senior journalist, clearly understood in terms of purpose, deadline, content, treatment and likely sources.

2 Is the briefing, if your own, clearly formulated.

3 Is your interpretation of the briefing properly attuned to the target readership.

4 Are the requirements of the briefing (particularly in intro and conclusion) clearly discernable in the finished piece.

Assessing information gathering (news)
1   Use criteria and sections under newsgathering, pages 151–5.

Assessing information gathering (wider ranging research)
1   Has the information been gathered by using, as necessary, criteria for interviews selected from newsgathering, pages 152–3.
2   Has the information been gathered by using, as necessary, criteria on written sources selected from newsgathering, page 154.

Assessing content
Has the feature got:

1   Content that accords with editorial policy.
2   Content appropriate to the target readership.
3   Content in accordance with legal and ethical constraints.
4   Examples, anecdotes and quotes appropriate to the theme or subject.
5   Accurate figures and statistics.
6   A text that makes good use of the gathered material.

Assessing structure
Has the feature got:

1   The appropriate balance (for the subject) of description, narration, exposition and argument.
2   A pace correctly judged for the circumstances that makes for impact and readability.
3   An intro that grabs the reader's attention.
4   A body that provides the necessary evidence for the thesis or viewpoint.
5   A conclusion that summarizes the points made, draws together the threads of the argument and follows convincingly from the body.
6   Analysis and argument that are clearly and convincingly organized.
7   Opinions properly backed by facts and evidence.

Assessing the style
Is it:

1   Readable.
2   Appropriate for the target readership.
3   Appropriate for the topic.
4   Accurate and convincing in the choice of language.

5   As clear, direct and concise as possible taking into account space considerations and the target readership.

6   Free of grammatical error, word misuse, cliché and jargon.

7   Regardful of house style and editorial policy.

PHOTOJOURNALISM

THE ELEMENTS of art and technical expertise in photojournalism bring in quite different skills criteria to those of any other form of journalism. Not only is a picture a piece of news or part of a feature that must obey editorial requirements and edition deadlines; it is also the product of artistic judgement and the skilful use of a piece of apparatus.

It is thus judged on two levels. On the one hand it needs to have merit as a photograph in terms of lighting, composition, tonal balance and correct exposure; on the other it needs to have relevance and illustrative value in terms of the news or features page for which it is chosen as reflected in the briefing given to the photographer.

However good a picture is as a piece of photography it is not much use to a newspaper or magazine unless it adds to a related story or tells a story itself with the aid of a caption. Indeed, a picture of less than ideal composition or exposure can sometimes have news value if it is the only one available and is vital to the text for which it is wanted.

Ideally, editors want pictures that are the best obtainable both in quality and relevance. There are, of course, those special occasions when fortune has smiled on the hard pressed photographer and resulted in pictures that are so good that they force their way into the page even when they were not asked for.

The following criteria are offered as a means of assessing success in picture assignments.

Photographic skills

IN TAKING your shot(s) did you:

1   Check your equipment before leaving for your assignment – i.e., what equipment, especially lenses, you need and the state of your equipment.

2   Check transmission arrangements for getting the picture back to the office.

3   Check your briefing and deadline plus any arrangements to be made to enable you to take your pictures, including permissions.

4   Take a choice of pictures, including close-ups and full lengths, and to suit horizontal or vertical use in the page.

5 Make a note of exposure, shutter speed and any other notes or technical details you might need to recall.
6 Have some means of verifying that your pictures are of the right person/object/scene, etc.
7 Check and note down appropriate caption details so that your picture and its contents can be correctly identified and captioned.
8 Write your own caption(s).
9 Notify the picture desk on job completion.
10 Produce a full set of contact prints plus your notes for picture desk use or for assessment.

Editorial skills

IN TAKING shots intended for publication, did you:

1 Study the use of pictures in your target publication, relating their treatment to the text that goes with them.
2 Familiarize yourself with the principles of cropping and scaling of pictures.
3 Examine the way your pictures have been cropped for use and also the reasons.
4 Study the principles and aims of page design and the use of pictures in page design.
5 Try to think up ways in which pictures can be used to extend a news story or feature, taking specimen assignments as examples.

SUBEDITING

ASSESSING standards in subediting is difficult because text editing is carried out for a variety of purposes. The sub might be reducing a huge amount of copy to a quarter of its size on a day when there is a good deal of news fighting for space or, on another day building up an important story to fill a given position from various text sources.

A young or inexperienced reporter might have turned in a good story with problems of spelling and syntax that need careful sorting; an urgently awaited page lead might prove to be bristling with legal pitfalls. Either text might need a rewrite or a partial rewrite.

The page one splash might be so well written by the reporter, and to the exact length required, that the highly skilled splash sub has only to check for spelling, punctuation and keyboarding errors. Another sub on the table might be sweating over half a column of news briefs in which each of ten stories has to be reduced to a fraction of its length to a polished informative paragraph by the edition deadline – not a job for the slow or the faint-hearted.

A story might need complicated editionizing with perhaps a version with a different intro and geography for each edition (some evening papers have seven or eight editions), or the task might be a running story with constant 'add copy' that needs changing and updating for every edition.

The headline alone is a specialized task. Not only has it to encapsulate the point or principal facts of the story so that the reader will be persuaded to read on; it must be of the right type, character count, balance and width to look right on the page.

Features subbing

FEATURES subbing has its own problems. While there is usually little cutting or collating required, the text often requires a good deal more display than a news story, with standfirsts, special quotes, perhaps a blurb for page one and a quite differerent, more subjective approach to headlines. The subeditor is more involved in what is being written and is helping to project the writer's message or ideas.

There is still the same need for watchfulness over facts, dates and quotations and for faults in grammar and spelling. Beware the expert who thinks he has remembered a famous quotation correctly or is unaware that all his life he has been confusing 'disinterested' with 'uninterested' or has never knowingly got the date of an Act of Parliament right.

The following criteria could apply to some or all subediting work and could be used selectively as a basis of assessment for the tasks in Chapter 5.

Accuracy

IN SUBBING your story to the briefing received, did you:

1 Check and correct the spelling as necessary.
2 Check and correct the grammar as necessary.
3 Check for misused words.
4 Put right any ambiguity or lack of clarity in the text.
5 Check the punctuation and simplify for the reader where necessary (i.e., avoid long sentences with many clauses – look out for misplaced commas leading to ambiguities).
6 Replace jargon, journalese and clichés (unless the clichés are short and lend colour to the text).

7 Check the spelling, meaning and accurate use of technical terms.
8 Spell out at first mention all but the most commonly used abbreviations.
9 Check any suspect facts (famous quotations, Acts of Parliament, titles of films, books, plays, songs, etc.).
10 Verify place names and geographical references, using gazetteers.
11 Check the names, addresses (if necessary to the story), style and title of people involved.
12 Check that spellings, names etc. do not vary through the text.
13 Check dates and figures where possible.
14 Ensure that any quotations used are properly and clearly attributed.
15 Ensure that house style is followed.

Cutting

IN CUTTING your story to the briefing received (mainly in news stories) did you:

1 If given a length in inches or centimetres, work out the number of words to aim at.
2 Shorten parts of the text where appropriate by rewriting more tightly.
3 Take out circumlocutions and long-winded phrasing.
4 Take out unnecessary adjectives.
5 Replace long words with shorter ones where appropriate.
6 Weigh up the facts of the story and reduce the length by progressively taking out the lesser important ones.
7 Ensure that remaining facts of lesser importance are at the end of the subbed story to make easy any last-minute cuts that might be needed.

Collating

IN COLLATING text for a story from several sources (mainly in news stories), did you:

1 Check for any byline or in-text attributions needed.
2 Ensure consistency of spelling of names and places in the reworked text.
3 Use the sources as a means of extending the story and for corroboration, while avoiding needless repetition.
4 Rewrite or paraphrase material to splice it together, where reasonable, to avoid excessive length, but keeping text and sources separate where appropriate.
5 Note and keep in any differences of geography, time or time scale that will be needed by the reader.

Legality

IN SUBBING the story to the briefing received did you:

1 Check the facts and quotations for any legal problems.
2 Check that you have not created new legal problems in text or headline as a result of your editing.

Headline writing

IN WRITING the headline, check that:

1 You based it on the main fact(s) of the story.
2 In getting the words to fit you did not distort the facts of the story.
3 You avoided all but the most commonly accepted abbreviations (i.e., BBC, TUC, Nato, etc.).
4 You kept it active by giving it a verb.
5 You avoided, where possible, the use of sub's jargon: boss, rap, row, probe, axe, chop, quiz, drama.
6 You avoided, in using figures, multiple noughts or odd numbers.
7 You kept punctuation to the minimum, or did without it.
8 You avoided asking the reader a question (he expects you to have the answers).
9 You avoided abstruse or foreign words (except where vital to the story).
10 You avoided ambiguous words, or words that could be taken equally for a noun or a verb or have more than one meaning.

To ensure that it has easy readability, did you:

1 Keep the wording uncomplicated.
2 Leave room for even spacing between the letters.
3 Avoid having wasteful or unwanted white around the type.
4 Achieve good balance of characters (i.e., avoiding lines of widely uneven width that can puzzle the eye).
5 Avoid having punctuation at the ends of lines (it is unsightly).

PLANNING AND DESIGN

SUCCESS in page design hinges on whether or not the page presents the chosen ingredients in a readable and attractive way within the format of the style used by the newspaper or magazine. This, in its turn, is determined by what is appropriate for the publication's readership. In terms of an overall mark this has to be a qualitative judgement based upon these considerations.

There are, nevertheless, in all cases general criteria for assessing the skills that have gone into planning and designing a page. The following list is offered as a basis of assessment either for the simulated page assignments in Chapter 6 based on cut-up material and for actual design exercises developed from them.

In planning and designing the page, did you:

1 Understand and put into effect the use of focal points in the overall design.
2 Take into account (to avoid clash) the content and visual display of any advertising on the page.
3 Take into account (to avoid clash) the content, whether editorial or advertising, and the visual effect of the page opposite.
4 Achieve a proper balance of type paying regard both to the relative importance of the items and the needs of the reader.
5 Make use, where necessary, of different sizes and 'weights' of type, and permitted variants, in order to achieve variety within the typographical format being used.
6 Crop and scale pictures to get the best possible out of them to suit the purpose of the text accompanying them and their placing on the page.
7 Locate the picture(s) to give the best possible visual effect, taking into account the other considerations above.
8 Measure accurately (with a print rule), and indicate on the page, the required text setting and picture sizes where these differed from standard column width.
9 Ensure that the page 'furniture' – any crossheads, bylines, stand-firsts, panel rules, etc. – were in keeping with the publication's type format.
10 In the case of colour ensure, from print-out, that the best possible colour balance has been achieved.

WORKSHOP PROJECTS

INDIVIDUAL marking and assessment are not easy to arrive at in group work where students or trainees interact with each other to achieve a result. However, it is desirable that projects of the sort outlined in the models given in Chapter 7 be more than just a practice run-through of skills and aptitudes to fill in course time.

Ideally, journalism being the sort of work it is, it is useful to have teamwork skills and aptitudes reflected in a percentage of the overall mark. For the guidance of tutors and instructors (and of students, too, for that matter) the following criteria are suggested as a means of assessing individual contribution to group projects. It is recommended that in the case of such projects each item (unless not applicable) be given a grading for the individual of 1 to 10, or alternatively a proportional weighting.

1 Co-operation with the team.
2 Ability to lead and delegate.
3 Ability to take delegation.
4 Organizing aptitude.
5 Creativity.
6 Originality.
7 Responsibility.
8 Resourcefulness.
9 Innovativeness.
10 Analytical powers.

STUDY PROGRAMMES

THE SORT of written work outlined in Chapter 8 would be expected to run alongside other course work with delivery at an agreed length to an agreed deadline, and with the mark being an agreed percentage of the final course mark.

The method of marking and the percentage weighting would depend on the course, but the following factors would need to be taken into account (depending on the subject) in assessing the mark.

1 Thoroughness of subject coverage in the period nominated.
2 Quality of supporting research and use of sources.
3 Structure.
4 Argument.
5 Factual accuracy.
6 Grammar and writing techniques.
7 Relevance and incorporation of quotations.
8 Readability.
9 Useful illustration (maps, charts, etc.).
10 Meeting deadline.

The last requirement should apply to any piece of journalism submitted during training, otherwise trainees will take the wrong message into the real world. The later that course work is submitted the higher should be the deduction of marks, with a final date after which work is not accepted.

REFERENCES AND FURTHER READING

Crone, T: *Law and the Media,* 3rd Edition (Focal Press, 1995).

Giles, V and Hodgson FW: *Creative Newspaper Design* (Butterworth-Heinemann, 1990).

Harris, G and Spark, D: *Practical Newspaper Reporting*, 2nd Edition (Focal Press, 1993).

Hennessy, B: *Writing Feature Articles*, 2nd Edition (Focal Press, 1993).

Hodgson, FW: *Modern Newspaper Practice*, 3rd Edition (Focal Press, 1993).

Hodgson, FW: *Subediting*, 2nd Edition (Focal Press, 1993).

Keene, M: *Practical Photojournalism* (Focal Press, 1993).

McNae, LCJ: *Essential Law For Journalists* (Butterworths, 1992).

10

Resources

AN ESSENTIAL part of a journalist's job is to know where and how to get information and who to ask.

In some ways the sourcing of materials has been made easier in recent years. Public access to databases has increased and the drive for openness in business and government has not been without success. But in other ways sourcing has been made more difficult: too many departments and press officers are as likely to conceal information as to dispense it.

Official publications are obtainable from the publishers, Her Majesty's Stationery Office (HMSO). Their bookshop, at 49 High Holborn, London WC1 (Tel: 0171-873-0011), has both a telephone and counter service, and there are agents throughout the country. They will tell you the nearest library where you can access the publications.

The *UK Press Gazette* has produced the *UKPG Contact Pro* disk (sponsored by Mercury Group), an electronic database for journalists, free for subscribers, sale price £29.50. This is a Microsoft Windows-compatible version of the Contact Pro program together with the database of 1400 contacts. It can easily be modified and extended. There are also versions for DOS and Apple Mac.

OFFICIAL INFORMATION

THE FOLLOWING is a selection of useful sources of information.

AGRICULTURE

Contacts: Local or county secretary of the National Farmers Union (NFU), Ministry of Agriculture, Fisheries and Food and its Horticultural Marketing Inspectorate.

The Farming Information Centre, NFU, Agriculture House, London SW1X 7NU. The information is on the politics of agriculture and union matters rather than technical aspects, and there is a picture library (farmland and machines). Telephone first: 0171-235-5077.

The Institute of Agricultural History and Museum of English Rural Life, University of Reading, Whiteknights, Reading RG6 2AG.

ANIMALS AND BIRDS

Contacts: Local inspector of the Royal Society for the Prevention of Cruelty to Animals (RSPCA), local officer of the Royal Society for the Protection of Birds (RSPB).

Animal Aid Society, Animal Health Trust, Animal Liberation Front (although their methods have been widely condemned). **Animal Welfare Trust**.

ARMED FORCES

Contacts: Press officer of the Ministry of Defence (MoD), PROs at district HQ and main camps/stations/barracks; press officers of recruitment centres.

Jane's Information Group publishes daily and weekly newsletters, weekly and monthly magazines, various books, including yearbooks, and databases. They are expensive. Most can be consulted in the British Library (see page 185). A free catalogue is obtainable from Jane's Information Group, Sentinel House, 163 Brighton Road, Coulsdon, Surrey CR3 2NX.

The Air Force List, The RAF Retired List, The Army List, and *The Navy List* are published annually by the HMSO, giving complete lists of senior service personnel.

ARTS

To obtain interviews with celebrities, the publicist for the relevant project is the best bet. How? Dogged persistence is needed to get past the barrier of agents, and a commission from a newspaper or magazine is usually necessary.

Contacts: The Arts Council, the British Film Institute (BFI), the main theatres, concert halls, the various unions, Secretaries of local societies (literary, theatre, etc.), curators of galleries and museums, librarians, organizers of festivals, managers of theatres and cinemas. See *The Guardian Media Guide* for a comprehensive list of contacts with telephone numbers and the *Media Organisations* and *Media Publications* sections in the Appendix of this book (pages 194-6 and 203-4).

The Arts Council of Great Britain, 14 Great Peter Street, London SW1P 3NQ. Supports all kinds of arts organizations. Information about regional arts councils and boards.

British Film Institute: Encourages the development of film, television and video in the UK. Divides into the National Film Archive, the National Film Theatre (NFT), Museum of the Moving Image. There is a library and information service, and a monthly magazine, *Sight and Sound*.

Architecture: Practising architects and firms, local council architect and planning officer, heritage and conservation pressure groups (see under *Environment*, page 173)

Royal Institute of British Architects, 66 Portland Place, London W1N 4AD. Houses the British Architectural Library.

BROADCASTING

Contact press officers of BBC's main radio and TV stations, PROs of ITV companies. *Blue Book of British Broadcasting* is the chief directory on the BBC and independent broadcasting organizations in the UK, and *The Guardian Media Guide* is a convenient guide to the telephone numbers (see media publications in the Appendix, pages 202-4).

British Broadcasting Corporation: Corporate HQ of the British Broadcasting Corporation (BBC) and of network radio: BBC, Broadcasting House, Langham Place, London W1A 1AA.

HQ of network TV with main production facilities: Television Centre, Wood Lane, London W12 7RJ.

HQ of BBC Enterprises, and broadcasting research: Woodlands, 80 Wood Lane, London W12 0TT.

HQ of regional broadcasting, educational broadcasting and some current affairs: White City, 201 Wood Lane, London W12 7TS.

Several TV departments, including documentaries, sport and arts: Kensington House, Richmond Way, London W14 0AX.

HQ of the World Service: Bush House, The Strand, London WC2B 4PH.

Contact press officers of BBC's main radio and TV stations, PROs of ITV companies.

CHARITIES

Most charities are bona-fide organizations, but cases have been recorded of charities cloaking dubious activities (with religious or political intent) under a respectable-sounding title. There are occasionally reports of misuse of funds, and controversy over the tax concessions given to some of them. Check the Companies House Index for those charities which are also limited companies. Contact the Charity Commission, which keeps local indexes of charities. Phone the Commission to ask for any file to be made available. Photocopies can be made, and you can deal with the Commission by correspondence. The Commission publishes various free leaflets. Your local library or local council can start you off on any investigation. See also the Registrar of Friendly Societies.

Charity Commission, St Alban's House, 57–60 Haymarket, London SW1Y 4QX.

CIVIL RIGHTS AND LIBERTIES

The Criminal Justice and Public Order Bill of 1994 brought together many dissenting groups, and various public demonstrations resulted in needed as well as unneeded publicity. The New Age travellers found themselves rubbing shoulders with rave-party organizers, the homeless of different sorts, Charter 88, the Law Society, Liberty, the Green Party and the No M11 Link Road Campaign. (See *Homeless,* page 176.)

Professional bodies of all kinds have departments that can be contacted to identify injustices. Many have ombudsmen to whom individual citizens can apply directly. The addresses below have been selected from those bodies for which identifying injustices is a primary concern, and which are likely to be of particular use to journalists.

Advance Party: Coalition of rave-party organizers against the Criminal Justice and Order Bill. It organized the May Day 1994 demonstration against the Bill, and published *The Right to Party*, with the Campaign against the Criminal Justice Bill.

Campaign for the Freedom of Information, 3 Endsleigh Street, London WC1H ODD. Campaigns for reform of the secrecy laws. Publishes the quarterly *Secrets.*

Campaign for Press and Broadcasting Freedom, 9 Poland Street, London W1V 3DG. It campaigns for more public access to the media and a right of reply, and against censorship of the media.

Community Rights Project, 5–11 Lavington Street, London SE1 0NZ. Campaigned for The Local Government (Access to Information) Act, 1985 to become law after drafting the Bill. The organization publishes a booklet *Guide to Councillors' Rights to Information*.

Commission for Local Administration:

England: 21 Queen Anne's Gate, London SW1H 9BU.

Wales: Derwent House, Court Road, Bridgend, Mid-Glamorgan CF31 1BN.

Scotland: 5 Shandwick Place, Edinburgh EH2 4RG.

Commissioner for Complaints, 33 Wellington Place, Belfast BT1 6HN.

Charter 88 Trust Ltd, 3 Pine Street, London EC1R 0JH.

European Commission on Human Rights, Council of Europe, 67006 Strasbourg Cedex, France.

Liberty (Formerly the National Council for Civil Liberties), 21 Tabard Street, London SE1 4LA. (Contact the General Secretary.) It has published several books on official secrecy. There is a network of groups in the UK.

National Association of Citizens' Advice Bureaux, 26 Bedford Square, London WC2. There are many local branches.

See also minorities and discriminations, page 179.

COMMERCE

Check information from different angles: get competitors'/opponents' viewpoints. Companies: write to the company secretary at the registered office to ask to see the registers, or consult the documents at Companies House. Company registers, accounts: annual reports are available from some reference libraries – or contact company's press office.

Contacts: Department of Trade and Industry (DTI), 1–19 Victoria Street, London SW1H 0ET, and regional press offices. Chamber of Commerce and local branches, district and county planning officers, company secretaries, press officers and managers, unions and workforces.

Kinds of sources: Company registers, accounts. Annual reports are available from some reference libraries – or contact PRO.
Companies House:
England: 55 City Road, London EC1Y 1BB.
Wales: Crown Way, Cardiff CF4 3UZ.
Scotland: 100–102 George Street, Edinburgh EH2 3DJ.
Northern Ireland: Companies Registration Office, IDB House, Chichester Street, Belfast BT1 4JX.

All companies must make an annual return to Companies House. Their files must reveal the names of all directors, the name of the company secretary, the shareholders, the kind of business carried on, accounts and balance sheets, and the company history.
Advisory, Conciliation and Arbitration Service (ACAS), 27 Wilton Street, London SW1.
Association of British Chambers of Commerce, 9 Tufton Street, London SW1P 3QB.
Confederation of British Industry (CBI), Centre Point, New Oxford Street, London WC1A 1DU. Represents all sectors of industry and lobbies energetically.
HM Customs and Excise, King's Beam House, 22 Upper Ground, London SE1 9PJ.
Department of Trade and Industry, 2 Marsham Street, London SW1P 3EB.
Monopolies and Mergers Commission, 48 Carey Street, London WC2A 2HX. Appointed by the Government, it advises on mergers that might affect free competition.
Office of Fair Trading: Field House, Breams Buildings, London EC4A 1PR. A statutory body that protects consumers in general.

CONSUMERS

Consumers' Association, 2 Marylebone Road, London NW1 4DX. The largest independent pressure group, it publishes *Which?* and other publications. It tests products and campaigns on issues.
National Consumer Council, 20 Grosvenor Gardens, London SW1W 0DH. A Government-funded organization, it lobbies on behalf of the consumer and produces various publications.

Statutory bodies set up to safeguard consumers' interests include the Audit Commission (the accounts of local authorities and the NHS), the National Audit Office (NAO) (the accounts of government departments and some public bodies), and the Office of Fair Trading (OFT) – see above.

The Institute of Trading Standards Administration. This is the professional body for trading standards officers.

CRIME AND CRIMINALS

Journalists writing about crime have to be fully acquainted with the law of libel (Crone: *Law and the Media* (Focal Press, 1995), Chapters 1 to 6). Some of the organizations most closely associated with crime are as follows. Others can be located in the *Directory of Voluntary Associations* and other directories.

Apex Trust, 9 Poland Street, London W1: It deals with prisoners' employment.

Criminal Injuries Compensation Board (CICB): Tay House, 300 Bath Street, Glasgow G2 4JR. A statutory body that pays compensation to those injured as a result of a crime.

Crown Prosecution Service (CPS), 50 Ludgate Hill, London EC4M 7EX.

Howard League for Penal Reform, 125 Kennington Park Road, London SE11.

Justice against Identification Laws, 271 Upper Street, London N1.

National Association for the Care and Rehabilitation of Offenders (NACRO), 125 Kennington Park Road, London SE11.

Preservation of the Rights of Prisoners (PROP), 339a Finchley Road, London NW3.

Prisoners' Wives and Families Society, 14 Richmond Avenue, London N1.

Rape Crisis Centre, PO Box 42, London N6.

Release, 1 Elgin Avenue, London W9. Advises on drug-related legal problems.

EDUCATION

Although the Local Government (Access to Education Act) makes available documents on all aspects of education policy, most schools are reluctant to allow any records to be seen.

Kinds of sources:

The *Education Yearbook* gives government departments, local education authorities, etc.

The Education Authorities Directory and Annual gives details of statutory education bodies, all secondary schools, universities and special schools. All further education establishments have their prospectuses. Other sources: *Independent Schools Yearbook, Municipal Yearbook*, Companies House Index, the Registry of Friendly Societies and the Index of Charities. Reference libraries stock many other publications listing details of courses, etc.

Contacts: Chief Education Officer in local authorities, local secretaries of the teachers' unions. The addresses of the following bodies will be found in the *Education Authorities Directory*:

Advisory Centre for Education
Association of British Correspondence Colleges
Campaign for the Advancement for State Education
Council for the Accreditation of Correspondence Colleges
Independent Schools Information Service
Pre-School Playgroups Association
Workers' Educational Association.

EMPLOYMENT

For unemployment figures, consult the *Ministry of Employment Gazette* at the local library.
Contact: The regional office of the COI.
The Training and Enterprise Council will give information on the state of youth employment. It provides training schemes to satisfy local needs in association with schools and further education colleges.
Employment Appeals Tribunal, 4 St James's Square, London SW1Y 4JU.

ENVIRONMENT

The following can be consulted on the various kinds of pollution, including noise, the spoiling of natural beauty, obstruction of building work, police involvement, demonstrations, tree preservation and houses due for demolition.
Council for the Protection of Rural England (CPRE), 4 Hobart Place, London SW1W 0HY. Advises on activities affecting the planning, improvement and protection of the countryside; briefs on the law.
The Countryside Commission, 19–23 Albert Road, Manchester M19. Publishes a free guide, *Out in the Country: where you can go and what you can do*, and *Rights of Way Manual*.

Friends of the Earth, 26–28 Underwood Street, London N1 7JQ. Publishes *The A to Z of local pollution: who to contact action guide* and *The Countryside Campaigner's Manual*.
The Green Party, 10 Station Parade, London SW1 9AZ.
The Open Spaces Society: The oldest of Britain's national conservation organizations. It advises on statutory rights, and publishes guides and information sheets.
The Ramblers' Association: Protects the landscape and footpaths. Publications include several on footpaths and rights of way.

FAMILY

When investigating family, particularly children matters, it is easy to get the law wrong. Check with *The Penguin Guide to the Law* (1993) and see Crone: *Law and the Media* (Focal Press, 1995), Chapter 9 on the operation of the various Children and Young Persons Acts.
Contacts: Education Officer, Director of Social Services, Chairman of Social Services Committee for Children in Care, Inspector of the National Society for the Protection of Children (NSPCC).

Children's Legal Centre, 20 Compton Terrace, London N1 2UN.
Family Rights Group, 35 Wellington Street, London WC2.

GOVERNMENT (CENTRAL)

In writing about Government (*see also politics*), you need to be voracious readers of the press releases, the counterblasts of opponents in various pressure groups, the range of quality and popular papers, political weeklies, etc. Deeper research, this side of the investigations of the Sunday quality teams, will normally involve going back to recent press coverage via the *British Humanities Index*, the *Clover Newspaper Index* and *Research Index*, all available in good reference libraries.

GOVERNMENT (LOCAL)

Local government is one of the areas where journalists might need to adopt investigative approaches (i.e. digging out information where there is an attempt to conceal). This is because there are such huge sums involved in local government and because scrutiny has been made easier by the Local Government (Access to Information Act) of 1985.

The local reference library or the council information centre (Town Hall) will indicate which documents and publications are available to the public. Notices of future council and committee meetings can be obtained. Write to a council officer or Chief Executive or Town Clerk to obtain access to particular information. A ward councillor or local MP can be contacted if the information is not forthcoming. Butterworth's *Encyclopaedia of Local Government Law* details the journalist's right to information.

Your local reference library might have many council documents on the shelves. Keep a record of your requests for information, with dates and times and names of council officials spoken to, so that if you are denied what is your right, you can take the matter further.

Associations of local authorities and county councils represent their members when lobbying nationally.

HEALTH

All organizations in the public health sector are listed in the *Hospitals and Health Service Yearbook*, together with essential information on finance, law, etc. District health authorities divide up into individual hospitals, health centres, community care services, ambulance services and community health councils. The Health Service Ombudsman reports directly to parliament. To investigate NHS policy locate Government reports in the *HMSO Monthly Catalogue*.

British Dental Association, 64 Wimpole Street, London W1M 8AL.
British Medical Association, BMA House, Tavistock Square, London WC1H 9JR. Literature on the Government's proposed reforms of the NHS. Publishes the *British Medical Journal*.
College of Health, 18 Victoria Park Square, London E2 9PF. A charity, it publishes *Consumer's Guide to Health Information* and *Guide to Hospital Waiting Lists*.
Community Health Councils (CHCs) (local health councils in Scotland, district committees in Northern Ireland): a network of independent consumer councils monitoring the NHS, enabled by law to attend meetings of health authorities.
District and Regional Health Authorities: contact the press office initially. To attend meetings, contact the district administrator under the name of the DHA in the telephone directory. There is no access, however, to meetings on confidential matters (complaints, etc.), and there is no law saying documents have to be made available.

General Optical Council, 41 Harley Street, London W1N 2DJ.
Health and Safety Executive, Baynards House, 1 Chepstow Place,
London W2 4TF.
The Health Service Ombudsman: details from (England) Church
House, Great Smith Street, London SW1P 3BW; (Wales) 4th Floor, Pearl
Assurance House, Greyfriars Road, Cardiff CF1 3AG; (Scotland) 2nd
Floor, 11 Melville Crescent, Edinburgh.

Hospitals

The Institute of Complementary Medicine publishes a *Yearbook*
that lists all the self-regulatory bodies in this area, which includes such
areas as homeopathy. Health Farm Publications publishes *The Directory
of Complementary and Alternative Practitioners*.

Private health care

The law provides for some opting out of the regular NHS administration.
Some hospitals have become registered companies (see Companies
House), some friendly societies and some charities. The main source of
reference is the *Directory of Independent Hospitals and Health
Services*. This has the law on private health services, lists of the
members of the Association of Independent Hospitals, and details of all
the hospitals and homes, and of pay beds in NHS hospitals.

Contacts: Hospital general manager, clinics' and departments' secretaries.

*See also medicine; mental health and handicap; physically handi-
capped*.

HOMELESS

Campaign for Single Homeless People, 5 Cromer Street, London
WC1H BL5.
Shelter National Campaign for the Homeless Ltd, 88 Old Street,
London EC1V 9BB.
Squash (Squatters Action for Secure Homes), 68 Bedford Road, London
E17 4PX.

Many of the current social problems are reflected in homelessness. The
demonstrations against the Criminal Justice and Public Order Bill in
1994 brought together housing organizations such as the National

Federation of Housing Associations (see under housing), as well as environmental and civil rights groups that normally make strange bedfellows (see civil rights).

HOUSING

Contact: Housing department of local councils, council architect/engineer/surveyor, estate agents and property developers, Chief Environmental Health Inspector, the Census, Citizens' Advice Bureau.

The National Federation of Housing Associations, 175 Gray's Inn Road, London WC1X 8UX.

HUMAN RIGHTS

(See also civil liberties.)
Amnesty International, International Secretariat, 1 Easton Street, London WC1X OD3; British Section, 99 Rosebery Avenue, London EC1 4RE. Various campaign literature. Campaigns for the release of 'prisoners of conscience', for an end to torture and the abolition of the death penalty. It is independent of political or religious creeds.

The Equal Opportunities Commission

(See minorities.)
European Commission on Human Rights, Council of Europe, 67006 Strasbourg Cedex.
Howard League for Penal Reform, 708 Holloway Road, London N19 3NL.
Legal Action Group, Publishers, 242 Pentonville Road, London N1 9NG.
Minorities Arts Advisory Service (MAAS), 26 Shacklewell Lane, London E8 2EZ produces *Artrage Magazine*.
Minority Rights Group, 379 Brixton Road, London SW9 7DE.

INTERNATIONAL AFFAIRS

Articles on aspects of international affairs can be researched in the indexes to publications in your reference library. For libraries and books to consult, see Ann Hoffmann, *Research for Writers* (A & C Black, 1992), Chapter 9.

European Parliament (London Office), 2 Queen Anne's Gate, London SW1H 9AA.
European Community Press and Information Office, 8 Storey's Gate, London SW1P 3AT produces much literature.
United Nations Association, 3 Whitehall Court, London SW1A 2EL publicises the work of the UN. The London Council of the UNA runs a bookshop, 23 New Quebec Street, London W1H 8DH.

LAND

Contact local parish and county records offices for property histories; current ownership, HM Land Registry. For rights of way/footpaths, contact local secretary of Ramblers' Association, the council or county surveyor, the clerk to the parish council, landowners and residents.

HM Land Registry, 32 Lincoln's Inn Fields, London WC2A 3PH.
The Housing Corporation, 149 Tottenham Court Road, London W1. Keeps a register of all housing associations.
Town and Country Planning Association, 17 Carlton House Terrace, London SW1Y 5AS. Gives free advice to groups and individuals, and publishes community manuals on planning.
Transport 2000, Walkden House, 10 Melton Street, London NW1 2EJ. Publishes guides on the transport aspects of planning.

LAW

The most comprehensive of law directories is *The Solicitors and Barristers Directory* published by Waterlow. It gives details of solicitors, barristers and firms, of the Law Society and the various institutions, and all civil and criminal courts in England and Wales.

Crone's *Law and the Media*, lists and discusses statutes and cases of most interest to the media. *The Guardian's Media Guide* lists the telephone numbers of courts from Crown Courts upwards and of legal bodies.

Law Society
England and Wales, 8 Bream's Buildings, London EC4A 1HP.
Northern Ireland, Royal Courts of Justice, Chichester Street, Belfast BT1 3JZ.
Scotland, 26–27 Drumscheugh Gardens, Edinburgh EH3 7YR.

MENTAL HEALTH AND HANDICAP

National Association for Mental Health (MIND), Granta House, Broadway, London E15 4BQ.
Royal Society for Mentally Handicapped Children and Adults (MENCAP), 123 Golden Lane, London EC1 3PP.

MINORITIES AND DISCRIMINATIONS

Equal Opportunities Commission, Overseas House, Quay Street, Manchester M3 3HN. The national body monitoring discrimination on sex or marital grounds. A civil claim for damages may be brought, but not a criminal prosecution. There are offices in Wales, Scotland and Northern Ireland.
England: Overseas House, Quay Street, Manchester M3 3HN.
Wales: Caerways House, Windsor Place, Cardiff CF1 1LB.
Scotland: 249 West George Street, Glasgow G2 4QE.
Northern Ireland: Lindsay House, Callendar Street, Belfast BT1 5DT.

Homosexuals

The age of consent has been reduced to 18, and a campaign continues to lower it to 16.

Albany Trust, 26 Balham Hill, London SW12 9EB. Counselling.
Campaign for Homosexual Equality, 38 Mount Pleasant, London WC1X 0AN.
The Terrence Higgins Trust, 52 Grays Inn Road, London WC1X. Has a helpline.
The London Lesbian and Gay Switchboard, BM Box 1514, London WC1N 3XX. Tel: 0171-837-7324. The main advice centre, operating 24 hours a day throughout the year. Both legal and medical advice available, and a list of gay groups and business services. A diary of events is prepared daily. There is also a separate Lesbian Line; Tel: 0171-837-8602. *See also women.*

Racial Minorities

Commission for Racial Equality, Eliot House, 10–12 Arlington Street, London SW1E 5EH. Monitors racial discrimination. A civil claim for damages may be brought, but not a criminal prosecution.
Institute of Race Relations, 2 Leeke Street, London WC1X 9HS.
Joint Council for the Welfare of Immigrants, 115 Old Street, London EC1V 9JZ.

POLICE

Police officers are local government officers, and the Local Government Act covers the right to inspect accounts and attend meetings of the police authority. The *Police and Constabulary Almanac* is the main source of information, giving details of every constabulary in the UK and of such organizations as the Home Office Police Department, the Forensic Science Service, the Police National Computer Organization. It also describes the policing at harbours, airports, etc.

The Home Office coordinates fifty-two separate police forces nationally through its Police Department: they are directly controlled by Chief Constables, responsible to the local police authority. The Home Office houses the Forensic Science Service, HM Inspectorate of Constabulary and the Police National Computer Organization. The Metropolitan Police of London is controlled by a Commissioner directly responsible to the Home Secretary. Intelligence services keep changing their telephone numbers. For MI5 (internal counter-subversion), contact the Home Office police press office; for MI6 (overseas intelligence agency), contact the Foreign Office press office.

Police forces HQs have press departments. Taped messages at many give details of incidents and regularly update during the day.

National Crime Intelligence Service, PO Box 8000, Spring Gardens, London SE11 5EN. An independent body that analyses serious organized crime on a national scale: for example football hooliganism, counterfeit currency and drug trafficking.
Police Complaints Authority, 10 Great George Street, London SW1P 3AB. Complaints against the police are investigated.
Statewatch is one of the independent information sources on the police. It has a large library on security and police affairs. It operates a public computer database, and publishes a bi-monthly journal. Tel: 0181–802–1882.
See also civil liberties, page 169.

POLITICS

MPs having other jobs and obtaining perks such as free travel are supposed to declare them in the *Register of Members' Interests*.

A complimentary copy of the *House of Commons Weekly Information Bulletin* and information on any Commons business can be obtained from the House of Commons Public Information Office (0171-219-4272). The number of the House of Lords Information Office is 0171-219-3107.

Cabinet Office, 70 Whitehall, London SW1A 1AA.
The Civil Service: The official guide, the *Civil Service Yearbook*, gives names and telephone numbers of key executives, and describes the workings of each government department, the Royal households, etc.
The Labour Research Department: 78 Blackfriars Road, London SE1 8HF. Although it investigates right-wing pressure groups and political donations by British companies, the LRD is quite independent of the Labour Party.

RELIGION

Contact clergy, bishops (or their secretaries or chaplains). For libraries and research centres, see Hoffmann: *Research for Writers*, Appendix 1. For general guidance on reporting religions, see Harris and Spark: *Practical Newspaper Reporting* (Focal Press, 1993), Chapter 12. Many religious organizations are limited companies, charities, housing associations and friendly societies. Information is therefore readily obtainable from the relevant registers.

The Church of England's activities and personnel are accounted for in the comprehensive *Crockford's Clerical Directory*. Other yearbooks are:

The Baptist Handbook
Buddhist Directory
Catholic Directory
Church of England Yearbook
Church of Scotland Yearbook
The Congregational Yearbook
Friends' Book of Meeting Yearbook
Jewish Yearbook
Salvation Army Yearbook.

SECURITY SERVICES

Information about the operations of MI5, MI6, the Special Branch and military intelligence is given in detail in the magazine *Lobster*, 214

Westbourne Avenue, Hull HU5 3JB. It was established in 1983. Their *Who's Who in the British Secret State* was published in 1985.

SpyBASE is an international database covering intelligence matters. (See *databases*.)

SOCIAL SERVICES

The main guide to social services departments is the *Social Services Yearbook*, which has sections on all departments and services and on the parliamentary committees that deal with social services. It also covers such aspects as community relations and advice and counselling. *Local contacts*: Town Hall departments, DHSS office.

TRADE UNIONS

General information from *The Trades Union Handbook*, the register of the Certification Office for Trade Unions and Employers Association, 27 Wilton Street, London SW1, and the *Directory of Employment Associations, Trade Unions and Joint Organizations* registered with the Department of Employment.
Trades Union Congress, Congress House, Great Russell Street, London WC1B 3LS.

TRANSPORT

Accidents

Contacts: Local police, ambulance station, doctors and eyewitnesses.

Airlines

Contacts: Operating companies, airport managers, tour operators, travel agents.
Civil Aviation Authority, CAA House, 45-59 Kingsway, London WC2B 6TE.

Buses

Contacts: Company managers, local councils.

Railways

Contacts: Railtrack, stationmasters, district managers, workshop managers, unions.

Roads and bridges

District engineer, county surveyor, regional office of Department of Transport, local office of the Automobile Association or the Royal Automobile Club.

Road transport

Local secretary of the Road Hauliers' Association, British Road Services, independent hauliers.

UTILITIES

Electricity

Contacts: Electricity generating companies, power station managers, regional boards (supply).

Gas

Contacts: Press officers: British Gas, Gas Consumers Council, Office of Gas Supply (Ofgas).

Telecommunications

Advisory Committee on Telecommunications (Oftel), Atlantic House, Holborn Viaduct, London EC1N 7HN.

Water

Contacts: Department of the Environment, which sets standards for water supply, the Drinking Water Inspectorate, local government environmental health officers. The privatization of the regional water authorities took place in 1990. The non-profit making services such as protection of the environment were taken over by the National Rivers Authority.

WOMEN

The Woman's Place, Hungerford House, Victoria Embankment, London WC2. Tel: 0171-836-6081. An advice centre, giving information and support to women. There is a useful library. A helpful organization, whatever the interest or the need.

London Women's Aid, 52–54 Featherstone Street, London EC1.

National Women's Aid Federation, 374 Gray's Inn Road, London WC1. Organizes refuges for battered women.

Onlywomen Press, 38 Mount Pleasant, London WC1.

Sheba Feminist Publishers, 488 Kingsland Road, London E8.

Silver Moon Women's Bookshop, 68 Charing Cross Road, London WC2.

Sisterwrite Women's Bookshop, 190 Upper Street, London N1.

LIBRARIES

INFORMATION services – researching, posting documents in microform, access to press cuttings libraries, use of researchers in them, and on-line and other database services – can be expensive. Check costs before committing yourself to using them.

Journalists who develop specialisms find most useful their own contacts and research sources recorded over the years of work, whether on cards or on a database. The advantage of the latter is that the records can be easily updated.

Aslib (The Association of Information Management) Directory British Archives. Lists libraries and record offices where public records are kept.

Information about specialist libraries is obtainable from the Library Association, which publishes the annual *Libraries in the United Kingdom and the Republic of Ireland*, providing names of librarians and telephone numbers.

ARTS

British Museum, Department of Printed Books and Music Library, Great Russell Street, London WC1B 3DG.

British Film Institute, 81 Dean Street, London W1V 6AA, where it houses its National Film Archive.

The Theatre Museum, 1e Tavistock Street, London WC2E 7PA.

Other information on theatre collections, libraries and museums is obtainable from *A Directory of Theatre Research*, edited by Diana

Howard, published by the Society for Theatre Research/Library Association.

COPYRIGHT LIBRARIES

Readers' tickets are needed for copyright and other important libraries such as those of the universities. Day tickets are usually available easily, but find out the rules before visiting. Libraries whose membership is by private subscription are listed in the yellow pages of telephone directories. The best known of these is the London Library, 14 St James's Square, London SW1Y 4LG.

British Library, Reference Division, Department of Printed Books, Great Russell Street, London WC1B 3DG.
Bodleian Library, University of Oxford, Broad Street, Oxford OX1 3BG. A national library as well as the library of the University of Oxford. The second largest library in the UK.

DEFENCE/MILITARY/SECURITY/TERRORISM

Home Office Information and Library Services, 50 Queen Anne's Gate, London SW1H 9AT. Civil defence and fire services, broadcasting, criminal law, criminology and penology are notable subjects. Information service available.
Imperial War Museum Library, Lambeth Road, London SE1 6HZ.
Ministry of Defence Library, Old War Office Building, Whitehall, London SW1A 2EU.
National Army Museum, Royal Hospital Road, London SW3 4HT. Tel: 0171-730-0717.
Public Record Office (see under government).
Royal Air Force Museum, Department of Aviation Records, Aerodrome Road, Hendon, London NW9 5LL.

GOVERNMENT AND OFFICIAL PUBLICATIONS

British Library Reference Division, Department of Printed Books, Official Publications Library, Great Russell Street, London WC1B 3DG.
Central Office of Information, Hercules Road, Westminster Bridge Road, London SE1 7DU.
House of Lords Record Office, House of Lords, Palace of Westminster, London SW1A 0AA.

Public Record Office, Ruskin Avenue, Kew, Richmond, Surrey; and Chancery Lane, London WC2A 1LR. Records of the Government and the Law Courts of England and Wales are kept, dating back to the eleventh century, the most recent ones at Kew. Records can be viewed after thirty years.
Public Record Offices of Northern Ireland, 66 Balmoral Avenue, Belfast BT9 6NY.
Scottish Record Office, General Register House, Edinburgh EH1 3YY.
House of Lords Record Office, House of Lords, Palace of Westminster, London SW1A 0AA.

MEDIA

The libraries of further education colleges and universities offering media studies and journalism courses contain books and periodicals on the media. For fuller information on the libraries and services offered, contact *Benn's Media Directory*, which includes all aspects of the media, including cable and satellite. Try your local libraries to see if they have subscribed to the directory.

British Library Newspaper Library, Colindale Avenue, London NW9 5HE. Historical collection of newspapers, and a reference library on newspapers.
Home Office Library (address on page 185): Contains a section on broadcasting.
St Bride's Printing Library, Bride Lane, Fleet Street, London EC4Y 8EE. Devoted to the history of printing.

NEWSPAPERS AND PERIODICALS CUTTINGS LIBRARIES

The national newspapers have useful libraries, including extensive press cuttings libraries, some of which can be consulted at a cost. Some will answer queries free on the telephone if they can be answered quickly. The BBC and the Financial Times have extensive paid for information services. Visits if allowed are normally charged, and researchers' time charged extra.

Staffs on newspapers can use the increasing number of computer-accessible databases and CD-ROMs (see *databases*). Since such on-line services as the *Financial Times Profile* are expensive, the research has to be carefully planned for relevance.

Many newspapers, however, restrict access to cuttings files and other materials in their libraries to their own staffs. Local newspapers' libraries will be worth consulting on local subjects. Professional and trade associations, charities and other voluntary associations and pressure groups keep cuttings libraries, and many will give access to them.

A word of warning. Press cuttings libraries of smaller organizations may not have been developed skilfully, and a campaigning zeal may result in a misleading picture with too many gaps. Also, errors tend to get repeated by journalists depending on cuttings being accurate and failing to double check. See also *research services*, *indexes* and *databases* below.

Press cutting agencies: Check on fees, how many newspaper and periodical sources cut, and on the time limits. See *Writers' and Artists' Yearbook* for UK and overseas services.
Press Association's News Library, The Press Association, 85 Fleet Street, London EC4P 4BE. Tel: 0171-936-2400. Over 14 million cuttings, from 1926. Fee depends on whether you use the library yourself or pay for a researcher's time.

PUBLIC RECORD OFFICES

See *government,* pages 174-5.

SCIENCE AND TECHNOLOGY

British Library Science Reference and Information Service (SRIS), 25 Southampton Buildings, London WC2A 1AW.

MISCELLANEOUS LIBRARIES

British Library of Political and Economic Science, London School of Economics, 10 Portugal Street, London WC2A 2HD.
London Library, 14 St James's Square, London SW1Y 4LG. A public subscription library. Has a postal service.

See *Yellow Pages* for important local subscription libraries.

RESEARCH SERVICES

British Library, Business Information Service, 25 Southampton Buildings, London WC2A 1AW. Tel: 0171-636-1544; brief enquiry service 0171-323-7454; charged online data base search service and business information service 0171-323-7979. The material includes reports, journals and trade catalogues as well as books and newspapers.
Benn's Editorial Media Information Service (BEMIS). Available to subscribers to *Benn's Media Directory* (see under books).
Celebrity Service Ltd, 93 Regent Street, London W1R 7TB. Publishes *Celebrity Bulletin, The Contact Book*, and *Celebrity Register*. Subscribers are given every fortnight news of the movements of celebrities, and of the hotels in New York, London or Paris at which they will be staying, and which press agent to contact.
Financial Times Business Information Service (BIS), 1 Southwark Bridge, London SE1 9HL. An extensive and expensive service, which makes use of the considerable business information resources of the FT, including its own specialized online databases and all main online systems.

There are many business publications to which the individual can subscribe.

PRINTED SOURCES

GENERAL

Advertisers Annual: Reed Information Services. Three volumes: agencies/ advertisers, UK media, overseas media. Known as the *Blue Book*.
Aslib Directory of Information Sources in the UK: Regularly updated.
Britain: An Official Handbook, HMSO.
British Library specialist source books: various.
Concise Guide to Reference Material, A J Walford (ed.), Library Association.
Directory of British Official Publications: A Guide to Sources, Stephen Richards, Mansell, 1981.
Freedom of Information Handbook, 2nd Edition, David Northmore, Bloomsbury Publishing, 1991. Explains why some information is hard to get, what you have a right to get, and how to get it. Covers individuals, companies, government departments, etc.
The Guardian Media Guide, Steve Peak (ed.) Fourth Estate, 1993. Comprehensive list of media organizations, with addresses and telephone numbers, plus telephone numbers of key contacts in government, police, etc.

A Guide to Library Research Methods, Thomas Mann, OUP, 1987.

Guide to Reference Material, A J Walford, (ed.), Library Association.

Library Resources, series published by the Library Association. Updated regularly.

Research for Writers, 4th Edition, Ann Hoffmann, A & C Black, 1992. Covers how to organize and carry out research, and lists many sources of information.

Whitaker's Almanack. Annual. General reference book which lists parliamentary constituencies, MPs and the peerage, government and public offices, official figures, and much more.

Writers' and Artists' Yearbook, A & C Black. Lists markets, agents, publishers and general advice and information for writers and artists.

The Writer's Handbook, Barry Turner (ed.), Macmillan 1900. Similar to the *Writers' and Artists'*. Gives names of features and section editors.

ORGANIZATIONS

CBO Research Ltd, Kent, publishes several directories of voluntary associations, including *Councils, Committees and Boards* (gives names of chairmen among details of organizations, and indicates fields of interest); *Centres and Bureaux* (expert advisory groups), and *Directory of British Associations* (see below).

The Charities Digest. The Charities Aid Foundation. Explains charity law and the operation of the Charity Commission. The Foundation also publishes *The Directory of Grant-Making Trusts*, which lists grant-making trusts, both large and small, from international to local.

Civil Service Year Book. Describes every section of government departments and gives names and telephone numbers of senior civil servants.

Environmental Information: A Guide to Sources, Helen Woolston and Nigel Lees (eds.), British Library, 1992.

Crockford's Clerical Directory. The best known of religious directories, giving details of who's who in the Church of England. See under *religious organizations* (page 181) for other directories and yearbooks.

Directory of British Associations: Published by Current British Directories (CBO) Research Ltd. Lists well over 8000 organizations – professional institutes, trade associations, voluntary associations, political groups and quangos, etc. CBO also publishes *Associations in Ireland*.

Directory of British Film and TV Producers. Producers' Alliance for Cinema and Television (PACT). Lists the main production companies and producers in detail.

Hollis Press and Public Relations Annual: Hollis Directories, Sunbury-on-Thames, Middlesex. Gives news contacts in the business world, official and public information sources and public relations consultancies.

Public Bodies. Annual. Gives brief notes on all nationalized industries and other public bodies and quangos.

Religious Yearbooks/Directories. See page 181.

Trade Associations and Professional Bodies in the United Kingdom. Gale Research International, Andover, Hants.

INDIVIDUALS

Blue Book of British Broadcasting. Tellex Monitors. Comprehensive lists for radio and TV: names, addresses and telephone numbers.

The British Film Institute Film and TV Handbook. Numerous facts, figures and contacts.

Directors' Guild Directory. Directors' Guild of Great Britain. Gives details of the work of broadcasting directors.

Dod's Parliamentary Companion. Dod's Parliamentary Companion Ltd, Herstmonceaux, East Sussex. Annual. It gives complete biographical details of MPs and members of the House of Lords. Information on government offices, etc.

Vacher's Parliamentary Companion. Brief details of MPs. Up to date – published quarterly.

Who's Who. Contains the names of all MPs, and selected prominent people. The first book you go to when you have to do a profile. Useful for obituaries, and for various kinds of contacts.

Who Was Who.

Who's Who in the Theatre, TV and Radio's Who's Who, International Who's Who. etc.

PUBLICATIONS

Benn's Media Directory. Volume 1: UK; Volume 2: International. Published by Benn Business Information Service. Gives magazines under subject headings.

Brad (British Rate and Data). Maclean-Hunter Ltd. Directory of all the media, with advertising rates.

Current British Directories. CBD Research Ltd. This lists most of the directories that give members of public bodies.

Current British Journals. British Library. Contains details of approximately 10,000 titles.

HMSO Monthly Catalogue. Index of all government publications, with descriptions.

Statutes and Statutory Instruments. Legal publications that indicate how organizations, including government department and agencies, have to operate.

Ulrich's International Periodicals Directory: a Classified Guide to Current Periodicals, Foreign and Domestic. Bowker, London and New York.

Willing's Press Guide: A Comprehensive Index and Handbook of the Press of the United Kingdom and Great Britain. Thomas Skinner Directories, East Grinstead. Annual.

ARTICLES

The British Library Newspaper Library has many indexes to articles, as do the national and many of the university libraries. Local reference libraries may have indexes of those local papers that publish them. Important papers in the UK that publish indexes are *The Times* (which includes material in the educational and literary Supplements), *Financial Times* and the *Glasgow Herald*. The chief papers in the USA do so, and some in Australia. Increasing numbers of newspaper indexes are appearing on microfilm or on disk, as are those of magazines. Check with your local librarian.

Specialist writers will also make use of the various *Abstracts* see Brendan Hennessy, *Writing Feature Articles* (Focal Press, 1993) chapter 8 on markets and ideas.

British Humanities Index. Library Association. Quarterly, with annual compilations. Lists articles under subject headings from broadsheet newspapers and selected magazines and journals.

The Clover Newspaper Index. Clover Publications, Bedfordshire. Quarterly. A detailed weekly bulletin covering events reported in national broadsheets. In looseleaf binder.

DATABASES

It is not only in libraries that electronic databases are replacing certain kinds of reference books, printed bibliographies and catalogue cards; databases are also replacing such aids in journalists' homes. Freelance journalists working from home are turning to on-line databases, accessed by means of an IBM-compatible computer or Apple Mac linked to the telephone line by a modem. Access to the entry points to the various databases are provided by using a linking service such as the Compulink Information Exchange (CIX) or Compuserve.

The possibilities are vast. Newsrooms access highly expensive database services, and have to make sure they are being used cost-effectively: researching in an unfocused way can waste time and money.

Journalists working at home, without having the benefit of expert researchers' advice at hand, need to work out carefully what equipment, software and access to databases they can afford. *UK Press Gazette* and *Writers' Monthly* keep readers up to date with the possibilities and pitfalls in electronic journalism, as does the Society of Authors' *The Author* and its quarterly supplement *Electronic Author* (see *media publications*, pages 202–4).

Many newspapers throughout the country now have in-house databases of their own editions and have stopped cutting to file.

British Broadcasting Corporation (BBC): The Library and Research Information Services contain 250,000 books, 22 million cuttings, research facilities, archives and databases. Many facilities and services are available outside staff.

British Library Automated Information Service (BLAISE): A computerized bibliographic service.

British Telecom Phone Base (Tel: 0800-919-199): An electronic form of the telephone book, allowing you to get numbers rapidly, and a quick way also of using Directory Enquiries. If you need this service for more than twenty calls a week, it is not expensive.

BT information Business Services, Freepost PP205, Network House, Brindley Way, Hemel Hempstead, Herts HP3 8BR. Tel: 0800-200-700.

Compulink Information Exchange (CIX): Suite 2, The Sanctuary,

Oakhill Grove, Surbiton, Surrey KT6 6DU. Tel: 0181-390-8446. A way in to many and varied databases in the UK and abroad.

Compuserve, PO Box 676, Bristol BS99 1YN. Tel: 0800-289378. Access possible to well over 1000 databases. American based. Its *Executive News Service* accesses daily news stories from such agencies as Associated Press (AP), United Press International (UPI), the *Washington Post*, and Reuters Financial News Service.

Financial Times Profile provides access to all national broadsheets and to an increasing number of tabloids.

SpyBASE: Available from Micro Associates, PO Box 5369, Arlington, VA 22205, USA. It is compatible with IBM and Apple-Macintosh. An international database of intelligence matters.

World Press Centre (WPC): 3 Parolles Road, London N19 3RE. Tel: 0171-263-63331. Information gathered from organizations and governments throughout the world. Includes background information and profiles, and all information is constantly updated.

Appendix

PROFESSIONAL ORGANIZATIONS

Advertising Association, Abford House, 15 Wilton Road, London SW1V 1NG. Federation of professional bodies representing advertisers.
Advertising Standards Authority, 2-16 Torrington Place, London WC1E 7HN.
Amnesty International Journalists' Network, St Michael's Studio, Queen Street, Derby DE1 3DX. Campaigns for media workers who have been imprisoned, disappeared, etc. Publishes newsletter.
Article 19 (International Centre Against Censorship), 90 Borough High Street, London SE1 1LL. Campaigns for the right to freedom of expression and information (Article 19 of the UN Universal declaration of Human Rights). Defends media against threats of censorship. Publishes bulletin.
Association of British Editors, 2 Common Lane, Hemingford Abbots, Huntingdon, Cambridgeshire PE18 9AN. Professional body covering editors in broadcasting, newspapers and periodicals. Publishes *The British Editor*.
Audit Bureau of Circulations, Black Prince Yard, 207 High Street, Berkhamsted, Herts HP4 1AD. Provides certified circulation data for newspapers and magazines.
Authors' Licensing and Collecting Society, 33 Alfred Place, London WC1E 7DP. Collects royalties for authors, and copywriting fees due for copying from periodicals and books; the latter via the Copyright Licensing Agency.
British Association of Industrial Editors, 3 Locks Yard, High Street, Sevenoaks, Kent TN13 1LT. Professional body for editors of companies'

in-house journals, etc. Publishes monthly *BAIE News*. Operates training programme.

British Association of Journalists, 97 Fleet Street, London EC4Y 1DH. Splinter group from the NUJ established in 1992.

British Guild of Travel Writers, Bolts Cross Cottage, Peppard, Henley-on-Thames, Oxon RG9 5LG. Publishes monthly newsletter. Annual directory of members.

Bureau of Freelance Photographers, 497 Green Lanes, London N13 4BP. Publishes monthly newsletter and annual handbook. Advises on picture agencies and publishing markets.

Campaign for Freedom of Information, 88 Old Street, London EC1V 9AR. Campaigns for right of access by law to public sector information, when it is of public interest. Publishes *Secrets*, a newspaper and information packs.

Campaign for Press and Broadcasting Freedom, 96 Dalston Lane, London E8 1NG. Campaigns for a media accessible to all, and for a Freedom of Information Act. Publishes *Free Press*, a bi-monthly journal.

Guild of Newspaper Editors, 74 Great Russell Street, London WC1B 3DA. Professional association of all newspaper editors. A lobby for the defence of press freedom. Publishes *Guild*, a journal, quarterly.

Institute of Journalists, 2 Dock Offices, Surrey Quays, London SE16 2XL. Member of the Federation of Professional Associations. Preserves standards, protects members' pay and conditions. Publishes *The Journal*.

Institute of Public Relations, 15 Northborough Street, London EC1V 0PR.

International Press Institute, Dilke House, Malet Street, London WC1E 7JA. Based in Switzerland, the association promotes freedom for the press and the free exchange of views. Various publications.

National Council for the Training of Journalists, Latton Bush Centre, Southern Way, Harlow, Essex CN18 7BL. Provides training courses, including correspondence courses.

National Council for Vocational Qualifications, 222 Euston Road, London NW1 2BZ. 'Lead' bodies organize for the council criteria and assessment procedures for the award of the qualifications. These bodies are, for journalism, the Royal Society of Arts, in partnership with the Newspaper Qualifications Council and The Periodicals Training Council.

National Union of Journalists, 14 Grays Inn Road, London WC1X 8DP. The main trade union for journalists. Publishes *The Journalist*, bi-monthly newspaper; and *Freelance Bulletin*, bi-monthly.

Newspaper Publishers Association, 34 Southwark Bridge Road, London SE1 9EU. Trade association for publishers of national newspapers.

Newspaper Society, 74 Great Russell Street, London WC1B 3DA. Trade association for publishers of all provincial newspapers and London local papers. Operates the Newspaper Conference, which deals with news gathering facilities in London for the regional press. Commercial side operates the PressAd database. Publishes journals and newsletters.

Periodical Publishers Association, 15 Kingsway, London WC2B 6UN. The trade association for magazine publishers. Lobbies, and organizes conferences, etc. It operates the Periodicals Training Council, providing training in magazine journalism. Various publications.

The Periodicals Training Council, Imperial House, 16–19 Kingsway, London WC2B 6UN.

Press Complaints Commission, 1 Salisbury Square, London EC4Y 8AE. Self-regulatory body of newspapers and periodicals. It investigates complaints about editorial matter and publishes reports monthly and annually.

Scottish Daily Newspapers Society, 30 George Square, Glasgow G2 1EG. Trade association of national papers in Scotland.

Scottish Newspaper Publishers Association, 48 Palmerston Place, Edinburgh EH12 5DE. Trade association and employers' organization for the weekly press in Scotland.

Society of Picture Researchers and Editors, BM Box 259, London WC1N 3XX.

Society of Women Writers and Journalists, 110 Whitehall Road, Chingford, London E4 6DW. Established 1894. Publishes *The Woman Journalist*.

Sports Writers Association of Great Britain, 43 Lime Grove, New Malden, Surrey KT3 3TP.

Thomson Foundation, 68 Park Place, Cardiff CF1 3AS. Registered charity providing training for overseas press and broadcasting organizations. Publishes a newspaper, *Scope*.

Women Writers Network, 38 Pagoda Avenue, Richmond, Surrey TW9 2HF. Support group, with monthly newsletter and annual directory of members.

BIBLIOGRAPHY

REFERENCE

Most of the following will be available in a good reference library. See Chapter 10 for key reference books, listings, contacts, organizations, publications, articles and libraries.

The Advertisers' Annual. Lists advertising rates of publications. Use with the NUJ Freelance Guide to determine fees paid by magazines for articles.

Atlas and Gazetteer of the British Isles.

Atlas of the World and World Gazetteer.

Annual Register, Longman. Surveys of countries and subject areas.

Authors' and Printers' Dictionary.

Bartlett's Familiar Quotations, Bartlett's Unfamiliar Quotations. L L Levinson (ed.), Allen & Unwin, 1992; 1972.

Benn's Media Directory, Benn Business Information Service. UK and international volumes. Gives magazines under subject headings.

The Blue Book of British Broadcasting, Tellex Monitors Ltd, 50 Grosvenor Street, London W1A 2DA. Annual. Contains over 1500 key personnel, including telephone numbers of the people working on programmes.

Britain: An Official Handbook, HMSO, annual.

British Rate and Data (BRAD), Maclean-Hunter, Maclean-Hunter House, Chalk Lane, Cockfosters Road, Barnet, Herts EN4 0B4. Gives circulation and readership figures, readership profiles, advertisement rates, etc. for newspapers and magazines in the UK.

Central Statistical Office: *Social Trends*, HMSO, annual. Charts the developments in the British way of life, with figures: population, various social groups and activities, trades unions, consumer expenditure, etc.

Chambers Biographical Dictionary.

Chronicle of the Twentieth Century, Longman, 1993.

Collins Dictionary and Thesaurus. Dictionary on the top half of the page and thesaurus on the bottom half, in the same alphabetical order, has its uses.

Concise Guide to Reference Material. A J Walford (ed.), Library Association.

Daily Mail Year Book. International events.

Dictionary of American Biography. American Council of Learned Societies.

Dictionary of National Biography.

Dictionaries of Dates. (Everyman, Chambers, etc.).

Dictionaries of quotations (Penguin and others).

Dictionaries of modern quotations (Penguin and others).

Encyclopedias. Discover the strengths of the various choices: Chambers, Penguin, etc. The most comprehensive is *The New Encyclopaedia Britannica*, 30 volumes.

Fowler's Modern English Usage. 2nd Edition, Sir Ernest Gowers (ed.), OUP 1978. Still the classic on the subject.

Guinness Book of Records.

Hansard's Parliamentary Debates: House of Commons and House of Lords, HMSO.

Hart's Rules for Compositors and Readers, OUP, 1983. Style, grammar and spelling for editors.

Hollis Press and Public Relations Annual, Hollis Directories, Sunbury-on-Thames.

Information, Press and PR Officers in Government Departments and Public Corporations, Central Office of Information (COI), Hercules Road, London SE1 7OU.

The International Dictionary of Twentieth Century Biography. Sidgwick Softbacks.

International Who's Who, Europa Publications. Annual.

International Yearbook and Statesman's Who's Who. Kelly's Directories Ltd.

Keesing's Contemporary Archives. Summarizes world news.

Keesing's Record of World Events.

Kelly's Handbook to the Titled, Landed and Official Classes, Kelly's Directories Ltd. Annual. Lists royalty, MPs, etc.

Kelly's Directories. Local history, etc.

Municipal Yearbook. For local government matters.

Newspeak: A Dictionary of Jargon, Jonathan Green, Routledge, 1987.

The Oxford Dictionary for Writers and Editors, OUP, 1981.

Penguin Paperback Dictionaries: arts, economics, history, politics, etc.

Research for Writers, Ann Hoffmann, A & C Black, 1992.

Slang Thesaurus, Jonathan Green, Pan Books, 1988.

The Spotlight Casting Directory and Contacts, Charles House, 7 Leicester Place, London WC2. Covers the world of entertainment, giving agents of actors.

The Statesman's Yearbook, Macmillan. Covers developments in countries and international organizations.

Titles and Forms of Address: A Guide to their Correct Use, A & C Black, 1990.

Webster's Guide to American History.

Whitaker's Almanack, J Whitaker and Sons Ltd. Annual. Government names, statistics and other information.

Whitaker's Books in Print, Book of the Month, Books to Come, Paperback Books in Print, Who's Who, Who Owns Whom, Who Was Who, Who's Who in the Theatre, etc. A & C Black. Annual.

Willing's Press Guide, Thomas Skinner Directories. Lists UK publications, with a section for magazines classified under subject headings. Lists important publications of other countries.

Writers' and Artists' Yearbook, A & C Black. Two main sections: markets for articles, fiction, scripts, photographs; and general information and guidance for the freelance writer and artist.

The Writer's Handbook, Barry Turner (ed.), Macmillan 1994. Similar to the W & A, it numbers more contacts on publications by name, and has useful double index: by companies and subjects.

GENERAL

Allaun, Frank: *Spreading the News – A Guide to Media Reform*, Campaign for Press and Broadcasting Freedom, 1988. An ex-Labour MP discusses the dangers and the possibilities.

Allen, R and Frost, J: *Daily Mirror*, Patrick Stephens, 1981; *Voice of Britain. The Inside Story of the Daily Express*, 1983.

Baistow, Tom: *Fourth Rate Estate. An Anatomy of Fleet Street*, Comedia, 1985.

Baynes, Ken: *Scoop, Scandal and Strife. A Study of Photography in Newspapers*, Lund Humphries, 1971.

Bleetman, Norman: *Britain's Newspaper Industry*, Jordan, 1987.

Bourne, Richard: *Lords of Fleet Street – The Harmsworth Dynasty*, Unwin Hyman, 1990. The Daily Mail family.

Bower, Tom: *Maxwell The Outsider*, Revised Edition, Mandarin Press, 1991.

Boyd-Barrett, Oliver: *The International News Agencies*, Constable, 1980.

Burchill, Julie: *Love it or Shove it*, Century Publishing, 1985. Collection of her iconoclastic columns.

Butler, Nancy: *Newspapers*. Hodder & Stoughton, 1989.

Carey, John: *The Faber Book of Reportage*, Faber & Faber, 1989. The reporters cover the years 400 BC to the 1980s.

Chippindale, Peter and Horrie, Chris: *Stick it up your Punter! The Rise and Fall of the 'The Sun'*, Mandarin Press, 1992.

Cohn, S and Young, J (eds.): *The Manufacture of News*, Sage Constable, 1981.

Crone, Tom: *Law and the Media*, 3rd Edition, Focal Press, 1995.

Crozier, Michael: *The Making of The Independent*, Gordon Fraser, 1988.

Dunnett, Peter: *The World Newspaper Industry*, Croom Helm, 1988.

Edwards, Robert: *Goodbye Fleet Street*, Coronet, 1989. From a former Fleet Street editor.

Evans, Harold: *Good Times, Bad Times*, Weidenfeld and Nicolson, 1983. The account of his editing of *The Times* and *The Sunday Times*.

Franklin, Bob and Murphy, David: *What News? The Market, Politics and the Local Press*, Routledge, 1991. An attack on the increase of commercial and political pressures on local newspapers.

Greenslade, Roy: *Maxwell's Fall. The Appalling Legacy of a Corrupt Man*. Simon & Schuster, 1992.

Greenwood, Walter and Welsh, Tom: *McNae's Essential Law for Journalists*. Butterworth, 1992.

Hamilton, Sir Denis: *Editor-in-Chief. Fleet Street Memoirs*, Hamish Hamilton, 1989.

Hart-Davis, Duff: *The House the Berrys Built*, 2nd Edition, Coronet, 1991. The history of the *Daily* and *Sunday Telegraphs*.

Hetherington, Alastair: *Guardian Years*, Chatto & Windus, 1981. The author was editor from 1956 to 1975. He discusses such questions as: What is news? How should it be handled? Who makes the decisions? How are they made? *News in the Region*, Macmillan, 1989.

Hobson, Sir Harold, Knightley, Phillip and Russell, Leonard: *The Pearl of Days: An Intimate Memoir of the Sunday Times, 1822–1972*, Hamish Hamilton, 1972.

Hollingworth, Clare: *Frontline*, Cape, 1990. One of the most highly respected foreign correspondents of recent times.

Jackson, Ian: *The Provincial Press and the Community*, Manchester University Press, 1971. Remains a valuable analysis.

Jenkins, Simon: *Newspapers. The Power and the Money*, Faber & Faber, 1979; *Market for Glory: Fleet Street Ownership in the Twentieth Century*, Faber, 1986.

Knightley, Phillip: *The First Casualty: The War Correspondent as Hero, Propagandist and Myth Maker*. Pan, 1987. One of the classic accounts of foreign reporting.

Kynaston, David: *The Financial Times: A Centenary History*, Viking, 1988.

Lake, Brian: *British Newspapers: A History and Guide for Collectors*, Sheppard Press, 1984.

Leapman, Michael: *Barefaced Cheek*, Hodder & Stoughton, 1983. Biography of Rupert Murdoch; *Treacherous Estate: The Press after Fleet Street*, 1992.

Lee, Alan: *The Origins of the Popular Press in England 1855–1914*, Croom Helm, 1980.

Linton, David and Boston, Ray: *The Newspaper Press in Britain. An Annotated Bibliography*, Mansell Publishing, 1987.

Littleton, Suellen M: *The Wapping Dispute*, Avebury Business School Library, 1992. The move of newspapers to Wapping; the dispute with the printing unions, and the impact on the national newspaper industry.

MacArthur, Brian: *Eddy Shah, Today and the Newspaper Revolution*, David and Charles, 1988. The start of the new technology in newspapers in the UK.

Medina, Peter and Donald, Vivien: *Careers in Journalism*, 6th Edition Kogan Page, 1994.

NCTJ/LGC Communications, *Essential Central Government*, 2nd Edition, 1993. See also Smith, Geoffrey.

Robertson, QC, Geoffrey and Nicol, Andrew: *Media Law – The Rights of Journalists and Broadcasters*, Penguin, 1992.

Shawcross, William: *Rupert Murdoch: Ringmaster of the Information Circus*, Chatto and Windus, 1992.

Smith, Geoffrey: *Local Government for Journalists*, 6th Edition, NCTJ/LGC Communications, 1993.

Snoddy, Raymond: *The Good, the Bad and the Unacceptable*, Faber & Faber, 1992. The media correspondent of the *Financial Times* critically analyses the British press.

Taylor, A J P: *Beaverbrook*, Hamish Hamilton, 1972. Historian's readable account of the life of the newspaper tycoon.

Taylor, John: *War Photography. Realism in the British Press*, Routledge, 1991.

Taylor, Philip: *War and the Media. Propaganda and Persuasion in the Gulf War*, Manchester University Press, 1992.

Taylor, S J: *Shock! Horror! The Tabloids in Action*, Bantam, 1991. The popular papers in the UK and the USA.

Tunstall, Jeremy: *The Media in Britain*, Constable, 1983.

Tunstall, Jeremy and Palmer, Michael: *Media Moguls*, Routledge, 1991. International in scope.

Winship, J: *Inside Women's Magazines*, Pandora, 1987.

Wintour, Charles: *Pressures on the Press: An Editor Looks at Fleet Street*, Andre Deutsche, 1972; *The Rise and Fall of Fleet Street*, Hutchinson, 1989.

Woods, Oliver and Bishop, James: *The Story of the Times*, Michael Joseph, 1985.

Zobel, Louis Purvin: *The Travel Writer's Handbook*, Writers' Digest Books, 1980.

TEXTBOOKS

Boyce, G Curran and Wingate, P: *Newspaper History: From the 17th Century to the Present Day*, Constable, 1978.

Black, S: *Introduction to Public Relations*, Modino Press, 1989.

Cumberbatch, G and Howitt, D: *A Measure of Uncertainty: The Effects of the Mass Media*, John Libbey, 1989.

Curran, J and Seaton, J: *Power without Responsibility*, Methuen, 1991.

Dutton, B: *The Media*, Longman, 1986.

Eagle, Selwyn: *Information Sources for the Press and Broadcast Media*, Bowker-Saur, 1991.

Glasgow University Media Group: *Bad News*, Routledge and Kegan Paul, 1976; *More Bad News*, RKP, 1980; *Really Bad News*, Writers and Readers, 1982; *War and Peace News*, Open University Press, 1985.

Hartley, J *et al*: *Making Sense of the Media*, Comedia, 1985.

Hollingsworth, Mark: *The Press and Political Dissent*, Pluto, 1986.

Jefkins, F: *Public Relations*, 4th Edition, Pitman/M & E Handbook, 1992; *Planned Press and Public Relations*, 3rd Edition, Blackie, 1993.

Kruger, S and Wall, I: *The Media Pack*, Macmillan, 1988.

Lewis, P and Pearlman, C: *Media and Power: From Marconi to Murdoch*, Camden Press, 1986.

McNair, Brian: *News and Journalism in the UK*, Routledge, 1993. Looks to the future.

McQuail, D: *Mass Communications Theory*, 2nd Edition, Sage, 1987.

Negrine, Ralph: *Politics and the Mass Media in Britain*, 2nd Edition, Routledge, 1994.

Tunstall, J: *The Westminster Lobby Correspondents*, Routledge, 1970; (ed.) *Media Sociology*, Constable, 1970; and *Journalists at Work*, 1971.

Veljanovski, Cento: *The Media in Britain Today*, News International, 1990.

Wall, I and Kruger, S: *The Media File*, Mary Glasgow, 1988.

Westmancoat, John: *Newspapers*, British Library, 1985.

Williams, Granville: *Britain's Media – How They Are Related*, Campaign for Press and Broadcasting Freedom, 1994.

MEDIA PERIODICALS

The Author. Society of Authors, 84 Drayton Gardens, London SW10 9SB. Quarterly. Available to non-members on subscription. Also *The Electronic Author*. Quarterly.

British Journalism Review, edited by Geoffrey Goodman. BJR Publishing Ltd, c/o Cassell plc, Villiers House, 41–47 Strand, London WC2N 5JE. Quarterly. Readable comment on the larger issues.

Campaign. Haymarket Publishing Group, 22 Lancaster Gate, London W2 3LY. Weekly. The main trade paper for the advertising industry. (See also *Marketing*, and *PR Week*.)

Financial Times Newsletters. Tower House, Southampton Street, London WC2E 7HA. Published by the *Financial Times*.

Freelance Market News. Freelance Press Services, Cumberland House, Lisadel Street, Salford, Manchester M6 6GG.

Free Press. Campaign for Press and Broadcasting Freedom. Bi-monthly magazine. Analyses of media ownership and related subjects.

Index on Censorship. Writers and Scholars International, 32 Queen Victoria Street, London EC4N 4SS. Reports on the struggles against censorship of all kinds of writing.

Jane's Defence Weekly. Jane's Information Group, Sentinel House, 163 Brighton Road, Coulsdon, Surrey CR5 2NH. The best-known publication of the group, it contains news on defence matters: military, political and industrial. Jane's catalogue gives full details of its journals. These include market intelligence reports for the arms industry.

The Journalist. National Union of Journalists, 314 Gray's Inn Road, London WC1X 8DP. Monthly newspaper of the NUJ.

The Journalists' Handbook. Carrick Publishing, 28 Miller Road, Ayr, Strathclyde, KA7 2AY. Quarterly journal with articles and lists of contacts.

Magazine News. Periodical Publishers Association, 15 Kingsway, London WC2B 6UN.

Media, Culture and Society, Sage Publications. Quarterly.

Media Law and Practice. Tolley Publishing, 2 Addiscombe Road, Croydon, Surrey CR9 5AF. Quarterly.

Media Week. EMAP Business Publishing, 33 Bowling Green Lane, London EC1R 0DA. A bridge between the media and advertising.

National broadsheets. *The Guardian* on Mondays, and *The Times* and *The Independent* on Wednesdays have a media page. Job advertisements.

The Photographer. British Institute of Professional Photography. Fox Talbot House, Anwell End, Ware, Herts SG12 9HN. The official journal.

PR Week. Haymarket Publishing Group, 22 Lancaster Gate, London W2 3LY.

The Publisher. Macro Publishing, Conbar House, Mead Lane, Hertford, Herts. Aimed at magazine production managers.

Two-Ten Communications, 210 Old Street, London EC1V 9UN provides
updated lists of editorial contacts in the press and broadcasting.

UK Press Gazette. Maclean-Hunter House, Chalk Lane, Cockfosters
Road, Barnet, Herts ENA 0BU. Tel: 0181–242–3000. Weekly. The
journalists' trade paper. Deals with the developments in the media,
including new technology, with emphasis on effects on journalists.
Job adverts. Regular list of press officers.

Writers' Monthly. 29 Turnpike Lane, Haringey, London N8 0EP. Aimed
mainly at the young freelance writer.

Writer's News. PO Box 4, Nairn, IV12 4HU, Scotland. Monthly for the
young freelance.

Writers' Newsletter. Writers' Guild of Great Britain, 430 Edgware Road,
London W2 1EH. Bi-monthly.

PRACTICAL GUIDES

Aitchinson, James: *Writing for the Press*, Hutchinson Education, 1989.
Straightforward guide to news writing.

Bagnall, Nicholas: *Newspaper Language*, Focal Press, 1993.

Barnard, Michael: *Inside Magazines: A Career Builder's Guide*,
Chapman & Hall, 1989; *Magazine and Journal Production*,
Chapman & Hall, 1990.

British Association of Industrial Editors: *Editor's Handbook*. Practical
advice in loose-leaf manual form, updated regularly.

Butcher, Judith: *Copy-Editing. The Cambridge Handbook*, 3rd Edition,
Cambridge University Press, 1992.

Butler, Harry: *Teeline Made Simple*. Butterworth-Heinemann, 1991.

Byrne, Padfield: *British Constitution Made Simple*, Butterworth-
Heinemann, 1987.

Byrne, Padfield: *Social Services Made Simple*, Butterworh-Heinemann, 1990.

Campbell, Morag: *Writing about Travel*, A & C Black, 1989.

Davis, Anthony: *Magazine Journalism Today*, Focal Press, 1994.

Dick, Jill: *Freelance Writing for Newspapers*, A & C Black, 1991.

Dobson, Christopher: *The Freelance Journalist*, Focal Press, 1992.

Evans, Hilary and Mary: *Picture Researchers' Handbook*, Chapman &
Hall, 1992.

Giles, Vic and Hodgson, F W: *Creative Newspaper Design*, Heinemann
Professional Publishing, 1990.

Gowers, Sir Ernest, revised by Sir Bruce Fraser: *The Complete Plain
Words*. One of the classics on style. Penguin Books, 1987.

Harris, Geoffrey and Spark, David: *Practical Newspaper Reporting*, 2nd
Edition, Focal Press, 1993.

Hines, John: *The Way to Write Magazine Articles*, Elm Tree Books, 1987.

Hennessy, Brendan: *Writing Feature Articles*, 2nd Edition, Focal Press, 1993.

Hodgson, F W: *Modern Newspaper Practice*, 3rd Edition, Focal Press, 1993. *Subediting*, 2nd Edition, Focal Press, 1993.

Hutt, Allen and James, Bob: *Newspaper Design Today: A Manual for Professionals*, Lund Humphries, 1989.

Jones, Graham: *The Business of Freelancing*, BFP Books, 1987. All aspects of organizing a freelance career.

Keeble, Richard: *The Newspapers Handbook*, Routledge, 1994.

Keene, Martin: *Practical Photojournalism*, Focal Press, 1993.

Kerton, Paul, with Greenand, Colin: *The Freelance Writer's Handbook*. Edbury Press, 1986. Fiction, broadcasting and print journalism.

Mitford, Jessica: *The Making of a Muckraker*, Quartet Books, 1981. Memorable tips on getting people to talk from a writer who wrote for the top US magazines.

Morrison, John: *Freelancing for Magazines*, Bureau of Freelance Photographers, 1991.

Northmore, David: *Freedom of Information Handbook: How To Find Out What You Want To Know*, Bloomsbury Publishing, 1993.

Purcell, Ann and Carl: *A Guide to Travel Writing and Photography*, Harrap Publishing, 1991.

Sellers, Leslie: *Doing it in Style*, Pergamon Press, 1968; *Keeping up the Style*, Pitman, 1975; *The Simple Subs' Book*, 2nd Edition, Pergamon Press, 1985.

Todd, Alden and Loder, Cari: *Finding Facts Fast*, Penguin Books, 1990. Basic research techniques.

Walker, Ronald: *Magazine Design*, Chapman & Hall, 1992.

Waterhouse, Keith: *Waterhouse On Newspaper Style*, Viking, 1989. Expanded, revised and updated version of *Daily Mirror Style*.

Watson, James and Hill, Ann: *Dictionary of Communication and Media Studies*, 2nd Edition, Edward Arnold, 1989.

Wells, Gordon: *The Magazine Writer's Handbook 1995/6*, Allison and Busby, 1994. Analysis of many magazine markets; *Writers' Questions Answered*, Alison and Busby 1986.

Whittaker, Kenneth: *Using Libraries*, Andre Deutsch, 1972.

Williams, Paul: *The Computerized Newspaper*, Butterworth-Heinemann, 1990.

Witt, Leonard (ed.): *The Complete Book of Feature Writing*, Writers' Digest Books, 1991.

NATIONAL UNION OF JOURNALISTS' CODE OF CONDUCT

1 A journalist has a duty to maintain the highest professional and ethical standards.

2 A journalist shall at all times defend the principle of the freedom of the press and other media in relation to the collection of information and the expression of comment and criticism. He/she shall strive to eliminate distortion, news suppression and censorship.

3 A journalist shall strive to ensure that the information he/she disseminates is fair and accurate, avoid the expression of comment and conjecture as established fact and falsification by distortion, selection or misrepresentation.

4 A journalist shall rectify promptly any harmful inaccuracies, ensure that correction and apologies receive due prominence and afford the right of reply to persons criticised when the issue is of sufficient importance.

5 A journalist shall obtain information, photographs and illustrations only by straightforward means. The use of other means can be justified only by over-riding considerations of the public interest. The journalist is entitled to exercise a personal conscientious objection to the use of such means.

6 Subject to the justification by over-riding considerations of the public interest, a journalist shall do nothing which entails intrusion into private grief and distress.

7 A journalist shall protect confidential sources of information.

8 A journalist shall not accept bribes nor shall he/she allow other inducements to influence the performance of his/her professional duties.

9 A journalist shall not lend himself/herself to the distortion or suppression of the truth because of advertising or other considerations.

10 A journalist shall only mention a person's race, colour, creed, illegitimacy, disability, marital status (or lack of it), gender or sexual orientation if this information is strictly relevant. A journalist shall neither originate nor process material which encourages discrimination on any of the above mentioned grounds.

11 A journalist shall not take private advantage of information gained in the course of his/her duties, before the information is public knowledge.

12 A journalist shall not by way of statement, voice or appearance endorse by advertisement any commercial product or service save for the promotion of his/her own work or of the medium by which he/she is employed.

PRESS COMPLAINTS COMMISSION'S CODE OF PRACTICE

The Press Complaints Commission is charged with enforcing the following Code of Practice which was framed by the newspaper and periodical industry and ratified by the Press Complaints Commission in April 1994.

All members of the press have a duty to maintain the highest professional and ethical standards. In doing so, they should have regard to the provisions of this Code of Practice and to safeguarding the public's right to know.

Editors are responsible for the actions of journalists employed by their publications. They should also satisfy themselves as far as possible that material accepted from non-staff members was obtained in accordance with this Code.

While recognizing that this involves a substantial element of self-restraint by editors and journalists, it is designed to be acceptable in the context of a system of self-regulation. The Code applies in the spirit as well as in the letter.

It is the responsibility of editors to co-operate as swiftly as possible in PCC enquiries.

Any publication which is criticized by the PCC under one of the following clauses is duty bound to print the adjudication which follows in full and with due prominence.

1 Accuracy

(i) Newspapers and periodicals should take care not to publish inaccurate, misleading or distorted material.

(ii) Whenever it is recognized that a significant inaccuracy, misleading statement or distorted report has been published, it should be corrected promptly and with due prominence.

(iii) An apology should be published whenever appropriate.

(iv) A newspaper or periodical should always report fairly and accurately the outcome of an action for defamation to which it has been a party.

2 Opportunity to reply

A fair opportunity for reply to inaccuracies should be given to individuals or organizations when reasonably called for.

3 Comment, conjecture and fact

Newspapers, while free to be partisan should distinguish clearly between comment, conjecture and fact.

4 *Privacy*

Intrusions and enquiries into an individual's private life without his or her consent including the use of long-lens photography to take pictures of people on private property without their consent are not generally acceptable and publications can only be justified when in the public interest.

Note – Private property is defined as any private residence, together with its garden and outbuildings, but excluding any adjacent fields or parkland. In addition, hotel bedrooms (but not other areas in a hotel) and those parts of a hospital or nursing home where patients are treated or accommodated.

5 *Listening devices*

Unless justified by public interest, journalists should not obtain or publish material obtained by using clandestine listening devices or by intercepting private telephone conversations.

6 *Hospitals*

(i)   Journalists or photographers making enquiries at hospitals or similar institutions should identify themselves to a responsible executive and obtain permission before entering non-public areas.

(ii) The restrictions on intruding into privacy are particularly relevant to enquiries about individuals in hospitals or similar institutions.

7 *Misrepresentation*

(i)   Journalists should not generally obtain or seek to obtain information or pictures through misrepresentation or subterfuge.

(ii) Unless in the public interest, documents or photographs should be removed only with the express consent of the owner.

(iii) Subterfuge can be justified only in the public interest and only when material cannot be obtained by any other means.

8 *Harassment*

(i)   Journalists should neither obtain nor seek to obtain information or pictures through intimidation or harassment.

(ii) Unless their enquiries are in the public interest, journalists should not photograph individuals on private property without their consent; should not persist in telephoning or questioning individuals after having been asked to desist; should not remain on their property after having been asked to leave and should not follow them.

(iii) It is the responsibility of editors to ensure that these requirements are carried out.

9 Payment for articles

Payments or offers for stories, pictures or information should not be made directly or through agents to witnesses or potential witnesses in current or criminal proceedings or to people engaged in crime or to their associates – which includes family, friends, neighbours and colleagues – except where the material concerned ought to be published in the public interest and the payment is necessary for this to be done.

10 Intrusions into grief or shock

In cases involving personal grief or shock, enquiries should be carried out and approaches made with sympathy and discretion.

11 Innocent relatives and friends

Unless it is contrary to the public's right to know, the press should generally avoid identifying relatives or friends of persons convicted or accused of crime.

12 Interviewing or photographing children

(i)   Journalists should not normally interview or photograph children under the age of 16 on subjects involving the personal welfare of the child, in the absence of or without the consent of a parent or other adult who is responsible for the children.

(ii) Children should not be approached or photographed while at school without the permission of the school authorities.

13 Children in sex cases

(1)   The press should not, even where the law does not prohibit it, identify children under the age of 16 who are involved in cases concerning sexual offences, whether as victims, or as witnesses or defendants.

(2)   In any press report of a case involving a sexual offence against a child –

(i)   The adult should be identified.

(ii) The terms 'incest' where applicable should not be used.

(iii) The offences should be described as 'serious offences against young children' or similar appropriate wording.

(iv) The child should not be identified.

(v)   Care should be taken that nothing in the report implies the relationship between the accused and the child.

14 Victims of crime

The press should not identify victims of sexual assault or publish material likely to contribute to such identification unless, by law, they are free to do so.

15 Discrimination

(i)   The press should avoid prejudicial or pejorative reference to a person's race, colour, religion, sex or sexual orientation or to any physical or mental illness or handicap.

(ii) It should avoid publishing details of a person's race, colour, religion, sex or sexual orientation, unless these are directly relevant to the story.

16 Financial journalism

(i)   Even where the law does not prohibit it, journalists should not use for their own profit financial information they receive in advance of its general publication, nor should they pass such information to others.

(ii) They should not write about shares or securities in whose performance they know that they or their close families have a significant financial interest, without disclosing the interest to the editor or financial editor.

(iii) They should not buy or sell, either directly or through nominees or agents, shares or securities about which they have written recently or about which they intend to write in the near future.

17 Confidential sources

Journalists have a moral obligation to protect confidential sources of information.

18 The public interest

Clauses 4, 5, 7, 8 and 9 create exceptions which may be covered by invoking the public interest. For the purposes of this code that is most easily defined as:

(i)   Detecting or exposing crime or a serious misdemeanour.
(ii) Protecting public health and safety.
(iii) Preventing the public from being misled by some statement or action of an individual or organization.

In any cases raising issues beyond these three definitions the Press Complaints Commission will require a full explanation by the editor of the publication involved, seeking to demonstrate how the public interest was served.

Comments or suggestions regarding the content of the Code may be sent to the Secretary, Press Standards Board of Finance, Merchants House Buildings, 30 George Square, Glasgow G2 1EG, to be laid before the industry's Code Committee.

Glossary

ABC   Audit Bureau of Circulations, the body that authenticates and publishes newspaper circulation figures.

Ad   Advertisement.

Ad dummy   The blank set of pages of an edition with the shapes and positions of advertisements marked in.

Ad rule   The rule or border separating editorial matter from advertisements on a page.

Add   Copy added to a story already written or subedited.

Advance   Printed hand-out of a speech or statement issued in advance to the press.

Advertising agency   An organization that prepares and designs advertisements for clients, and buys advertising space.

Agony column   A regular feature giving advice on personal problems to the mainly young; hence agony aunt.

Alts   Alterations made to copy or set matter.

Angle   A particular approach to a story.

Angling   Writing or editing a story from a particular angle, i.e. to bring out a particular aspect of its news content.

Art   Pertaining usually to design and layout of pages, the use of pictures and typography in newspaper display.

Art desk   Where page layouts are drawn in detail and the pictures edited.

Art editor   The person responsible for the art desk and for design of the newspaper.

Artwork   Prepared material for use in newspaper display.

Ascender   The part of a letter that rises above its x-height, as in h, k, l and f.

Assignment   A story which a journalist has been assigned to cover: a briefing.

Author's marks   Corrections or amendments by the writer on an edited story, either on screen or on proof.

Advertorial   Advertising disguised as editorial material.

Back bench   The control centre for a newspaper's production, where sit the night editor and other production executives.

Backgrounder   A feature giving background to the news.

Back numbers   Previous issues of a newspaper.

Bad break   Ugly or unacceptable hyphenation of a word made to justify a line of type. *See Justify*.

Banner   A headline that crosses the top of a page – also *streamer*.

Bastard measure   Any type setting of non-standard width based on columns.

Beat   An exclusive story or one that puts a newspaper's coverage ahead of another's.

Big quotes   Quotation marks larger than the typesize they enclose, used for display effect.

Big read   A long feature covering many columns – usually an instalment of a series.

Bill   A newspaper poster advertising the contents of the paper at selected sites.

Black   A copy or carbon of a story, an electronic duplicate of a story; also used to describe certain boldface types.

Blanket   Newspaper page proof.

Bleach-out   A picture overdeveloped to intensify the blacks and remove the tones – useful in producing a motif to use as a display label on a story.

Blobs Solid black discs used in front of type for display effect, or for tabulating lists.

Blow-up Enlargement of a picture or type.

Blurb A piece of self-advertisement composed of type, and sometimes illustration, used to draw a reader's attention to the contents of other pages or issues to come.

Bodoni A commonly used serif type, noted for clean lines and fine serifs.

Body The space taken up by the strokes of a letter – the density of a letter.

Body matter The reading text of a newspaper.

Body type The type used for reading text.

Bold Name given to type of a thicker than average body.

Border A print rule or strip used to make panels for stories, or for display effects in layout – used in stick-on tape form in paste-up pages.

BOT Type reversed as black on tone background.

Box A story enclosed by rules on all four sides – also *panel*.

Break 1 Convenient place to break the text with a quote or crosshead; 2 The moment news happens.

Breaker Any device such as a quote or crosshead which breaks up the text in the page.

Break-out A secondary story run on a page with a main story, usually on a feature page. Also: a sidebar.

Brief A short news story, usually one paragraph.

Briefing Instructions for a journalistic assignment.

Bring up An editing instruction meaning use certain material earlier in a story.

Broadsheet Full size newspaper page approximately 22 in by 15 in, as opposed to tabloid, half size.

Bromide Emulsioned stiff paper on which photographic material is printed; any photographically printed material.

Bucket Rules on either side and below tying in printed matter to a picture.

Bureau   The office of a news agency; in the US any newspaper office separate from the main one.

Buster   Headline whose number of characters exceed the required measure.

By-line   The writer's name at the beginning, or near the top, of a story.

c & lc   Capital letters and lower case of type.

Cablese   Abbreviated text used in copy transmitted by telegraph, i.e. to save transmission costs.

Caption   Line(s) of type identifying or describing a picture.

Caps   Capital letters of type.

Caslon   A traditional-style seriffed type face used for headlines.

Cast off   To edit to a fixed length; (n) the edited length of a story as estimated.

Catchline   Syllable taken from a story and used on each folio, or section, along with folio number, to identify it in the typesetting system.

CD-Rom   Compact disk read-only memory used to hold computer-accessible data.

Centre spread   Material extending across the two centre-facing pages in a newspaper. *Spread*: any material occupying two opposite pages.

Centred   Type placed equidistant from each side of the column or columns.

Century   Much used modern seriffed type with bold strokes.

Change pages   Pages that are to be given new or revised material on an edition, or on which advertising material is being replaced.

Characters   The letters, figures, symbols, etc. in a type range, hence *character count*, the number of characters and spaces that can be accommodated in a given line of type.

Circulation   The number of copies of a newspaper sold, i.e. in circulation; hence *circulation manager*, the executive in charge of distributing copies and promoting circulation, also *circulation rep* (representative).

City editor   Editor of financial page; in US the name given to the editor in charge of news-gathering in main office.

Classifieds   Small adverts gathered into sections.

Clean up   Editing instruction to improve tone of copy.

Cliché   A well-worn, over-used phrase.

Cliffhanger   A story that still awaits its climax or sequel.

Close quotes   Punctuation marks closing quoted material.

Close up   To reduce space between words or lines.

Col   Short for column.

Colour   Descriptive writing.

Column   Standard vertical divisions of a newspaper page; hence column measure.

Column rule   Fine rule marking out the columns.

Columnar space   Vertical space separating one column of matter from another.

Command   A keyboarded instruction to a computer.

Comp   Compositor; a printer who composes typeset material or makes up a page.

Compo   Composite artwork made up of type and half-tone.

Condensed type   Type narrower than the standard founts; hence *extra condensed* and *medium condensed*.

Contact book   A reporter's record of useful personal contacts and their telephone numbers.

Content   Material in a newspaper.

Contents bill   Bill or poster advertising a story or item in a newspaper.

Copy   All material submitted for use in a newspaper.

Copy-taker   Telephone typists who take down reporters' copy on a typewriter or VDU (US telephone reporter).

Copy-taster   Person who sorts and classifies incoming copy in a newspaper.

Copyright   Ownership of written or printed material.

Corr   Short for correspondent.

Correct   To put right typesetting errors.

Correction   Published item putting right errors in a story.

Count   The number of characters in a line of type.

Coverage   The attendance at, and writing up, of news events; also the total number of stories covered.

Credit   Usually the photographer's or artist's name printed with an illustration; hence *credit line*.

Crop   To select the image of a picture for printing by drawing lines to exclude the unwanted area.

Crosshead   Line or lines of type to break the text, placed between paragraphs.

Cross reference   Line of type referring to matter elsewhere in the paper.

CRT   Cathode-ray tube, used as a light source to create the type image in a photosetter.

Cursive   Any flowing design of type based on handwriting.

Cursor   Electronic light 'pen' on VDU screen, used to manipulate text during writing and editing.

Cut   To reduce a story by deleting facts or words.

Cut-off   A story separated from the text above and below by type rules making it self-contained from the rest of the column; hence *cut-off rule*.

Cut-out   Half-tone picture in which the background has been cut away to leave the image in outline.

Cuttings   Catalogued material from newspapers cut out and stored in a cuttings library for future reference (in US clippings).

Cuttings job   A story based on cuttings.

Cypher   A type character which represents something else, i.e. ampersand (&) and £ and $ signs.

Database   The material to which a computer gives access.

Dateline   Place and date of a story given at the top.

Dead   Matter discarded and not to be used again.

Deadline   Latest time a story can be filed, accepted or set.

Deck   One unit of a headline.

Decoder   A device for turning transmitted material into usable form, i.e. pictures or text.

Define   To specify on a computer screen the material a command is intended to cover.

Delayed drop   An intro which reserves the point of a story till later.

D-notice   An official instruction to editors that a story is subject to the Official Secrets Act and therefore should not be used.

Descender   The part of a letter that projects below the x-line.

Diary   1 The newsroom list of jobs for the day or week; 2 A gossip column in a newspaper.

Direct input   The inputting of material into a computer by writers for the purpose of screen editing, i.e. by the use of VDUs.

Directory   A list of stories of a given classification held in a computer and available to those with access.

Disaster caps   Large heavy, sanserif type, used on a major (usually disaster) page one story.

Disclaimer   A printed item explaining that a story printed previously has nothing to do with persons or an organization with the same or similar name as used in the story.

Display ads   Advertisements in which large type or illustration predominate.

District reporter   Reporter working from a base away from the main office.

Double   The same story printed twice in the paper.

Double-column   Across two columns.

Dress   Redress or revision of a story; also *rejig*.

Drop letter   An outsize initial capital letter on the intro of a story; also *drop figure*.

Drop quotes   Outsize quotes used to mark off important quoted sections in a story.

Dummy   Blank copy of the paper, sometimes half size, showing the position and sizes of the advertisement and the space available for editorial use; also mock-up of editorial pages as preparation for a new format.

Edit   Prepare copy for the press.

Edition   An issue of the paper prepared for a specific area; hence *editionize*, to prepare such.

Editor   Chief editorial executive who is responsible for the editing and contents of a newspaper.

Editorial   The leading article or opinion of the paper.

Editorialize   To insert, or imbue with, the newspaper's own opinion.

Editor's conference   Main planning conference of a newspaper.

Egyptian   A type family which has heavy 'slab' serifs.

Ellipsis   Omission of letters or words in a sentence, represented by several dots.

Em   Unit of type measure based on the standard 12 pt roman lower case letter 'm'; also called a *mutton* (in US a pica).

Embargo   Request not to publish before a nominated time.

En   Half an em – based on the standard roman lower case letter 'n'.

Exp   Expanded (of type).

Execute   Computer command meaning to put into effect.

Facsimile   Exact reproduction of an original, as in facsimile transmission of pages from one production centre to another by electronic means.

Family   All the type of any one design.

Feature   Subjective articles used in newspapers, as opposed to objective news material; newspaper material containing advice, comment, opinion or assessment; sometimes any editorial content other than news.

File   A reporter's own computer input; to send or submit a story; a writer's or agency's day's output.

Files   Back issues.

Filler   A short news item of one or two paragraphs.

Filmset type   Photoset type.

Fit-up   Artwork involving several elements joined together.

Flash   Urgent brief message on agency service – usually an important fact.

Flashback   A story or picture taken from a past issue.

Flatbed press   Small, mostly old-time, press that prints from a flat surface, i.e. not rotary.

Flimsy   Thin paper carbon copy of story.

Flush   Set to one side (as of type).

Fold   Point at which the paper is folded during printing; hence *folder*, a device attached to the press which does this.

Folio   Page.

Follow-up   A story that follows up information in a previous story in order to uncover new facts.

Format   1 The shape and regular features of a newspaper; its regular typographical appearance; 2 Any pre-set instruction programmed into a computer.

Forme   The completed newspaper page or pair of pages when ready to be made into a printing plate (in old technology).

Fount   All the characters in a given size of any type.

Frame   The adjustable easel at which paste-up pages are made up from photoset and photographic elements.

Freebie   Free trip, services, entertainment offered to a journalist.

Freelance   Self-employed person, i.e. journalist.

Free sheets   Newspapers that rely solely on advertising income and are given free to readers.

Front office   Usually the advertising and editorial part of a newspaper office to which the public are admitted.

Fudge   Part of the front or back page of a newspaper where late news is printed from a separate cylinder 'on the run', sometimes called the 'stop press', i.e. the presses are stopped so that the late news can be fudged in.

Full out   Typeset to the full measure of a column.

Galley   Shallow long metal tray on which metal type was gathered and proofed before being taken to the page; hence *galley proof* (still used).

Gatekeeper   Sociologist's name for the copy-taster.

Gatherers   Journalists who gather and write material for a newspaper – a sociological term.

Ghost writer   One who writes under another's name; one who writes on behalf of someone else.

Good pages   Pages that do not have to be changed for later editions.

Gothic   Family of sanserif type with a great variety of available widths – medium condensed, extra condensed, square, etc.

Graphics   Usually any drawn illustrative material used in page design.

Grot   Abbreviation for Grotesque, a family of sans headline type.

Gutter   The margin between two printed pages.

Hack   Slang term for journalist – sometimes used by journalists.

Hair space   The thinnest space used between letters in typesetting systems.

Half lead   The second most important story on a page.

Half-tone   The reproduction process, consisting of dots of varying density, by which the tones of a photograph are reproduced on a page.

Handout   Pre-printed material containing information supplied for the use of the press.

Hanging indent   Style of typesetting in which the first line of each paragraph is set full out and the remaining lines indented on the left.

Hard copy   Typewritten or handwritten copy, as opposed to copy entered into a computer.

Hard news   News based on solid fact.

Head, heading   Words for headline.

Header   The part of a VDU screen in which commands and basic instructions are entered, and in which the computer communicates with the user.

Heavies   Name sometimes given to the quality or serious national press as opposed to the popular press; newspapers that specialize in serious news.

H & J   Computer term for 'hyphenated and justified', meaning that the material has been prepared on the screen in the length and sequence of equal lines in which it will be typeset.

Hold   To keep copy for use later; also *set and hold*.

Hold over   To keep typeset matter for later, also to *HO*.

Hood   Lines of type above a picture or story and attached by rules top and side.

Hook   A term used in some computer systems for a queue or desk to which stories can be sent after tasting to await possible use.

Horizontal make-up   Page design in which stories and headlines cross the page in several legs as opposed to being run up and down.

Hot metal   The traditional printing system in which type was cast from molten metal into 'slugs' for assembly into pages.

House style   Nominated spellings and usages used to produce consistency in a given newspaper or printing house.

Imprint   Name and address of the printer and publisher, usually found at the bottom of the back page of a newspaper.

Indent   Material set narrower than the column measures, leaving white space either at the front or at both sides.

Ink fly   A fine spray that can hang in the air in rotary printing operations.

Insert   Any copy inserted into a story already written or typeset.

Intro   The introduction or beginning of a story.

Investigative journalism   A form of reporting in which a news situation is examined in depth by a team of reporters under a project leader, i.e. as an investigation of all aspects.

Issue   All copies of a day's paper and its editions.

Italic   Type characters that slope from right to left.

Jack line   *See widow.*

Job   A journalistic assignment.

Journalese   Newspaper-generated slang; shoddy, cliché-ridden language.

Justify   To space out a line of type to fit a nominated width.

Keyboard   The panel of keys on a typewriter or VDU by which copy is entered on to paper or a screen.

Kicker   A story in special type and setting that stands out from the main part of the page.

Kill   To erase or throw away a story so that it cannot be used.

Label   A headline without a verb.

Layout   The plan of a page.

Lead (pronounced leed)   The main story on a page; the page lead.

Lead (pronounced led)   The space between lines of type under the hot metal system, achieved by using strips of metal, or leads, of set points width (term still used on computer systems).

Leader   Editorial opinion, or leading article.

Leg   Any portion of text arranged in several columns on the page.

Legal kill   A legal instruction not to use.

Legman   A journalist who assists with gathering the facts but does not usually write the story; hence leg work.

Letterpress   A method of printing from a raised or relief surface, as with metal or polymer stereo plates on rotary presses.

Letter-spacing   Space the width of an average letter in a given type.

Lift   To use, and keep in a page, matter that has appeared in a previous edition.

Light box   A device consisting of a ground glass screen illuminated from below through which pictures can be viewed face downwards so that they can be cropped and scaled on the back.

Light face   Type of a lighter weight or character than standard.

Lineage   Computation of lines used as a basis of payment to writers; sometimes used for payment of non-staff newspaper contributors.

Line block   An engraved plate, as in the hot metal printing system, which reproduced the lines of a drawing in continuous black, as opposed to the half-tone block which rendered tones by means of dots of varying density.

Line drawing   Drawing made up of black strokes, as with a cartoon or comic strip.

Literals   Typographical errors.

Lithography   Printing by means of ink impressed on a sheet.

Local corr   A district correspondent.

Logo   Name, title, recognition word, as of a regular column or section of newspaper.

Long primer   Old name for 10 pt type; also 1p.

Lower case   Small, as opposed to capital, letters of an alphabet.

Make-up   The act of making up a page, sometimes the page plan.

Masking   Excluding part of a photograph by paper overlay to indicate area to be printed.

Master   The basic type shape inside a photosetter from which printed type is generated.

Masthead   The name or title of a newspaper at the top of page one.

Measure   Width of any setting.

Medium   A weight of type between light and bold, or heavy.

Memory   The part of a computer that retains information fed into it; where written and edited stories are stored.

Merchandizing   Information about price and place of purchase in consumer journalism features.

MF   Abbreviation for more to follow.

MFL   More to follow later.

Milled rule   A Simplex rule or border with a serrated edge as on the edge of a coin.

Montage   A number of pictures mounted together.

Mood picture (or shot)   A picture in which atmosphere is more important than content.

Mop-up   A story that puts together information already used in separate ways, or on separate occasions.

Morgue   Old name for newspaper picture and cuttings library.

Motif   Drawing or picture used to symbolize a subject, or to identify a feature or story.

MS   Manuscript of any text before printing.

Mug shot   Picture showing only a person's head.

Must   An item that must be used, and containing *must* in its instructions.

Mutton   Printers' old name for an em.

Nationals   Newspapers on sale all over the country.

New lead   A version of a story based on later information.

News agency   An organization that collects, edits and distributes news to subscribing newspapers.

News desk   The newsroom, where the collection of news is organized, and where reporters are based (in US, city desk).

Nibs   News in brief.

Night editor   The senior production executive of a daily paper.

Nose   The intro or start to a story; hence to *re-nose*.

NS   Newspaper Society, an association for provincial newspaper proprietors in Britain.

Nuggets   Small items of news; separate sections of a story.

NUJ   National Union of Journalists (in Britain).

Nut   Printers' name for an en; hence *nutted*, type indented one nut, or nut each side.

Obit   Obituary item.

Offset   Printing by transferring the page image from smooth plastic printing plate to a rubber roller which then sets it off on to paper.

Off-stone   When a page is ready to be made into a printing plate.

Open quotes   Punctuation marks denoting the start of a quoted section.

Overline   A line of smaller type over a main headline; also a *strapline*.

Overmatter   Left-over printed material not used in the edition.

PA   Press Association, home national news agency in Britain.

Page facsimile transmission   Method by which completed pages are digitized and reduced to an electronic signal for transmission by wire or satellite to another printing centre for simultaneous production.

Pagination   The numbering of pages; the number of pages of a publication.

Panel   Story enclosed in rules or borders; see *box*.

Paste-up   The method of making up pages from photoset material by attaching them to a page card.

Personal column Regular column signed by writer (i.e. with a by-line).

Photoset The name usually given to photocomposed type under computerized printing systems; hence *phototypesetter*.

Pica 12 pt type; unit of measurement based on multiples of 12 points (pica = one em).

Picture desk Where collecting and checking of pictures is organized; hence *picture editor*.

Plate Printing plate, of metal or plastic, derived from the page image.

Platen Surface which holds the paper in a typewriter or printing press and presses it against an inked surface.

Point Unit of type measurement. The British-American point is 0.01383 in, or about one seventy-second of an inch. The size of type is measured by depth in points.

Populars Mass circulation newspapers of popular appeal.

Press release Official announcement for use by press.

Print Total number of newspapers printed of one issue; also a picture or bromide printed from a photographic negative.

Print order The number of copies of an issue ordered to be printed.

Print-out A copy of material in a computer printed out for reference in advance of actual typesetting. Print-outs sometimes show the type as it will look when set.

Printing plate The plate, metal or polymer, from which the page is printed.

Processor The part of a typesetter that produces the bromide print of the type for paste-up; or produces the print from a photographic negative.

Projection The display and headline treatment given to a story in the page.

Promotion Any form of planned publicity that has a specific aim.

Proof An inked impression taken from typeset material.

Proof reader Person who reads and corrects proofs to ensure that copy has been accurately followed; hence *proof marks*, corrections marked on a proof.

Publishing room   Where the newspapers are counted, wrapped and prepared for distribution.

Puff   An item in a newspaper which publicizes something or somebody.

Pull-out   Separate section of a newspaper that can be pulled out, often with separate pagination.

Pundit   A regular newspaper columnist who dispenses opinion.

Qualities   Serious, as opposed to popular, newspapers.

Queue   A collection, or directory, of stories held in a computer – features queue, newsroom queue, etc.

Quire   Unit of freshly printed, ordered newspapers, usually twenty-six copies.

Quotes   Raised punctuation marks to indicate quoted speech.

Qwerty   Standard keyboard layout as on a typewriter or VDU, based on the first five characters of the top bank of letter keys.

Ragged (left or right)   Copy set justified on one side only, sometimes used in captions.

Range   The number and variety of characters available in a type.

Rate card   List of newspaper advertising charges based on specific sizes and placings.

Reader   A proof reader.

Reader participation   Editorial material or items which involve contributions by readers, such as readers' letters, competitions and articles based on invited opinions.

Readership   The total number of people who read a newspaper – not the number of copies in circulation. The estimated number of readers per copies of magazines and newspapers can vary considerably.

Readership profile   A tabulated analysis of the sorts of readers that buy a newspaper or magazine.

Redress   *See rejig.*

Reel   Spindle holding a roll of newsprint; sometimes, a roll of newsprint; hence *reel room*, where rolls of newsprint are stacked for use.

Register   The outline of printed matter as it appears on the paper; important in colour printing where the main colours are printed separately on to the picture image.

Rejig   The revision of a story in the light of later information, or a change of position in the paper, often between editions.

Release   The date or time handout material becomes available for use.

Re-nose   To put a new intro on to a story, using different material or a different angle.

Re-plate   To replace a printing plate to allow a later version of a page on to the press.

Reporter   Person who gathers and writes up news.

Retainer   Periodic payment made to retain someone's services, as with local correspondents; *see stringer*.

Retouching   Improving the quality of a photographic print by the use of a brush or pen.

Reuters   British based international news agency.

Revamp   General change given to a story or page in the light of a reconsidered approach.

Reverse   Type printed white on a black or tone background; can be done in a photosetter as *reverse video*.

Reverse indent   *See Hanging indent.*

Review   Assessment of arts production.

Revise   To check and correct, or improve, edited material.

Rewrite   To turn a story into new words rather than to edit on copy.

RO   Run on (on typed copy).

Roman   The standard face of a type.

ROP   Run of press. For instance spot colour is printed during run of press rather than as a separate or additional process.

Rota picture   A news picture obtained under the rota system, in which limited coverage of an event by newspapers is allowed on a shared basis.

Rotary press   Traditional press in which newspapers are printed by the letterpress method from curved metal or polymer relief plates.

Rough   Outline sketch of page layout.

Rule   A printed border of varying width.

Run   Length of time taken to print an issue of a newspaper.

Running story   A story that develops and continues over a long period.

Run on   To carry on printing without changing plates for an edition.

Rush   Second most urgent classification of news agency material after *flash*; hence *rushfull*, a full version based on rushes.

Sans   Sanserif-types without tails, or serifs, at the end of the letter strokes.

Satellite printing   Printing at subsidiary production centres by the use of page facsimile transmission.

Scaling   Method of calculating the depth of a picture to be used.

Scalpel   Used to lift, cut up and place material in paste-up pages.

Schedule   List of reporting or feature jobs to be covered for use in an issue of a newspaper.

Scheme   To plan and draw a page; also a *page layout*.

Scoop   Exclusive story.

Screamer   Exclamation mark.

Screen   The density of dots in half-tone reproduction of photographs.

Screen   The part of a VDU on which stories held in the computer are projected for reading or editing; hence *screen subbing*, subbing by electronic means by use of a cursor.

Scroll (up or down)   To display material on to a VDU screen so that it can be read in sequence.

Seal   Standard words, often in spot colour, at the top of a page indicating the edition; also a logo.

Section   A separately folded part of a newspaper; hence sectional newspapers.

Send   A command to transfer material in a computer to another queue or desk, or to the typesetter.

Separation   The separate elements of a colour picture by which the colour is transferred to the page.

Sequence   The order in which a story is presented (in subbing).

Series   Range of typesizes, or of types.

Serif   Type characterized by strokes that have little tails or serifs.

Service column   An advice, or consumer, column.

Set and hold   Put into type for use later.

Set flush   To set full to the margin.

Set forme   The last forme (of page or pair of pages) to go to press.

Set solid   To set without line spacing.

Setting format   Setting of a nominated size, width and spacing that is programmed into the computer, i.e. where such setting is regularly used.

Shorts   Short items of edited matter, usually of one, two or three paragraphs.

Sidebar   Story placed alongside a main story to which it relates.

Side-head   A headline or cross-head set flush left, or indented left.

Sign-off   The name of the writer at the end of a story.

Situationer   A story giving background to a situation.

Sizing   *See scaling.*

Slab-serif   Type with heavy square-ended serifs.

Slip   To change a page between editions, hence *slip edition.*

Slug-line   Catchline (in US).

Snap   Piece of information in advance of full details in news agency story.

Spike   Home for unwanted stories. Computers also have an electronic *spike* to which stories can be sent.

Spill   To run down and fill space (of type).

Splash   The main page one story.

Split screen   The use of a terminal to display two stories at once.

Spot colour   Non-processed colour applied to the page during run of press.

Spread   A main story that crosses two adjoining pages.

Squares   Black or open, a species of type ornament used to mark off sections of text.

Stand-first   An explanation in special type set above the intro of a story, i.e. it stands first.

Stand-up drop   An initial letter in large type that stands above the line of the text at the start of a story.

Star   Type ornament; hence *star-line*, a line of stars.

Star-burst   Headline or slogan enclosed in star-shaped outline, used in blurbs and advertising.

Start-up   When the presses begin to print.

Stet   Proof reader's mark means 'as it stands'.

Stock bills   Newspaper display bills on fixed subject such as 'today's TV', 'latest scores', etc.

Stone   Bench where pages were made up under hot metal system; hence *stone sub*, the journalist who supervised this work; *stone-hand*, the printer who worked on the stone (term still used in cut-and-paste page make-up).

Stop press   Late news printed from a separate cylinder on to the page while on the press, or afterwards.

Strap-line   Headline in small type that goes above the main headline; also *overline*.

Streamer   Headline that crosses the top of the page, also a *banner* headline.

Stringer   A local correspondent.

Subeditor   Person who checks and edits material for a newspaper to fit set space, and writes the headline (US deskman).

Subhead   Secondary headline.

Subst head   Headline in place of another.

Syndication   The means by which a newspaper's material is offered for a fee for use in other publications or countries.

Tabloid   Half size (newspaper).

Tag-line   An explanatory line or acknowledgement under the bottom line of a headline.

Take   A piece of copy, part of a sequence.

Tear-out   A picture printed with a simulated torn edge, usually a flash back of a printed picture, or a part of a document; also *rag-out*.

Telephoto lens   Camera lens that magnifies an image telescopically.

Teleprinter   Machine that prints text received by telegraphic signal.

Terminal   The part of a video display terminal on which electronically-generated text is displayed and monitored; also any VDU or VDT.

Textsize   A broadsheet, or full-size newspaper page.

Tie-in   A story that is connected with one alongside.

Tie-on   A story that is connected with the story above.

Tip-off   Information from an inside source.

Top   A top of the page story; mostly any story that merits a good headline and of more than three paragraphs in length.

Trim   To cut a story a little.

Turn head   A head covering a story that has been continued from another page (US a *jump head*).

Typebook   Catalogue of types held.

Typechart   A tabulated list giving character counts for given types.

Underscore   To carry a line or rule under type.

Update   To work in later information.

Visualize   To plan and work out how a page or display will look.

VDU   Video display unit, a device with a screen and keyboard used to display and enter text into a computer; also VDT, video display terminal.

Web-offset   A system of printing in which the inked page image is transferred from a smooth printing plate on to a rubber roller and then offset on to paper, as opposed to being printed directly on to paper by relief impression.

Weight   The thickness of a type.

Widow   A short line left at the top of a column of reading type (usually avoided in page make-up).

Wing in   To set a headline within the top rule of a panel or box, leaving a piece of rule showing on either side.

Wire   A means of transmitting copy by electronic signal which requires a receiver or decoder; hence *wire room*, where such copy is transmitted or received.

Word processor   Electronic system by which text can be keyboarded into a computer, stored, edited, amended and finally printed (i.e. processed) when required.

Work station   A special video display terminal used at a distance from the computer, with access and facilities to enable work to be done away from the main centre.

WOB   White on black type.

WOT   White on tone type.

x-height   The mean height of letters in a type range, exclusive of ascenders or descenders.

Index